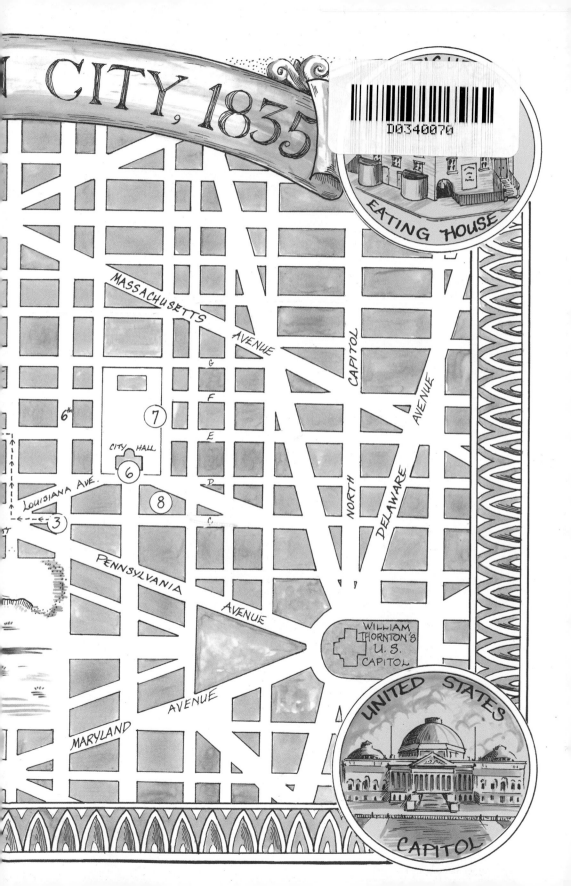

SNOW-STORM IN AUGUST

ALSO BY JEFFERSON MORLEY

*Our Man in Mexico: Winston Scott and the
Hidden History of the CIA*

Washington City in 1834, as seen from the south.

SNOW-STORM IN AUGUST

Washington City, Francis Scott Key, and the
Forgotten Race Riot of 1835

Jefferson Morley

NAN A. TALESE | DOUBLEDAY
New York   London   Toronto   Sydney   Auckland

Copyright © 2012 by Jefferson Morley

All rights reserved. Published in the United States by Nan A. Talese/Doubleday,
a division of Random House, Inc., New York, and in Canada
by Random House of Canada Limited, Toronto.

www.nanatalese.com

DOUBLEDAY is a registered trademark of Random House, Inc. Nan A.
Talese and the colophon are trademarks of Random House, Inc.

Pages 321–22 constitute an extension of this copyright page.

Book design by Michael Collica
Jacket design by Michael J. Windsor
Jacket photographs: Landscape © Historic Map Works LLC / Getty Images;
People © After William Ludlow Sheppard / The Bridgeman Art Library /
Getty Images; Capitol Building © Everett Collection / Superstock
Endpapers map by Ellisa Mitchell

Library of Congress Cataloging-in-Publication Data

Morley, Jefferson.
Snow-storm in August : Washington City, Francis Scott Key, and
the forgotten race riot of 1835 / Jefferson Morley.—1st ed.
p. cm.
Includes bibliographical references and index.
1. Washington (D.C.)—Race relations—History—19th century. 2. Race riots—
Washington (D.C.)—History—19th century. 3. Free African Americans—Washington
(D.C.)—History—19th century. 4. Slavery—Washington (D.C.)—History—
19th century. 5. Trials (Attempted murder)—Washington (D.C.) 6. Key, Francis Scott, 1779–1843. 7. Bowen, Arthur, b. 1816? 8. Thornton, Anna Maria Brodeau,
1775?–1865. 9. Washington (D.C.)—History—19th century. I. Title.
F198.M67 2012
305.8009753—dc23
2011042032

ISBN 978-0-385-53337-9

MANUFACTURED IN THE UNITED STATES OF AMERICA

1 3 5 7 9 10 8 6 4 2

First Edition

For my mother and father,
Jane Augustine and Tony Morley

We rejoice that we are thrown into a revolution where the contest is not for landed territory but for freedom. Let no man remove from his native country, for our principles are drawn from the book of divine revelation, and are incorporated in the Declaration of Independence, "that all men are born equal."

—*Declaration of the Fifth National Negro Convention, Philadelphia, 1835*

"The Star-Spangled Banner"

Francis Scott Key

O say, can you see, by the dawn's early light,
What so proudly we hail'd at the twilight's last gleaming?
Whose broad stripes & bright stars, through the perilous fight,
O'er the ramparts we watch'd, were so gallantly streaming?
And the rockets' red glare, the bombs bursting in air,
Gave proof through the night that our flag was still there.
O say, does that star-spangled banner yet wave
O'er the land of the free & the home of the brave?

On the shore dimly seen through the mists of the deep,
Where the foe's haughty host in dread silence reposes,
What is that which the breeze, o'er the towering steep,
As it fitfully blows, half conceals, half discloses?
Now it catches the gleam of the morning's first beam,
In full glory reflected, now shines on the stream
'Tis the star-spangled banner: O, long may it wave
O'er the land of the free & the home of the brave!

And where is that band who so vauntingly swore
That the havoc of war & the battle's confusion
A home & a Country should leave us no more?
Their blood has washed out their foul footstep's pollution.
No refuge could save the hireling & slave
From the terror of flight or the gloom of the grave:
And the star-spangled banner in triumph doth wave
O'er the land of the free & the home of the brave.

O thus be it ever when freemen shall stand,
Between their lov'd home & the war's desolation!
Blest with vict'ry & peace, may the heav'n-rescued land
Praise the Power that hath made & preserved us a nation!
Then conquer we must, when our cause, it is just,
And this be our motto—"In God is our Trust"
And the star-spangled banner in triumph shall wave
O'er the land of the free & the home of the brave!

Contents

Author's Note

All the people described in this story were real living persons.

All events occurred as documented and described by contemporaneous sources and eyewitnesses. Nothing has been made up.

All dialogue denoted by quotation marks comes from contemporaneous accounts. In some cases, identified in the Notes, this language has been edited for clarity. No dialogue in quotes has been invented.

Part I

The Disciple of Epicurus

A view of Washington City in the 1830s
looking east toward the Capitol.

BEVERLY SNOW DID not look like trouble, not hardly. He was a mild-mannered fellow of mixed-race heritage—in the lingo of the day, a mulatto. The admixture of African and European blood in his veins gave an air of incongruous humor to his countenance. His language was learned, if a little extravagant, for he knew his way around a kitchen and loved to pass cooking time in conversation. To the patrons, white and colored alike, who gathered at his oyster house in the tobacco town of Lynchburg, Virginia, Beverly held forth more as a Creole raconteur than discontented bondsman. In the autumn of 1829, he was certainly better known for his way with words and white men than for any sort of difficulty. He humored the hungry with a steady stream of jokes and japes while doling out fat James River oysters and dispensing a variety of sage epigrams, dubious puns, and enigmatic epiphanies at no extra charge. The fare was salubrious, the conversation light, the prices lighter. That was Beverly's way.

While it was true that not all white men approved of a colored man doing business in the heart of town, it was more true that Beverly's friends, John and Susannah Warwick, approved of his enterprise. In Lynchburg that was enough. John was the son of Major William Warwick, a Revolutionary War veteran turned banker who had served as the first mayor of the settlement around John Lynch's ferry landing back in 1805. Susannah was the daughter of Captain William Norvell, a veteran of Valley Forge and the village's first clerk. John and Susannah Warwick owned Beverly Snow, but ownership hardly described Susannah's relationship to him. Beverly was also her friend, almost a big brother.

Beverly had lived for at least a few years in Captain Norvell's mansion on Federal Hill, the most distinguished enclave in the growing town. Nothing is known of Beverly's parents other than that one of them, probably his father, was white. Unusually for an enslaved person, Beverly learned to read and write at an early age, perhaps because Captain Norvell had helped establish the first public school in Lynchburg. Along the way, Beverly might have glimpsed one of the great men of the day, former president Thomas Jefferson, who sold a plot of land to William Norvell in 1812. Legend has it that Jefferson visited their house. Beverly, as a servant and cook, might have prepared his meals, perhaps even overheard his conversation. The servant and the statesman would come to share at least one pastime. Jefferson often digressed on his admiration for Epicurus, the ancient Greek philosopher who espoused a creed of pleasurable moderation in the third century before Christ. Before long, Beverly Snow would do the same.

Susannah Norvell, five years younger than Beverly, came of age eating his food and laughing at his jokes. A sensitive dark-haired beauty, she married John Marshall Warwick, the son of her father's friend, when she was seventeen years old. She endowed her husband's mustachioed placidity with the drive of self-improvement, and the young couple flourished. John Warwick had worked in the family dry-goods business since boyhood. As early as 1816, his name appeared on a bill of sale to Jefferson. At age twenty-one John obtained his merchant's license and turned his attention to tobacco, the cash crop of the hilly counties surrounding Lynchburg. The leafy plant was grown in abandon, bundled into fifteen-hundred-pound hogsheads, inspected, and sold to traders who shipped the leaf to Europe, where segars and pipe smoking were all the rage. Enslaved Africans did most of the work to create this pleasure. White men reaped all of the profits. John Warwick did better than most. He was a rich man well before his thirtieth birthday. His wife had a harder time. Susannah Warwick gave birth to four children, three of whom died before the age of three. In her sorrow, she liked to write and dream of a better world. She loathed the institution of slavery and was unafraid to say so. "It is a stain upon the character of Virginians," she wrote in her journal, "and one which I hope will not long remain."

In 1824, Susannah's father prepared his will. At the time, Captain Norvell owned several Negro families, including twenty-six people. He granted each of his six children the right to take possession of any two.

Susannah chose Beverly. By the next year, he had moved in with the Warwicks. In 1826, the couple announced their success to Lynchburg society by building a Federal-style brick house on Court Street along the high bluff overlooking the James River. Beverly perfected his cooking skills in the basement kitchen. He also took a wife, a soon-to-be-free colored girl six years his junior who was known to white people as Judy. She called herself Julia.

Beverly and Julia Snow lived in the same house as John and Susannah Warwick, sharing something of their prosperity and of their sadness. Beverly saw how John coped with the loss of his babies: by serving others. When Lynchburg formed its first board of health in 1828, John became a member. Eventually, John Warwick, like his father, would become the mayor of Lynchburg. With John and Susannah's support, Beverly and Judy opened the oyster house on Lynch Street to serve customers and workers at John's nearby tobacco warehouse and others who thronged the busy wharf. It was the kind of informal agreement between owners and bondsmen not unknown in well-established families in Virginia. Beverly, while still the property of his mistress, had permission to keep at least some of the money his customers handed over.

Beverly's wit soon set the people of Lynchburg to laughing. One tale concerned the Cargills, a strolling family theatrical company that had arrived in 1828. Beverly was not alone in admiring their considerable style. The Cargills arrived in carriages and buggies, while their wardrobes came in baggage wagons. As stage performers, the Cargills were truly distinguished, the locals agreed, not at all resembling the disreputable Crummieses, the acting family lampooned in Charles Dickens's just-published novel *Nicholas Nickleby*. Mr. Cargill was a gentleman, and Mrs. Cargill was ladylike and educated. Their daughter, the beautiful Mary, was comely, beloved, and respected. They delighted the town with their comic and tragic performances for much of a year.

Then one morning, Lynchburg awoke to find the Cargills had vanished. The stunned townspeople discovered they would have to pay for their happy suspension of belief about the Cargills' dramatis personae. The strolling actors had strolled off without a nod to friends or creditors. The young studs who lamented the loss of the phenomenal Mary did not suffer long. But the Cargills' many business associates did. Those who had provided food and drink, bed and board to these consummate actors could only shake their unpaid bills in impotent fury. When one man wondered aloud how the spendthrift thespians had escaped, Beverly nodded toward the James River.

"I believe, sir," he sighed, "that the play-actors have concluded to glide smoothly down the stream," which was certainly one of the greatest euphemisms ever uttered in Lynchburg.

Beverly Snow tasted politics in the summer of 1828 when Secretary of State Henry Clay came to Lynchburg. John Warwick formed a welcoming committee to hail the Kentucky statesman who would pursue the presidency of the United States of America without success for the next three decades. John supported Clay's "American System," in which the national government in Washington would use tax and tariff revenues to build roads and canals and make other internal improvements that would enable the people of the young republic to wrest a living from the virgin forests and rolling plains once occupied by the native Indians. To many Lynchburg merchants, Henry Clay's plan was common sense. New roads and canals would fortify the town's position as a commercial center between the eastern seaboard and the western frontier.

Beverly Snow, it is safe to say, was less enamored of the slick operator some called "Harry of the West." When it came to people of color, Clay was a supporter of African colonization. This was a popular scheme of the day that proposed to end the blight of chattel slavery in the United States of America by freeing the enslaved and sending them to settle the western coast of Africa. While the supporters of colonization prided themselves on their humanitarianism toward Negroes, theirs was a benevolence wrapped in a prejudice that Henry Clay voiced as well as any man. Clay especially reviled those Africans in America who had managed to gain their legal freedom. "Of all classes of our population, the most vicious is that of the free colored," Clay liked to say. "Contaminated themselves, they extend their vices to all around them."

Beverly had no use for such insults. He planned to obtain his freedom within two years and he had other destinations in mind besides Africa. Despite the practice of slavery and the common condescension articulated by the likes of Clay, Beverly was not eager to leave the country where he was born. Truth be told, he often enjoyed life in these United States. In central Virginia, the families of slaves and masters had been intertwined for generations. Countless children of African and European blood, like Susannah Norvell and Beverly Snow, had grown up as siblings, playmates, friends, rivals, and every other human bond. By the early 1800s, the bonds of decency and familiarity, combined with the revolutionary ideology of the War for Independence, had prompted a growing number of white men to let their bondsmen buy their freedom. Some whites freed their slaves in their wills. Others promised freedom to their children. Those were the terms that Beverly had been born into: with a promise of manumission when he reached the age of thirty.

Beverly Snow embodied the reality of America's race-mixing ways. While the "amalgamation" of whites and blacks was often abhorred, it was also indulged. To cite but one common practice among white people, most white mothers preferred African women to Irish women as wet nurses for their children, finding them altogether more agreeable, affectionate, and trustworthy than their Hibernian counterparts. White men, alas, had baser impulses. They wanted women of color as mistresses, concubines, whores, and occasionally as wives. Beverly, along with plenty of other people, knew the story of Richard Mentor Johnson, a famous Indian fighter turned U.S. senator from Kentucky. Johnson lived openly with a mulatto woman named Julia Chinn, who bore him two daughters of whom he was quite proud. Johnson offended the finer ladies of Frankfort, Kentucky—and made news nationally—by attempting to introduce the two girls at a Fourth of July cotillion in 1828. They were rejected by the other white mothers over Johnson's indignant protests. When Chinn died, Johnson took up with another enslaved African woman named Parthene. While scandalous to the moralists of press and pulpit, Johnson's domestic arrangements did not impede the upward arc of his political career. And colored men wanted white women. They risked brutal punishment or death for observing, much less sampling, the charms of white women, which didn't mean that more than a few black fools didn't try. Among the lowest classes of whites, some women were notorious for favoring Africans as lovers. The less scrupulous among them used their wiles to extract money favors from the duller Negroes. Even the white man's most savage treatment of these aspiring Othellos—and the white woman's shaming of their sisterly Desdemonas—could not extirpate such forbidden desires. Coupling and procreating had a stubborn pride that disregarded taboo and teaching. It was natural that Beverly Snow's mother had named him after a white man, Beverley Randolph, who had served as Virginia's eighth governor in 1788. By heritage and upbringing, Beverly lived in a racially mixed society that pretended it was anything but.

The question facing Beverly in 1829 was whether he should stick around Lynchburg or seek his fortune elsewhere. Beverly needed no reminder that his thirtieth birthday was approaching. If the good news was that he would soon be free, the bad news was that the Commonwealth of Virginia required his removal. According to an 1806 statute, any enslaved person of African descent who obtained his or her freedom had to leave the state within a year or else "be apprehended and sold" back into slavery. Beverly could remain in Lynchburg only if a white man petitioned the state legislature for permission. With an owner as friendly as Susannah Warwick, Beverly might have been able to stay if he wanted. Instead he made plans to depart.

Lynchburg had little to offer a free man of color. The slave traders supplying the tobacco planters with coerced Negro laborers dominated the town's life. A carpenter from the area named Pleasant Roane summed up the appalling difficulties he faced at that time. The free black man, Roane said, was "denied the use and enjoyment of many of the most valuable rights and privileges of freemen [and] subjected in all cases of offences to the most vigorous exactions of penal law." As a result, he added, most free blacks sank into "a state of contempt and degradation."

Beverly figured Washington City could not treat him worse than that. The capital lay in the District of Columbia, located 180 miles northeast of Lynchburg, a ride of several days by coach. Such proximity generated some awareness of its attractions and dangers. Yes, the capital city was known as a perennially indebted municipality of dubious morals. Yes, its haphazard streets and well-hidden charms evoked laughter among European tourists and Virginia squires alike. And yes, there were stories of free colored men who had visited the capital of liberty only to be kidnapped and sold into slavery. But the capital was changing. In the recent presidential election, General Andrew Jackson, hero of the Battle of New Orleans in January 1815, had won more votes than incumbent John Quincy Adams. The first westerner elected to the presidency, Jackson was inaugurated in March 1829 before a vast and adoring crowd. If nothing else, Beverly and Julia could live and work there legally. The capital beckoned not as a promised land but as a refuge, a haven where a colored man just might have room enough to prove himself.

In November 1829, Beverly's day came. Susannah Norvell Warwick did her part to end the stain of slavery on herself and her state by agreeing to manumit her bondsman. Beverly and her husband walked two blocks to the Lynchburg courthouse, where John handed the justice of the peace a handwritten deed of freedom. The justice of the peace copied its standard language into a big bound volume. In exchange for five dollars, John Warwick attested that he did "emancipate, set free, and relinquish all Manner of right to the personal Services of my man Slave Beverly, commonly called Beverly Snow."

John Warwick signed the deed and set his seal in red wax. Snow walked out onto Court Street a free American.

2

BEVERLY AND JULIA aimed to reach Washington City in time for the fall races. In central Virginia, a land known for horses and gambling, this annual autumnal event in the nation's capital was much discussed, and it became Beverly's destination. The journey north was neither difficult nor comfortable. The stagecoach left Lynchburg three times a week; the fare was seventeen dollars. Beverly and Julia would have traveled east on the Lexington Turnpike to Richmond, then north. The carriages were indifferent to the frailties of the human skeleton. "They may be likened to the car portion of the swings at an English fair," wrote Charles Dickens, who made the trip a few years later. They are "roofed, put upon axle-trees and wheels, and curtained with painted canvas. They are covered with mud from the roof to the wheel-tire, and have never been cleaned since they were built."

The broad road on which the coaches bounced was a highway to a less bucolic world. Most of the coach drivers were flamboyant free black men. They dressed in coarse pepper-and-salt suits, excessively patched and darned, particularly at the knees. They wore gray stockings, enormous unblacked high-low shoes (a poor man's boot), and very short trousers. One driver sported mismatched gloves while wielding a short whip and wearing a low-crowned, broad-brimmed black hat. Dickens thought him an insane imitator of an English coachman. The man was right at home on the road to Washington City.

Fredericksburg came as a relief. It was a neatly laid-out town of three thousand people on the Rappahannock River. Founded in 1728, Fredericksburg was older and more genteel than Lynchburg. A boomtown fifty years before, it had settled into stately respectability. Slaveholding plantation owners lived within its gates while cultivating their lands in the adjacent countryside. Fredericksburg also had a substantial community of free colored people, who were, by reputation, religious in tendency, church-going in practice, and Baptist in creed. Beverly Snow was none of those things.

Like many a sore passenger disembarking in Fredericksburg, Beverly and Julia probably staggered down to the dock in search of gentler transport. The daily steamboat that went down the Rappahannock and up the Potomac to Washington City for three dollars and seventy-five cents offered vistas and ease unknown to the rattled prisoners of stage-coaches. After a few soothing hours, the ship docked in Alexandria, the southernmost city in the District of Columbia. At Gadsby's Tavern they boarded another coach, which took them to the Long Bridge, a rickety wooden structure that crossed the Potomac in a northeasterly direction. The planked road, passing just ten feet above the river's turbid waters, was lined with men wielding fishing rods and blunderbusses. Oblivious to the passing horses, these bystanders took aim at the clouds of ducks flying overhead and fired. Fowl fell from the sky as the newcomers sped by in their carriage.

Washington City stood on the far side of the bridge. Barges, barks, and flat-bottom boats lined the northern shore. Over the waters to the south one could see the outline of the new penitentiary and the finer homes of Greenleaf's Point. Beyond that flowed the Eastern Branch, also known as the Anacostia River. To the north, one could glimpse the spires of Georgetown College in the distance. Closer was the opening of Tiber Creek, a channel that allowed small boats to sail into a dock at Eighteenth and B streets (a location now under the pavement of Constitution Avenue). And, from almost anywhere, one could see, on a hill to the east, the magnificent white building of the U.S. Capitol, home of the Congress and citadel of American democracy. The building did not yet have the distinctive dome that was added in the 1860s, but its massive profile impressed nonetheless.

The National Metropolis, as optimistic boosters dubbed it, was promiscuous in its realities. It was the national capital for the slaveholding states of the South. Yet no other American city, with the possible exception of New Orleans, offered free colored people more opportunities. Unlike in Virginia, slavery was receding and liberty growing in the capital city. Between 1800 and 1830, the number of enslaved Negroes had grown faster than the number of free blacks in every southern state. The opposite was true in Washington City. In the year of its founding, 1800, enslaved people had outnumbered free blacks by four to one. When Beverly Snow arrived thirty years later, free Africans outnumbered the enslaved for the first time. Freedom was coming to the federal district.

Yet the number of white men in Washington trafficking in people was growing too. With the frontier states of the South and West opening up for cotton cultivation, distant landowners contracted with brokers to send them enslaved and able-bodied Negroes who could be forced to do the hard work. White families in the Upper South who owned property in people found they could sell their bondsmen, especially healthy young people, for higher prices. In Alexandria, the firm of Franklin and Armfield, located on Duke Street, ranked as the single largest slave-trading syndicate in the nation. When a northerner called on the proprietor, John Armfield, he was surprised to find him "engaging and graceful." Buying and selling humans was a respectable business in Washington City.

There were regular auctions of people at Jesse Brown's Indian Queen Hotel, which occupied most of the block between Sixth and Seventh streets on Pennsylvania Avenue in the heart of the city. "Forty Negroes for sale, in Families," read one advertisement in the *National Intelligencer* newspaper. Africans were held in J. W. Neal & Company's unobtrusive slave prison in the Centre Market. Black people languished at the notorious Yellow House, run by the legendarily cruel William H. Williams, at Seventh Street and Maryland Avenue on the south side of the city. Colored people were sold at a slave pen at Third Street and Pennsylvania Avenue, others taken in chains from the alley behind G Street, just north of City Hall. When one white man first saw such a coffle of slaves he could not help but stare, and a passing colored hack driver called out to him, "See there. Ain't that right down murder? Don't you call that right down murder?"

Many people did. Most did not.

The city itself was the result of a dinner table conversation about slaves and money that had taken place just forty years before. In September

1790, Secretary of the Treasury Alexander Hamilton and Secretary of State Thomas Jefferson dined in Philadelphia and came to an agreement about the location of the country's capital city. The new government of the United States of America, then based in Philadelphia, was struggling for survival. Hamilton, who had the keenest financial mind of any of the nation's founders, wanted the national government to assume the debts incurred by the various states during the War for Independence from Great Britain. The southern states understood that such a move would empower the national government and the bankers of Philadelphia and New York rather more than they wanted. Jefferson told Hamilton that southerners in Congress would oppose his debt plan unless the northerners would assent to establishing the national capital in a more southern location.

The southerners disliked Hamilton's assumption-of-debts scheme, but they disliked even more the standing proposal to move the capital to a district along the Susquehanna River in southern Pennsylvania in 1800. The problem was that, under the liberal influence of Benjamin Franklin and Quaker merchants, Pennsylvania had largely abolished Negro slavery by 1790. No southern man could ignore the implications. If the new capital stood on Pennsylvania soil, they might not be able to bring their servants to the seat of government. A capital free of African slaves might also be taken as prescriptive, a signal of disapproval of slavery elsewhere in the nation. As they ate their dinner Jefferson told Hamilton the southerners in Congress wanted the site of the future capital moved farther south, to a lightly populated ten-mile square along the Potomac River to be carved out of Maryland and Virginia, both states where slavery was legal. Hamilton had no objection. High finance and human slavery were reconciled in the coordinates of the new capital city.

Northerners and southerners alike had expected a grand metropolis to emerge on the spot. To that end, President George Washington asked Pierre Charles L'Enfant, a French engineer of impressive ego, to lay out a plan for the city. Influenced by his time in Paris, L'Enfant designed a series of broad boulevards radiating out from the city center. The first president also sponsored a public competition to design a building to house the

Congress. The sketches of architect William Thornton, a liberty-loving emigrant from Britain via the West Indies, impressed both Jefferson and Washington, and his design was selected. As constructed in the late 1790s, the grandeur of Thornton's Capitol inspired visions of a grand metropolis. "I doubt not it will be the most splendid and beautiful City in the world in a few years," William Thornton wrote to a friend in 1796.

He was off by only a century or two. Within a few years Thornton's premature optimism gave way to a run-down reality. After its founding in 1800, the capital attracted a transient population of congressmen and senators who lived in hotels and dingy boardinghouses along Pennsylvania Avenue and who returned to their home states when Congress was not in session. Amidst the scattered dwellings, pockets of prosperity emerged. A society of ladies and gentlemen took shape in the presidential mansion at Sixteenth Street and the nearby homes of his cabinet secretaries, as well as the opulent residences of the diplomats of England, France, and Russia. A community of clerks and shopkeepers grew up to serve government officials and local landowners. But the speculative dreams of George Washington and his cronies who envisioned a booming city with rising property values suffered expensive disappointment. Few Americans moved to the capital. The roads were primitive, the accommodations cramped, the attractions minimal, the summers infernal. The speculators went bankrupt, the locals made do, and the contrast between the city's ambitions and realities often startled visitors.

"I saw the dome of the Capitol from considerable distance at the end of a straight road," wrote Harriet Martineau, a popular English author of the day who visited not long after Beverly Snow arrived. ". . . I was taken by surprise on finding myself beneath the splendid building, so sordid are the enclosures and houses on its very verge. We wound round its base, and entered Pennsylvania Avenue, the only one of the grand avenues intended to centre in the Capitol which has been built with any completeness."

Three decades after the capital's founding, Washington was eager to escape its village past. Among the peculiarities of local speech was the term "Washington City." "We no longer say London town or Paris city," observed the editors of the *National Intelligencer*. "Whether this addition be more necessary in the case of Washington, whose claim to it might be forgotten, we do not know." Dickens thought the motley metropolis resembled a western frontier town in its unkempt appearance and erratic weather. A typical day in Washington, he complained, was "scorching hot in the morning, and freezing cold in the afternoon, with an occasional tornado of wind and dust." Here and there rows of buildings sprang up, but by far the greater number of the houses stood far apart. The streets were unusually wide and unusually empty. "The whole affair," said another visitor, "looks as if some giant had scattered a box of his child's toys at random on the ground."

Yet the core of an incipient city was visible. Pennsylvania Avenue between the Capitol and the presidential mansion was lined with Lombardy poplar trees that shaded hotels and shops, boardinghouses, taverns, apothecaries, bookstores, grog shops, faro banks, jewelers, and tailors. The surrounding blocks were lined with wood-frame and brick houses, hardware stores, milliners' shops, horse stables, and the anonymous slave pens. To the west, in front of the executive mansion, stood President's Square, now lined with grand homes. Two blocks north of the Avenue on Seventh Street stood the Patent Office, the Land Office, and St. Patrick's Church, constituting an almost grand square (in the area now known as Gallery Place). To the east, between Fourth and Sixth streets, the massive unfinished edifice of City Hall anchored Judiciary Square. And above it all, on the eastern hill, stood the ever-present spectacle of the Capitol.

"The mists of the morning still hung around this magnificent building when it first broke upon our view," wrote Frances Trollope in her best-selling book *Domestic Manners of the Americans,* "and I am not sure that the effect produced was not the greater for this circumstance. It stands so finely too, high, and alone."

This was the view from Beverly Snow's new neighborhood.

Upon their arrival, Beverly and Julia most likely stayed with friends who had migrated from Virginia before and knew the ways of the capital, which were certainly different from those of Lynchburg. Not only were there some four thousand free people of color living and working in Washington City, but also the fortunes of their friends and family who were enslaved varied widely. Washington was not a plantation where hard labor was ruled by brutality. The owners of slaves often hired them out to work in other places. Slaves for hire worked as waiters in the hotels on Pennsylvania Avenue and as masons on the construction of public buildings like City Hall. They helped dig the new Chesapeake & Ohio Canal. While their owners received payment for their labor, the bondsmen enjoyed a degree of independence unknown among people enslaved anywhere in the southern states.

Beverly and Julia might have noticed that women outnumbered men in the city among the free people of color. In the finer homes, black women worked as domestics and seamstresses. The free men of color earned their money as hack drivers, cooks, and laborers and spent it on their families or favorite pastimes. Many of the free people of color were poor and shiftless. Some were prosperous, and others were getting there. Seventy-five colored people paid taxes in Washington City in 1830, triple the number just six years earlier. A handful of them owned more than one thousand dollars in personal property. The ablest among them enjoyed positions of trust and confidence with powerful white people.

Colored men, for example, found a particular niche as messengers in the government offices. The city's burgeoning class of cabinet secretaries, auditors, and officeholders increasingly conducted business in documents delivered by the notoriously insecure U.S. Postal Service. The art of intercepting and reading a gentleman's letters had reached new levels of refinement. The careful public servant might avoid a world of trouble—even save his own job—by finding a trustworthy colored man to assist him at a salary less than the white messenger's $350 a year.

Capital life could be hard for any newcomer, much less a free man of color, but it had consolations too, including many taverns serving endless draughts of gin slings, gin cocktails, sherry cobblers, mint juleps, snakeroot bitters, timber doodle, and eggnog, not to mention Madeira wine from Portugal and hock wine from Germany. All in all, Washington City exuded a certain common charm for small-town folk like Beverly and Julia. It might not have loomed as large as legend had it in Lynchburg. The capital did, however, have an amiable virtue: One could easily get drunk there.

3

IT DID NOT take long for Beverly to adopt the customs of Washington City. His goal was to work at the fall races, which were sponsored by the Jockey Club, a conclave of local horsemen. If a free man, white or colored, wanted to set up an ordinary—a stand selling food or drink—at the racetrack, he had to get a license. They sold for three dollars, payable to the clerk of the circuit court.

Beverly made his way to the courthouse, which stood on Louisiana Avenue (later renamed Indiana Avenue) between Fourth and Sixth streets. The building, spanning 252 feet across its front, exceeded anything Beverly had ever seen, both in size and shabbiness. The fragrance of a nearby hog-fattening operation did not improve the atmosphere of the place. When Beverly finally arrived, he was too late to obtain a license for the races that opened on October 20. He had to settle for a license for the November 5 races.

All the while, Beverly was scouting out possible locations for a more permanent oyster house, something like his operation in Lynchburg, but better. One possibility was Centre Market, which occupied a vast plaza on the south side of Pennsylvania Avenue between Seventh and Ninth streets. It was home to dozens of farmers' stalls offering a cornucopia of produce: raspberries, melons, pumpkins, squash, corn, rutabagas, and the newly popular "love apples," otherwise known as tomatoes. There were also at least ten butchers on the premises. Slave dealer J. W. Neal had an office there as well, peddling a different sort of flesh. On market days—Monday, Wednesday, Friday, and Saturday—the place ran thick with people, white and colored alike. Beverly wanted something in the vicinity.

Another factor in Beverly's calculations: proximity to the hotels. The biggest was the Indian Queen, Jesse Brown's four-story palace graced by a large swinging sign featuring the brown-eyed, ruby-lipped visage of Pocahontas, the legendary Indian maiden. Brown's hotel was a destination for every kind of traveler from around the country, and for good reason. Brown was an exuberant hotelier of corpulent girth. Beverly was an experienced cook who knew how to prepare a fine table, but he could learn something from this showman of the carving board.

Jesse Brown would march out onto the hard-packed dirt of Pennsylvania Avenue with extended hand to greet his arriving guests as they descended from their coaches. In his huge dining room on the second floor, Brown boasted of fresh vegetables every day and carved the meat himself. He announced the excellencies of his offerings—fish, beef, or fowl—while inviting those seated at the tables around him to send up their plates.

"I have a delicious quarter of mutton from the Valley of Virginia," Brown would proclaim in stentorian tones above the clatter of the crockery and the din of steel forks and knives.

"Let me send you a rare slice, Mr. A."

"Colonel B, will you not have a bone?"

"Mrs. C, send up your plate for a piece of kidney."

"Mrs. D, there is a fat and tender mongrel goose at the other end of the table."

Beverly, fresh from the frontier, faced some serious city competition in his dream of setting up an eating house. Fortunately for him, most hotel-keepers were not so capable as Jesse Brown. Boardinghouse guests scared away by the bloody carcasses and soggy legumes spread before them on some dismal sideboard would surely take to the streets of the city to find something edible. Beverly planned to be ready for them.

When the races finally opened over the course of several lustrous weekends in the fall of 1830, Beverly imbibed Washington City at its most opulent. Delegations of sporting men crowded into the Indian Queen, the National, and other hotels along Pennsylvania Avenue. Planters from Maryland, Virginia, and the Carolinas prosecuted the business of the turf as a pastime. To them cost was nothing. They bought stallions at staggeringly large prices, arranged for studs, wagered with gusto, and enjoyed society like English noblemen. The big event took place at the Jockey

Club's racetrack on Meridian Hill. The track consisted of a long dirt oval, one mile in circumference, fifty feet wide, and a low-slung viewing stand. In the company of his fellow barkeeps, Beverly set up an ordinary in a wooden booth in the middle of the racing oval. While customers perched on the roofs to watch the horses, he worked the crowd, dispensing ale, selling food, pocketing coins, and taking stock of his new customers.

"You must not be astonished at hearing that a number of beautiful females were present, sitting exposed on the tops and boxes of carriages, and in other conspicuous seats," wrote one European visitor, delighted to see America's reputation for puritanical propriety was overblown. To his astonished eyes it seemed that "every line of separation is so entirely obliterated that where there are men you are sure to meet women." Indeed the Jockey Club races attracted people of all description—white, African, mulatto, dandy, mechanic, lady, and lad. They cheered, clapped, shouted, hugged, and cursed. There was laughter, quarreling, drinking, and fighting.

Not all of Washington society approved of this gay scene. In recent years, a new religious fervor had infused much of the nation and the capital too. Around the city, men organized temperance societies, dedicated to curbing their consumption of spirits. In the surrounding countryside, camp meetings, sponsored by flamboyant traveling preachers, offered salvation to growing crowds of men and women, both black and white, who wanted a holy presence in their lives. The idea of reform had taken root, but it hardly dampened the popular passion for the horses.

President Jackson's arrival at the fall races in October and November 1830 was memorable. He came sauntering up Fourteenth Street astride his favorite gray steed, wearing a high white fur hat with a broad band of black crepe. As he and his entourage swept into the grounds of the racetrack they found their spot amidst murmurs and congratulatory shouts. The old general loved a crowd and he loved wagering large sums of money with full confidence in his mastery of the equestrian arts, a delusion that was both costly and incurable. In the main event, Mr. Burwell's horse bested all comers in the two-mile race, and Jackson's pony wasn't even close. Crestfallen, the president went home with a thinner purse.

The fall races closed for good a few days later, but Beverly would not go out of business for long. He let his newfound friends and customers around town know that he would soon open an oyster house on Seventh Street.

In this first venture, Beverly knew what he wanted to serve: a variety of cooked birds dressed with sauces and served with champagne or wine. What he didn't know was where he should advertise. He had two choices. The longest-lived newspaper in town was the *National Intelligencer,* which had an office around the corner on D Street. Edited by two gentlemen of good standing, William Seaton and Joseph Gales, the *Intelligencer'*s editorials treated Negroes with some respect. But the newspaper that everybody seemed to be talking about was the *United States' Telegraph,* edited by a pugnacious and profane former army general named Duff Green, who worked out of a print shop on E Street. The *Telegraph* was as scrappy and aggressive as its irascible owner. Every issue came emblazoned with Green's creed, "Power is always stealing from the many to the few." When debating the issues of the day, Green proved a cantankerous philosopher. His arguments in defense of slavery and states' rights included learned references to pistols, canes, and cowhide. One particularly frank exchange with a political opponent left Green with several broken bones and a dislocated leg. The *Telegraph,* needless to say, had a lot of readers.

Beverly did not have to care that Duff Green defended the slave masters. Most white men did. What mattered to the newcomer from Lynchburg was that people read his sheet. The way Beverly looked at it, no matter what words came out of the white man's mouth, some food had to go in. Slavers or not, they were all potential customers. So Beverly gave his dollar to Duff Green's printer, who typeset the handwritten text in hot lead, and the ad appeared in the *Telegraph* the next day:

BEVERLY SNOW
7th Street, a few doors south of the Patriotic Bank,

Respectfully informs his friends and the public generally, that he has opened an establishment at the above place where he will be ready to accommodate them on the shortest notice. He has made arrangements with the Steamboats to supply with Canvas-Back Ducks, Venison, Norfolk Fish,

Oysters, and every other luxury which the market affords.
His table will be furnished with Chafing Dishes and West
India Jellies.

With this elegant missive Beverly injected himself into Washington
City life, like no colored man ever had. Regardless of race, his enterprise
was original. The ordinaries and inns of Washington served one or two
meals a day at a fixed time and price, at a common table. The underpaid
cooks were indifferent to the quality of their fare, and the customers were
expected to help themselves to whatever landed in front of them. This
arrangement, common in hotels as well, worked well for assertive men
seated near the middle of the table. It could be frustrating for those with
more particular tastes, as well as for women and children, not to mention
for the wayfaring stranger, or anyone seated at the far corners.

Beverly's new place resembled more what the French called a *table
d'hôte,* or restaurant. These were a new sort of eating places, already common in Paris, that served a standard daily meal, usually roasted meat, at
a communal table. The term "restaurant" had first come into popular use
in France as the name of a *table d'hôte* serving light restorative (*"restaura-
tif"*) dishes such as beef broth. By the late eighteenth century the Parisian
restaurant had become a refectory that offered seating at private tables and
single servings of food from a somewhat varied menu.

Beverly Snow was the first culinary entrepreneur in the capital city to
offer this new restorative experience. How many people in Washington
City had a skilled cook who could serve them canvasback duck, a bird
renowned for the subtlety of its taste, at a cozy table with a chafing dish to
warm their victuals? Not many. Beverly offered a dining room like those
in the finest Virginia homes, like the one he grew up in, and he offered it
to anyone who could pay. For aspiring people in a sometimes coarse city
such an offer of comfort constituted an unusual treat, especially when the
price was right. Beverly's customers had a tendency to return.

B EVERLY PAID ATTENTION to the peculiar eating habits of Americans. "They consume an extraordinary quantity of bacon," observed Mrs. Trollope, duly appalled. "Ham and beef-steaks appear morning, noon, and night. In eating they mix things together with the strangest incongruity imaginable. I have seen eggs and oysters eaten together; the sempiternal ham with apple-sauce, beef-steak with stewed peaches and salt fish with onions." She complained of a "great want of skill in the preparation of sauces," a paucity of second courses, and a general want of intelligent conversation because men and women rarely dined together.

Beverly intuited that a more coordinated and convivial repast might appeal. He and Julia probably lived in an apartment above his eatery on the west side of Seventh Street, just south of D Street. Their customers came from the neighborhood: lamblike tourists looking for the Patent Office, strutting senators, dour clerks, and ladies in their carriages. Before long the better sorts of people stopped in. Mrs. Julia Seaton, the wife of William Seaton, coeditor of the *National Intelligencer,* became a patron. So did William Bradley, president of the Patriotic Bank at the corner of Seventh and D, which disturbed Anne Royall, the capital's only female editor. As sole proprietor of a crusading independent publication called *Paul Pry,* Royall was a scourge of Christianity, temperance, abolition, and other right-thinking causes. She was appalled that a free man of color like Snow could become Bradley's "particular friend."

As his next newspaper advertisement made clear, however, Beverly welcomed attention:

LOOK AT THIS!
The subscriber takes this method of informing his friends
that he has just received a fresh supply of very fine VENISON
which will be served up in the best style for the accommoda-
tion of his customers.

BEVERLY SNOW

It did not hurt Beverly's prospects that his doors opened just one block
north of Centre Market, the commercial hub of the city. The surrounding
streets housed dry-goods dealers, glassblowers, tanners, dealers in coal
and firewood, and two wool mills, not to mention assorted butchers and
greengrocers.

This parade of humanity gave lie to the outdated joke that Washington was but a swampy village. The National Metropolis was beginning
to live up to its billing, with a diverse population from all corners of the
young republic. The southerners of Washington City carried themselves
with ease and frank courtesy, observed Harriet Martineau, while the New
Englanders were deferential to, if not cowed by, rivals who carried guns.
"One can tell the New England member [of Congress] in the open air by
his deprecatory walk," Martineau observed. "He seems to bear in mind per-
petually that he cannot fight a duel, while other people can." As for visitors
from the West, they beggared description. "One had a neck like a crane
making an interval of inches between stock and chin," Martineau reported.
"Another wears no cravat, apparently because there is no room for one."

The growing city also attracted another group of newcomers, the
young white men known as "mechanics." In America at the time any
manual laborer, skilled or unskilled, might be called a mechanic, but in
Washington City, the term seemed reserved for unskilled foreign workers, often Irish or German, who were brought in by the boatload from
northern European ports, lured by contractors hired to pave Pennsylvania
Avenue and dig the Chesapeake & Ohio Canal. When a cholera epidemic
struck in late summer 1832, more than four hundred and fifty people succumbed to the disease within three months, with white mechanics and
free blacks, who often lived in unsanitary conditions, suffering the most.

Along with the influx of new immigrants came Americans with new
ideas that some considered shocking, if not dangerous. Some residents,

black and white, had begun to denounce slavery, not merely as unfortunate or cruel but as illegal, a violation of human rights. The liberal-minded whites who favored African colonization found themselves facing a new argument: that America should simply abolish the practice of enslaving people of African descent. Beverly did not identify himself as one of the so-called abolitionists, but he soon enough fell in with those who did.

He and Julia befriended a barber, Isaac Newton Cary, who owned the Emporium of Fashion barbershop on Sixth Street across from John Gadsby's newly renovated National Hotel on Pennsylvania Avenue. Cary, who hailed from Fredericksburg, was the son of a prosperous free black man, Thomas Cary Sr., who admired Sir Isaac Newton and named his son in his honor. Known for his excellent sense and scrupulous conduct, Isaac Cary seemed to enjoy the respect of all who knew him, white and black. In his business, Cary touted himself to gentlemen staying at the nearby hotels as a "Professor of Shaving and adept at Hair-Cutting." With a fellow barber, John Fleet, he was planning to open a second tonsorial emporium at Twelfth Street and Pennsylvania Avenue.

Isaac Cary did not advertise the fact, but he and his brother Thomas Jr. were also active opponents of slavery who sought to undermine the institution of racial bondage at every opportunity. Isaac Cary sold subscriptions to *Freedom's Journal*, the first antislavery newspaper published by black men. When it ceased publication, he became an agent for another antislavery sheet, called the *Genius of Universal Emancipation*. In the summer of 1830, Cary had supported the National Negro Convention in Philadelphia, the first gathering of free black men from all of America. Cary did not attend the meeting but welcomed the convention's declaration denouncing slavery and African colonization, and he agreed to serve on the local committee to advance its work, an audacious and potentially dangerous undertaking. In the slaveholding capital, Snow's new friends, Isaac and Thomas Cary, qualified as subversives.

So did Cary's friend John Francis Cook, also from Fredericksburg. Trained to be a shoemaker, Cook had come to the capital in 1826 when his aunt, Lethe Tanner, a light-skinned free black woman who ran a vegetable stand in President's Square, bought his freedom. At eighteen years of age, Cook enrolled in a school for blacks near the corner of Fourteenth and H streets, run by teacher and antislavery activist John Prout. As Cook learned to read and write, his capacious intelligence became evident, and not just to colored people. He soon obtained a job in the Land Office, housed in a grand building on Seventh Street, where he worked for a white man named John Wilson, who became his friend for life. Cook's "indefatigable application" was "a matter of astonishment" to Wilson, who said he had "seen nothing in all his observation to surpass and scarcely to equal it."

Before long Cook was acting on his irrepressible lifelong imperative to educate, organize, and improve the lives of his fellows. When banker William Bradley manumitted one of his slaves in 1831, Cook organized a celebration with other young black men featuring the reading of antislavery poetry and tracts. Cook would go on to organize what he called the Philomathean Talking Society, also known as the Young Man's Moral and Literary Society, where he condemned slavery and encouraged young black men to prepare themselves for freedom. Some white men viewed Cook with mistrust, but among black folks he was widely admired as a prodigy.

Beverly probably shook hands at some point with a friend of Isaac Cary's named Benjamin Lundy, a white man who often came visiting from Baltimore. At forty-one years of age, Lundy was the itinerant editor and publisher of the *Genius of Universal Emancipation*. The *Genius*, as it was known, attracted loyal readers among free blacks and some whites because its pages exposed and denounced every aspect of the American slave system. Lundy reported the stories of injustice that the capital's respectable newspapers—the *Intelligencer, Telegraph*, and *Globe*—rarely mentioned.

Lundy had grown up without much formal education in a Quaker family in New Jersey. As a young man he moved to Wheeling, West Virginia, where he roomed with a gambler and consorted with "wild and fashionable" friends. But when he glimpsed a coffle of enslaved people being forcibly transported south, he was stunned and disturbed. He decided to dedicate his life to fighting the slave system. He organized an antislavery society in Ohio and in 1821 started publishing the *Genius* wherever he happened to live. He moved to Tennessee, and then, in 1828, to Baltimore, where he supported himself and his family back in Ohio with the sale of subscriptions. "One dollar per annum," he told his customers, "always to be paid in advance."

The *Genius* was an early gem of American journalism. Barely four inches wide and eight inches tall, each issue came emblazoned with the words of Thomas Jefferson's Declaration of Independence: "We hold these truths to be self-evident: that all men are created equal, and endowed by their Creator with certain inalienable rights; that among these are life, liberty, and the pursuit of happiness." In its tiny pages Lundy reported on the terrible realities of continental slavery. He catalogued the depredations of slave traders, the ingenious methods of escape used by bondsmen, the regrettable quiescence of leading churchmen, the struggle against slavery in England, and so on. Despite the living nightmare of its subject, the *Genius* managed to exude a hearty outrage that reflected the editor's tenacity and good humor.

As Lundy's radically simple proposal for immediate emancipation of America's two million enslaved Africans gained currency in the late 1820s, the *Genius* gained readers faster than ever. With subscriptions growing, Lundy could afford to hire another editor. He chose a headstrong former printer's devil from Massachusetts named William Lloyd Garrison and imbued him with his own conviction to do constant battle against slavery.

"Nothing is wanting . . . but the will," Lundy told Garrison. He frequently published a sketch of a slave coffle under the title "Hail Columbia," the name of a popular patriotic anthem of the United States, with the injunction "LOOK AT IT, again and again." The very idea of the United States of America was at stake, Lundy insisted. His new assistant editor was captivated by the clarity of his mentor's moral vision. "Garrison sought a cause," said one of his biographers. "Lundy had found one."

Their profession was hazardous. One of Lundy's stories in the *Genius* exposed Austin Woolfolk, Baltimore's leading dealer of enslaved persons, as a beast who regularly destroyed families by selling off children for the sake of cash profit. This innovative example of investigative journalism did not go over well. Woolfolk responded by waylaying Lundy on the street and beating him severely. Lundy pressed charges. A Baltimore judge ruled that slave trading was a beneficial activity and that "Lundy had received no more than merited chastisement."

Lundy went back to work. His fearless example helped launch Garrison's career as one of nineteenth-century America's most influential journalists. Lundy taught Garrison how to channel his passion into reporting:

how to find stories, to tell them, and to name names. When Garrison likened another transporter of slaves, Francis Todd, to a highway robber in the pages of the *Genius,* city authorities charged him with libel. Garrison was convicted and fined a thousand dollars. He left for Boston with no intention of returning or paying the fine. The outstanding bill imperiled Lundy's livelihood, so the editor amicably parted ways with his protégé, expressing respect for his passion, if not his prudence. Garrison retreated to the safety of Boston to launch his own publication, *The Liberator,* which would become the leading abolitionist publication in America for the next three decades, until the slave system was abolished.

As Garrison headed north in the fall of 1832, Lundy headed the other direction. He moved south to Washington with an audacious plan: to publish the *Genius of Universal Emancipation* in the seat of the U.S. government. He enlisted Jacob Janney, a young Quaker, to sell subscriptions.

Lundy did not hide his purpose. By relocating to the capital, he told his readers that he hoped "to become more generally acquainted with intelligent and influential men from every part of the Union, and thus to increase the facilities of collecting and disseminating important information" about American slavery. He rented an office on E Street, near Tenth Street, just a few doors down from the print shop where Duff Green's *Telegraph* rolled off the presses daily. Soon Lundy was nose to nose with Green, arguing about the morality of the slave system.

The editors of the *American Spectator,* a popular monthly magazine, faintly praised Lundy as a "warm-hearted philanthropist" who was more than a little light in the head. Talking about slavery in Washington City "must be done with . . . caution and circumspection," warned the *Spectator.* Otherwise "the lighted match is applied to a train of gun-powder." They advised Lundy that his "airy dream" of advocating abolition of slavery in Washington City might be blown "sky high."

Lundy scoffed at such cringing sentiments.

"Shall American Statesmen fear to look this evil in the face, while it is yet in its infancy?" he asked in the next issue of the *Genius.* His answer was no. It was such outspoken decency that touched the likes of Beverly Snow, Isaac Cary, and John Cook. When Lundy came to Washington they lodged and fed him. In the eyes of the law, they were all subversives, black or white.

Politics and slavery aside, Beverly Snow could see the possibilities of Washington City. Some of the colored men around him already had more money than the average white man. Lynch Wormley, a native of the polyglot African island of Madagascar, ran a popular livery stable at Fourteenth and G streets. He and his four children owned more than a dozen lots of property all over town. David Jones, a colored shoemaker, had two houses on G Street and a third on F Street. A black man named Moses Hepburn was building a home on E Street worth almost three thousand dollars. When Beverly met a capable black fellow named William Walker, who owned a house north of President's Square, he made him a business partner. Beverly Snow was making more plans.

5

B EVERLY'S FIRST WINTER in Washington was a season of cold reflection. The Potomac River froze solid and the draymen could drive their carts across the ice, the first time that had happened in thirty years. The snow drifted knee deep around the presidential mansion, and construction of the Chesapeake & Ohio Canal ceased. One day in February, an eclipse of the sun brought an eerie dusk to the white landscape of the city for three hours. Beverly and Julia stayed warm by tending the fires of his kitchen stove.

The latest affliction facing colored people was the white man's enthusiasm for African colonization. The Fourteenth Annual Meeting of the American Colonization Society, held in the Capitol on January 19, 1831, provoked more than a little discussion in the boardinghouses and the hotels. According to a sympathetic account in the *Intelligencer,* dozens of leading gentlemen attended, including senators, congressmen, judges, and clergymen. The meeting passed high-toned resolutions calling for renewed efforts to promote the migration of freed American slaves to a colony on the west coast of Africa called Liberia. The society, its leaders declared, had already made much progress. In the past year, they had collected more than $27,000 and sent two boatloads of black people to Liberia.

African colonization for free black Americans was a venerable idea, enjoying wide support among educated white Americans uncomfortable with the contradiction between America's revolutionary ideals and American slavery. Colonization had been first proposed almost fifty years before by William Thornton, the late architect of the Capitol. As a young man, Thornton had seen the workings of slavery at his family's plantation on the island of Tortola in the West Indies. In the late 1780s, he traveled up and down the eastern seaboard touting the idea to free people of color and interested whites. He attracted some support but never succeeded in getting anyone to actually emigrate. His family in Tortola virtually disowned him, and he soon dropped the notion in favor of his idea of designing the Capitol.

Thornton's idea was revived around 1810 by Paul Cuffe, a black sea captain who lived in Westport, Massachusetts. Convinced that the black people needed to get away from whites if they were to have any peace and happiness, Cuffe organized an initial expedition to Sierra Leone, where a small community of free blacks was established. Colonization gained credibility and prestige among whites in 1817 with the founding of the American Colonization Society in Washington. The society attracted gentlemen, from both the North and South, determined to do something about the practice of slavery, which all agreed was a blot on America's democratic aspirations. The founders included William Thornton, Henry Clay, Senator Theodore Frelinghuysen of New Jersey, and Bushrod Washington, a justice on the U.S. Supreme Court and nephew of the first president.

In Washington City, most of the gentlemen friendly to colored people also supported the idea. William Bradley, friend and patron of Beverly Snow, was a colonization man. So was William Seaton, the editor of the *Intelligencer.* So was Francis Scott Key, the Georgetown attorney famed as author of the popular song "The Star-Spangled Banner."

The discussion of colonization warmed with the weather in early 1831, not the least among those who would be most affected. On a windy Wednesday evening in late April, a large and respectable crowd of colored people gathered at the African Methodist Episcopal Church on South Capitol Street. The church belonged to a network of black Methodist congregations founded in Philadelphia in the 1790s by a former slave named Richard Allen, who had tired of mistreatment by white clergymen. Colored Methodists from Maryland to Maine followed his example, and by 1831, the AME churches constituted the largest black institution in the country, with ten thousand parishioners in every northern state and several southern ones.

The meeting, open to the public, was chaired by John Prout, headmaster at the school for colored children on H Street. The assembled crowd passed a series of resolutions addressed to the American Colonization Society. The free people of color in Washington City announced that they viewed the society's efforts with "distrust." They affirmed their ties to the United States, insisting "the soil which gave them birth is their only true and veritable home." In a nod to Ben Lundy (who probably was there) and William Lloyd Garrison (who was not), the attendees approved a resolution recommending that people of color subscribe to and read the *Genius of Universal Emancipation* and *The Liberator.* The meeting, as reported in the *Intelligencer,* signaled a new development. African American political action had come to the nation's capital for the first time.

Beverly Snow, more interested in cooking than colonization, forged ahead with his business ambitions. In the fall of 1832 he and William Walker prepared to move their eating house on Seventh Street to a more central location. Among Beverly's new acquaintances was a white man named John Withers who promised something better. Withers, at age fifty-five, was nearly twenty-five years older than Beverly. A liberal-minded businessman from Alexandria, he used the profits of his mercantile firm to buy no less than seventeen different pieces of real estate up and down Pennsylvania Avenue. He also engaged in philanthropy and eventually became the greatest benefactor of the Colombian College (which evolved into today's George Washington University).

Beverly eyed with the most interest a three-story brick building that Withers had just constructed on the northwest corner of Sixth and Pennsylvania, at the cost of twelve thousand dollars. This fresh edifice rose between the imposing bulk of Jesse Brown's Indian Queen Hotel on the Avenue and its chief rival, John Gadsby's National Hotel around the corner. A drugstore already occupied the corner shop, between Mr. Handy's Hat Store and his friend Isaac Cary's Emporium of Fashion. Beverly liked the company.

On the sidewalk in front there was an outdoor stairwell surrounded by a cast-iron guardrail. The stairs descended to a basement door, behind which lay several large, gloomy, and empty rooms. Beverly envisioned this underground lair as the home of his new eating house. He would set up a basement kitchen, just like he had in the Warwicks' house in Lynchburg.

It was a novel idea. A basement was about the last place you would expect to find respectable people eating dinner. Slaves and servants, maybe. Ladies and gentlemen, rarely. But John Withers went along, agreeing to provide Beverly and his partner with tables and chairs to furnish the dining rooms and bar. In the farthest recesses of the basement, Beverly installed a kitchen and larder. On the wall outside the entrance, William Walker hung a large sign, hand painted in red and black, which announced "Refectory: Snow and Walker's."

At the same time, Beverly wanted his customers to know the place by a different and more evocative name with a classical theme. In a round of advertisements placed in the *Intelligencer,* the *Globe,* and the *Telegraph* in October 1832, Beverly announced a grander name for his new establishment:

SNOW's EPICUREAN EATING HOUSE
The proprietor has spared neither pains nor expense to secure the comfort of his guests, and, if a decided disposition to oblige, coupled with a choice and well-stored Larder and bar, can command patronage, he confidently challenges competition.

Beverly invited "the citizen and the stranger alike" to call on his service, pledging himself to "their good entertainment." His basement eatery soon filled with new and old customers.

Beverly, it seems, had read some ancient Greek philosophy over the years (not hard to do in Washington) and had come to admire Epicurus, the philosopher of pleasure and virtue, whose thinking so appealed to Thomas Jefferson. The former president, who had died in 1826, had called Epicurean thought "the most rational system remaining of the philosophy of the ancients, as frugal of vicious indulgence and fruitful of virtue as the hyperbolic extravagancies of rival sects."

Like Jefferson, Beverly found in Epicurus a kindred spirit. The Athenian sage held the unique view that happiness was proof of a virtuous life, which was rather different from what most Christians believed. Thus the name had its risks. In a city where evangelical Christianity was fast becoming the dominant religion and a country where many prided themselves on republican simplicity, the word "Epicurean" often evoked corrupt indulgence. When Alexander Hamilton called Jefferson "an Epicurean" he may have been alluding to the not-quite-secret fact that Jefferson kept a slave mistress, Sally Hemings. He certainly did not speak as a friend. An epicure, in common usage, was an immoral atheist, devoted to sensualism, or, more loosely and less negatively, a gourmand devoted to pleasures of the table. Beverly did not accept the former charge, nor dispute the latter. Like other contemporary admirers, he did not recognize Epicurus as hedonistic or corrupt. Anyone who read his maxims knew that Epicurus was among the least indulgent of the ancients. "The Wise Man ought never to drink to Excess," he advised his followers. "Neither must he spend the Nights in Reveling and Feasting."

The name of Beverly's new place appealed to a common sentiment emerging in the forward-thinking middle class: Epicurus had something to offer to the people of America. The same month Beverly lit his new stove, the lead story in *The New-England Magazine*, a popular national publication, declared, "Of all the philosophers of antiquity, whose tenets are frequently and familiarly referred to, Epicurus is the least understood in his moral doctrine and the most unjustly reproached in life and character."

The author, a physician named Charles Caldwell, emphasized the man's modernity. "The virtue of Epicurus was not that of the ancient Stoics or Cynics nor of the modern Puritans," he wrote. "It was, however, greatly preferable to either; because it was much more conformable to the constitution of human nature."

The spiritual appeal of Epicurus for Beverly is not hard to conjure. Epicurus lived in a time of tyranny. So did Beverly. Epicurus did not take much interest in the religion of his day, saying the gods had little interest in the affairs of mortals. Beverly could see that the Christian god did not worry much about the suffering of Africans in America. Epicurus counseled avoidance of public affairs and the illegal use of women, prudent advice for a free man of color in slaveholding Washington City. For Beverly the hardy Epicurean precepts offered protection from the drink and sloth that enervated so many former bondsmen when they gained their freedom. Yet Epicurean thinking did not require him to subscribe to the white man's Puritan asceticism or his self-righteous patriotism. Epicurus joined pleasure and virtue and invited all men to pursue both. His way of thinking was natural and easy, which had been Beverly's style since Lynchburg. He was proud to call himself an Epicurean. Many Americans were.

"No word has more censurably been perverted from its original and proper signification than the word EPICUREANISM," declared the *Boston Masonic Mirror* in October 1830. "So far from being, in its proper sense, luxury or sensual enjoyment it is derived from the name of a sage of transcendent genius . . . EPICURUS, who lived three hundred years before Christ and was the most philosophical and temperate, if not the most abstemious, Grecian of his time." Epicurus, said the *Masonic Mirror*, "dared to expose the absurd theology of his day, and in his life and doctrines gave a perpetual rebuke to vice and immorality of every kind. . . . Such was Epicurus, and what rational man would not be his disciple?"

Beverly must have asked himself that very question, because in June 1833, he provided a direct answer in another advertisement in the *Globe*:

> BEVERLY SNOW: THE DISCIPLE OF EPICURUS
> And grand Caterer to the good taste of a kind public . . .
> will, THIS DAY at 11 o'clock serve up a splendid GREEN TURTLE in Soup, dressed in Port Wine.

Beverly's whimsy mixed self-confidence with self-deprecation:

> Mr. SNOW feels certain he can give universal satisfaction, and his Champaigne, though it may offend the purse can never affect the head. . . . His bills of fare can only be surpassed by his bills of cost, which to make a bad pun, are generally very fair things. Without further comments on his own merits, he will close with a promise to be liberal.

It is safe to say that no black man, free or enslaved, had ever dared to speak so freely and publicly to the white people of Washington City. The man from Lynchburg turned the insult of Epicureanism into a compliment and a calling card for his new eatery. His gambit was not only intellectually bold. It was commercially astute.

The Epicurean Eating House constituted one of the first true restaurants in Washington City, if not the very first. Of course, there had long been oyster houses, the fast-food outlets of their day. There were ordinaries, serving simple food and drink, like the one Beverly ran at the racetrack. And there were other cooks feeling the French influence. Ben Perley Poore, a newspaperman who chronicled capital life in the nineteenth century, credited Belgian cook Joseph Boulanger with operating Washington's first restaurant on G Street during the Jackson administration. But Boulanger was still a steward in Jackson's kitchen in 1832, when the Epicurean Eating House opened its doors.

The truth was Beverly had no rivals in the sophistication of his table service. He offered the basic features of a Parisian-style restaurant to the capital when few did so. He was among the first cooks to seat groups of patrons at their own tables; to serve meals at unspecified times; to provide a menu from which customers made their own choices; and to tout health and ambiance as part of the eating experience. He was at the forefront of creating a new sort of public place, a comfortable setting open to all, where people could go to eat and drink privately. Beverly Snow was helping to invent an institution that endures to this day: the Washington restaurant.

At the time, it was a dangerous idea.

PART II

FRANK'S SONG

Francis Scott Key, witnessing the British bombs bursting in air over Fort McHenry in Baltimore Harbor on September 14, 1814, the day he wrote "The Star-Spangled Banner."

6

As Beverly Snow welcomed diners to the Epicurean Eating House at Sixth and Pennsylvania, Francis Scott Key often passed by his corner on foot or in a carriage. At fifty-two years of age, Key was the sort of gentleman whom Beverly hoped to attract. An attorney-at-law, Key often argued cases at the courthouse up the street in Judiciary Square or down the Avenue at the U.S. Supreme Court in the basement of the Capitol. A longtime resident of nearby Georgetown, Key was known about Washington City for his philanthropy, piety, ambition, and, of course, his famous song, "The Star-Spangled Banner," whose lyrics he had composed some eighteen years before. The stirring anthem launched by the words "O say, can you see" made Key famous in his own lifetime, serving as background music for an eventful career in law, politics, and public service that is oddly omitted from American memory.

Key wore the fame of his song lightly. He, his wife, Polly, and their ten children occupied a two-story brick home at the far end of Bridge Street (now M Street) in Georgetown, where the little ones frolicked in terraced gardens and a lawn that sloped down to banks of the Potomac River. By 1830, his two oldest daughters, favorite Elizabeth Phoebe and free-spirited Maria, had grown and married, as had his oldest son, Francis Jr. Ann, a sensitive nineteen-year-old, had just married and moved out. They all lived in Maryland, while John Ross, a dutiful twenty-year-old, attended a boarding school in New York. Remaining at home was the volatile fourteen-year-old Daniel; twelve-year-old Philip Barton, who would prove the most intelligent of them all; as well as three children under ten—Ellen, Mary Alicia, and Charles Henry. Key tried to instill religious feeling in them, not always successfully. He clashed with Maria and Daniel, who did not take to the Bible and skipped their prayers.

Another child, Edward, had died tragically in 1822 at the age of eight when he was pulled under by the Potomac's tricky currents while playing in the shallow waters near the family house. Key, away on a business trip, returned to comfort himself and his wife with the belief that "such an awful shock as this is never ordered by a merciful God, but for some wise and good purpose."

On weekdays, Key walked to his nearby law office or took a carriage to the courthouse in Washington. His practice, representing claimants to the War Department and the Land Office, was lucrative, especially when bankrolled by Alabama landowners who routinely paid a thousand dollars for his services. In the evenings, Key attended meetings of various philanthropic and religious causes. On Sundays he prayed in pew 40 of Christ Church of Georgetown, located at Congress and Beall streets. In his later years he would undertake at least four sensitive political missions on behalf of President Jackson. On occasion, he spent time with his family.

Key was no Epicurean; he renounced luxury in all of its forms. But he might well have dined at Snow's new restaurant. He certainly passed by Snow's corner often enough. As an attorney he met out-of-town clients at Brown's Hotel and caught the coach to Annapolis in front of Gadsby's. Snow's place offered a natural rendezvous for him and his associates, not that Key would have much cared for the mulatto proprietor. Key prided himself as a humanitarian and as a young lawyer relished defending individual colored people in court. Some even called him "the Blacks' lawyer." At the same time, Key shared a general view of the free people of color as shiftless and untrustworthy: a nuisance, if not a menace, to white people. He spoke publicly of Africans in America as "a distinct and inferior race of people, which all experience proves to be the greatest evil that afflicts a community." He nurtured a vision, expressed in deed (though not song), in which African colonization would solve the problem of the free blacks by helping them emigrate to Liberia. Key had worked ceaselessly and ineffectively on behalf of this dream for more than twenty years. He was, as one biographer admitted, a distressingly serious man.

Humanitarian ambition drove him. In his younger days, Key often left Polly and their growing brood to travel throughout the mid-Atlantic promoting the establishment of what were known as Lancaster schools, institutions of learning open to all white children, which evolved into the region's first public schools. He attended the annual General Convention of the Episcopal Church, where he denounced popular amusements like gambling. While some of his coreligionists chafed at his harsh pronouncements, none doubted his piety. Said his friend John Randolph, the brilliant and eccentric Virginia senator, "His whole life is spent in endeavors that do good for his unhappy fellow-men." Randolph, an iconoclastic bachelor fond of opium and poetry, admired Key's benevolence but did not entirely trust it.

In his relations with enslaved people, Key was decent by the standards of the day. He had grown up on his family's plantation in the hills of northern Maryland surrounded by slaves and an ethic of service. His mother read the Bible to the blacks in residence. Family lore held that his grandmother had been blinded by smoke while rescuing a black family from a fire. Key abhorred the mistreatment of bondsmen and the sundering of families by slave dealers. A prim man, he was incapable of brutality. Condescension came more easily. During his lifetime, Key freed seven of his slaves. He said that all but one of them—whom he did not identify—had thrived in freedom. But in general, Key expressed disappointment at the results of his efforts on behalf of colored people. "I have been thus instrumental in liberating several large families and many individuals," he told a contemporary. "I cannot remember more than two instances, out of this large number, in which it did not appear that the freedom so earnestly sought for them was their ruin." Key concluded Negroes could not handle the responsibilities of liberty in America. When they moved back to Africa, the United States would then be free of slaves (and former slaves) and could thus fulfill its destiny as a "land of the free" for white people.

Key was a colonization man. He had helped organize the first meeting of the American Colonization Society in 1817, unquestionably sincere in his belief that African emigration would bring about the end of chattel slavery in America, perhaps within a century. He had served as one of the group's twelve managers, or agents, ever since. But what had he achieved? In the fourteen years of Key's service, the society arranged transportation for no more than two thousand freed American slaves. Those numbers showed that colonization could succeed, Key said to many a meeting room, often to applause. Critics like Benjamin Lundy pointed out that during the lifetime of the society the enslaved population in America had grown by nearly four hundred thousand people. Numerically speaking, colonization had failed to diminish slavery in any way. Key did not waver. When Congress balked at funding the scheme, Key took on the chore of fund-raising—"the begging business," he called it—for the selfless cause of sending the blacks back to Africa.

So when Isaac Cary, John Cook, and other free blacks spoke out against colonization at the AME church meeting in April 1831, Key probably took exception. Their avowed "distrust" of the American Colonization Society could have only irked his sense of benevolence. But Key preferred not to respond to the critics of colonization. And at that moment, he had a rather more important matter to ponder:

President Jackson wanted to see him personally.

Key had made the trip from Georgetown to the president's house many times before and he knew the route well. His carriage went down Falls Street, which turned into Bridge Street, which took him over Rock Creek and into Washington City. He continued down Pennsylvania Avenue as the fields gave way to houses and then past the popular Franklin House on Twenty-First Street. From there it was a short jaunt to President's Square. The carriage pulled into the semicircular driveway of the executive mansion. As Key entered the building through the north portico, a Negro servant, dressed in a blue coat with brass buttons, a white shirt, and white breeches, ushered him in.

Inside some of the rooms looked elegant, carpeted with tapestries displaying national emblems. Others stood almost empty, thanks to a penurious Congress. Key mounted the stairs and passed through a large square audience room where the president received petitioners and other business callers. He arrived at Jackson's personal office, which featured silk curtains crowned by gilded-eagle cornices and a long table once owned by Thomas Jefferson.

Key found the president looking tired and a bit worn. At sixty-four years of age, Andrew Jackson was a tall, spare rooster of a man with a high forehead and brushed-back gray hair. He had keen eyes, and on occasions like this—important decisions in the offing—a good-natured, almost childlike expression about his mouth. He smoked a reed pipe and did not waste time.

"I want to tell you confidentially that I wish to offer Taney the place of Attorney General," Jackson began. "Would that be acceptable to him?"

THE LARGELY FORGOTTEN friendship of Francis Scott Key and Roger Taney would soon shape the life of the United States and Washington City in profound ways. Taney, with Key's help, would become the attorney general and then the chief justice of the Supreme Court and eventually the author of the *Dred Scott* decision, which hastened the coming of the Civil War. Key, in constant contact with Taney, would go on to serve the Jackson administration and the people of Washington through a seven-year stint as district attorney. The fraternal bond that sustained Key and Taney through the political wars of the Jackson era subjected them to danger, controversy, and tragedy. It also elevated them to positions of power in a formative period of the country's political life. Not only did the modern two-party system of American politics originate during the Jackson administration, so did the "red-blue" dynamics that still animate partisan political conflict in the twenty-first century. Francis Scott Key and Roger Taney flourished as recognizably modern men. They were founding fathers of the enduring American political tradition that might be called "red patriotism."

Key and Taney first met in the late 1790s. Both had grown up on bucolic slaveholding plantations in Maryland. Both read law in Annapolis, hoping to become lawyers in the Maryland courts. Key, a graduate of St. John's College, got by on charm and quick intelligence. Taney, a more studious graduate of Dickinson College in Pennsylvania, benefited from the profane tutelage of a brilliant, hard-drinking lawyer named Luther Martin. When Key and Taney were admitted to the Maryland bar, they started practicing law in Frederick Town, a growing manufacturing center in central Maryland near the Key family estate.

The two young men meshed in their differences. Roger was a gaunt, homely, dark-haired fellow, as lean as a Potomac herring (or so they said) and as shrewd as the shrewdest, despite the fact he could not see very well. Francis was almost pretty in his dreamy blond handsomeness. Taney was meticulous; Key impulsive. Taney was determined; Key vacillating. Taney knelt daily to pray but did not regard a whiskey or a wager as self-indulgence. Key was more abstemious and more popular with the ladies. The two men were already friends when Taney started courting Key's only sibling, his younger sister Ann. In 1806 Roger Taney and Ann Key married in a lavish ceremony at the Key family estate known as Terra Rubra. Francis and Roger drew as close as brothers.

Taney was impressive in an odd way. He was, in the words of a friend, "a tall, square shouldered man, flat breasted in a degree to be remarked upon, with a stoop that made his shoulders even more prominent." He had "a face without one good feature . . . [and] discolored and irregular teeth, the gums of which were visible when he smiled." Taney always dressed in black, "his clothes sitting ill upon him, his hands spare with projecting veins—in a word, a gaunt, ungainly man."

After his marriage Taney stayed in Frederick Town pursuing what he admitted was an "ambition for legal eminence—not so much for the emoluments it would bring, as for the high rank and social position which were in that day attached to it." He soon became known as one of the leading lawyers in the area. He was democratic in his politics, probably because he was a Catholic. In an early political venture, he favored giving Jews in Maryland the right to vote. In 1819 he defended a white preacher named Gruber charged with inciting slaves to rebel. Preaching to a huge outdoor revival meeting attended by hundreds of blacks and whites, Gruber had declared that slavery was a sin. Taney argued that as long as the man did not urge the slaves to rebel, his sermon did not violate the law. The preacher was acquitted.

Meanwhile, Key had married Mary Tayloe, a pretty girl from another wealthy slaveholding Maryland family. He called her Polly and they moved to Georgetown to take over the law practice of his uncle Philip

Barton Key, a retired congressman. Key soon established himself as a capable, even eloquent advocate in the courtroom. Polly bore their children and took care of them with the help of various slaves.

Taney eventually made his way to Baltimore, where he developed an expertise in maritime and insurance law and became a director of the Union Bank of Maryland, then the state's largest financial institution. Taney's connections and work ethic gained him a reputation for probity, and in 1827, the governor of Maryland appointed him to be the state's attorney general.

Unlike Taney, Key avoided politics for a long time, taking pride that "The Star-Spangled Banner" transcended the country's political divisions. He told his friend John Randolph, "The worst men of a party will be uppermost in it." (The acidulous Randolph replied: "You will put down party spirit when you put down whiskey drinking.") But Taney's sympathy for the presidential ambition of General Jackson proved contagious. In 1828, Key embraced the democratic charisma of General Jackson and discovered his own political ambition.

Frank, as Key was known to his political cronies, found Jackson capable and heroic. He offered the hope of shaking up a country that Key lamented was succumbing to "luxury," a materialism that undermined faith and decorum. In 1828, Key held a barbecue for Jackson supporters in Frederick County where the liquor flowed freely. His hopes were fulfilled at Jackson's inauguration in March 1829, when thousands of people jammed Pennsylvania Avenue to welcome the new president. Key thrilled to the crowd's energy and deportment. "It is beautiful," he exulted. "It is sublime."

He might have been speaking of his own prospects. Key had come to professional maturity in the capital in the early 1800s, watching as clans of aristocratic gentlemen from Virginia and Massachusetts dominated the councils of government. They had effortlessly excluded men like himself. With Jackson's arrival, the old order finally seemed to give way to a vigorous new democracy in which Key might play a leading role.

He offered his services to the new administration. He agreed to act as a special prosecutor in the case of Tobias Watkins, a government auditor in the Adams administration who had allegedly embezzled money from navy accounts. Some thought the prosecution a maneuver to justify Jackson's plans for "rotation in office," which many feared meant replacing civil servants with political hacks. Key's nonpartisan reputation helped convince a jury otherwise. Watkins was convicted.

President Jackson had called Key to his office in the spring of 1831 and asked him about Roger Taney because he needed a new attorney general. In fact, Jackson needed an entirely new cabinet because his administration, from its very first day two years earlier, had been hobbled by a social and political debacle that came to be known as the Eaton Affair. Key had proved helpful once before in this matter, and the president wondered if he might be again.

The Eaton Affair blossomed in the early days of 1829 as the prototypical Washington sex scandal, a moralistic and vicious struggle for power. It began, as such scandals usually do, with rumors of a promiscuous woman. The lady in question was Margaret Eaton, the wife of John Eaton, Jackson's secretary of war. Eaton, a handsome but not quite brilliant protégé of the president's, had proven himself both fighting Indians and winning votes. Elected senator from Tennessee, he came to Washington and fell in love with Margaret, who had grown up playing hostess in her father's hotel, the Franklin House tavern at Twenty-First Street and Pennsylvania Avenue. Margaret's flirtatious style, lovely brown curls, and reputation for bedding the occasional swain deranged an entire government. By her own admission she was "the wildest girl that ever wore out a mother's patience . . . as gay as a lark, full of fun and nonsense . . . sometimes, maybe, a little original and lawless." In the eyes of one male admirer Margaret Eaton exemplified a strain of Irish beauty that combined the best of the Greek and the Spaniard. Margaret Bayard Smith, the matronly confidante of every first lady since Martha Washington and leader of Washington society, bristled at such masculine flapdoodle. Margaret Eaton was "very handsome," she conceded. She was also "one of the most ambitious, violent, malignant, yet silly women you ever heard of."

The ladies of Washington, including the wives of Jackson's other cabinet secretaries, regarded Mrs. Eaton as little better than a whore. They felt obliged to snub her socially, refusing even to stay in the same room with her at state dinners, diplomatic balls, and punch-bowl receptions, where much of the business of government actually took place. Jackson regarded John Eaton almost as a son and reflexively defended his bride from the gossips. From the start he demanded that Vice President John Calhoun tell his wife to accept a visit from Mrs. Eaton, as capital protocol required. Calhoun, a brilliant but emotionally obtuse man, refused to get involved in what he dismissed as "a ladies' quarrel." Jackson, for whom loyalty was paramount, never trusted Calhoun again.

Jackson took the snubbing of the Eatons personally. During the campaign of 1828, his wife, Rachel, had been savaged by Jackson's foes as an adulteress because she had lived with Jackson before getting divorced from her abusive first husband. After his election she died suddenly in December 1828. In defending Margaret's honor he was honoring the memory of his late wife, who had also been traduced. Now abandoned by his vice president and thwarted by the ladies of society, the old general defended the Eatons all the more adamantly. To one clergyman who questioned Margaret's virtue, Jackson famously roared, "She is as chaste as a virgin," a sentiment perhaps more sincere than accurate.

Key and his wife, Polly, did not have to see the Eatons socially, so they could stay aloof from the conflict around her at least for a while. But then the Reverend John Nicholson Campbell, minister of the Second Presbyterian Church on Fourteenth Street, told friends he had proof of Margaret's immorality. The Eatons heard of his aspersions and confronted him in his parsonage. John Eaton wanted to challenge the offending divine to a duel with pistols, but his wife insisted on defending herself. Margaret took a swing at the reverend, and in the ensuing fracas suffered a bruise on her face. As John Eaton pulled her away, she promised to sue Campbell for libel. Rev. Campbell, previously known only for his turgid sermonizing, realized he was at risk of public scandal. He retained Key as his attorney. Under the sacred tenet of lawyer-client confidentiality, Campbell conceded he had no evidence of any moral transgressions by Mrs. Eaton, only the same rumors everyone else had heard: that she made love outdoors, that she boasted of cuckolding her first husband, that she did not recognize a past lover at a social occasion, and so on.

Key's counsel was uncomplicated. Publicly, he played for time, issuing a statement that the reverend would present the evidence to the appropriate authorities. Privately, Key advised Campbell to meet with the president and withdraw the accusation. Campbell did so in such obsequious fashion that Jackson loathed him all the more.

As the impasse endured, Jackson dispatched his friend Senator Richard Mentor Johnson to talk to other cabinet members who were deferring to their wives in what had become known as "the Petticoat War." Johnson was a war hero in the mold of Jackson, legendary for having killed the great chief Tecumseh in battle and popular with working-class voters for crusading against imprisonment for debt and opposing laws that curbed consumption of liquor on the Sabbath. Johnson had reason to share Jackson's fervent belief that a man's choice of women was nobody's business. He had what some regarded as his own sex scandal in Julia Chinn, his mixed-race companion back in Kentucky, whom he regarded as a wife even though they were not married. Despite his popularity, Senator Johnson failed to persuade anyone in Washington to see the Eatons.

After two years of frustration Jackson decided to dissolve the Eaton impasse by simply purging the entire cabinet. The president let it be known he wanted the resignations of all the cabinet secretaries, including John Eaton. The unprecedented plan stunned Washington and so did the details of its origins. In April 1831, the well-connected Duff Green reported in the *Telegraph* that the idea of the cabinet purge originated with Secretary of State Martin Van Buren, the canny political boss from New York whose brilliant wardrobe adorned a body seemingly devoid of any principle, belief, or conviction save the accumulation of power. His willingness to resign as secretary of state ingratiated him with Jackson, and it was indeed a masterstroke, ensuring that the president would take on Van Buren as his vice presidential running mate in 1832 and replace Calhoun as Jackson's heir apparent.

As Jackson collected resignation letters from his cabinet, the last obstacle was the incumbent attorney general, John Berrien, who declined to take the hint. Berrien was a Georgia politico who compensated for a second-rate legal mind with first-class oratory.

As a widower, he paid special attention to the feelings of his two daughters, both of whom wanted to snub Mrs. Eaton. He supported them and did not want it thought that he endorsed Jackson's efforts to impose Mrs. Eaton on Washington society. While the other cabinet men shuffled off to new jobs, Berrien played for time by going to Georgia. The much-annoyed Jackson decided Berrien needed a push, and Frank Key was just the man to provide it.

In June 1831 Key traveled to Georgia on behalf of the president, ostensibly to mediate a dispute between white settlers and displaced Indians. On the return trip, Key arranged to travel in the same stagecoach as Berrien. As soon as the door closed Berrien sensed doom.

"I expect that I am supposed to resign," he said to Key, "although I would remain if the President is so inclined. What are people saying and thinking?"

As a gentleman, Key dissembled. He told Berrien that he might not have to quit.

"I know Taney agrees," Key added. This was kindly but wholly erroneous. Taney was back in Baltimore angling hard for the attorney general's job. Berrien was not fooled.

"I'm afraid Van Buren requires me to be included in his arrangement," he said, sighing. "Who do you think will be my successor?"

Taney's name had been mentioned, Key allowed, which was accurate. "But I don't think the job will be offered to him," he added—which was not.

"Would Taney accept?" Berrien asked.

"Possibly," Key replied. "That is, if he sees a prospect of things going well."

Berrien got the point. He would have Key's support for keeping his job right up until the moment Taney was offered the position. He changed the subject.

When the stagecoach reached Washington City many hours later, Jackson immediately summoned the exhausted Key again. It was after nine o'clock at night when Key arrived in the candlelit offices. Jackson told him he was going to replace Berrien with Taney. Key fumbled for words, then assured the president that his brother-in-law would accept. Key went home to notify Taney of the good news. Berrien resigned in the morning.

On June 23, 1831, Roger Brooke Taney was named the new attorney general of the United States of America. Before long he was a trusted confidant of the president, his influence exceeded only by Van Buren's. In the process, Francis Scott Key achieved a new measure of influence with President Jackson.

Francis Scott Key had ridden the immortal "rockets' red glare" to fame and power. Yet as he rose in Washington he was modest about how he came to write "The Star-Spangled Banner," and for good reason. His memorable composition was the culmination of a disastrous series of events embarrassing to Key and the country. Only the enduring popularity of Key's song redeemed the ignominy that preceded it.

The story of the "Banner" begins in 1812. At the behest of the U.S. Congress, President James Madison had reluctantly declared war on Great Britain. The so-called war hawks of Capitol Hill cited a variety of British provocations, ranging from punitive tariffs to the impressment of American seamen into the British navy. Led by the thirty-four-year-old Henry Clay, then the Speaker of the House of Representatives, the hawks disdained diplomacy as inadequate to the threat against American interests. Once the fighting began, the hawks discovered neither their government nor their constituents were as ready for war as they had assumed. When U.S. forces attempted to seize Canada in 1813, the British had repulsed them. The Americans had more success annihilating the Indian tribes who had allied themselves with the English. In early 1814, the British navy took the offensive with a series of raids on the eastern seaboard. In August, British commanders moved a flotilla of warships carrying some five thousand soldiers up the Chesapeake Bay to the Patuxent River.

By the middle of the month, the people of Washington City, less than fifty miles away, woke up to the possibility of an attack by an experienced expeditionary force of the most powerful country in the world. Almost as frightening, the British commanders were offering freedom to enslaved Africans who helped them. Already more than a thousand slaves had run away from their white owners to join the British forces, with some black men serving as scouts to help the invaders navigate the countryside. President Madison, a reticent man with no military experience, appointed General William H. Winder to organize the capital's defense. Winder, who had never commanded a force of more than a thousand soldiers, rallied a motley army of some ten thousand men. Militias came from the towns around the Chesapeake and descended from the hills of Virginia, Maryland, and Pennsylvania. Francis Scott Key, a young gentleman lawyer, mobilized with the Georgetown militia in which he served as a lieutenant.

As the British forces advanced, Winder decided to take his stand on a hill above the town of Bladensburg in Maryland, just outside the District of Columbia. If the British wanted to attack the capital, they would have to pass through the town, cross a narrow bridge, and then advance uphill against a larger American force. The Americans had the superior terrain, the British the superior soldiers. Major General Robert Ross, leader of the British ground forces, had battled Napoleon's legions in Europe, while Winder was an overwhelmed gentleman leading a band of ill-educated farmers, undisciplined mechanics, and inexperienced scions exemplified by one Francis Scott Key. As the American forces mobilized for the big battle, General Winder did not appreciate the lieutenant's unsought battlefield advice. "Mr. Francis Key informed me that the troops coming from the city could be most advantageously posted on the left and right," General Winder noted in his journal, impressed by the uselessness of Key's recommendation.

As the British forces approached the American lines at Bladensburg, Winder's artillery started to rain shells down on them. The British flanks did not break as the soldiers absorbed the explosions and mounted the slope, firing steadily at the Americans as they advanced. When the novices in the American front lines saw the implacable advance of British bayonets, some started to panic. Their officers, such as Key, did not command much respect and could not calm them. One line of soldiers broke and ran, then another. As the troops started to flee the battle zone, their hapless officers joined them, causing still more soldiers to bolt. As the gunfire intensified, the Americans took flight by the hundreds and then thousands. Most simply ran back toward Washington, including Lieutenant Key, who chugged down the dirt road looking sweaty and ridiculous in his blue uniform. Wags and cartoonists would soon dub this mass retreat the "Bladensburg Races," a derisive term that did service as a punch line for decades. In the Bladensburg Races, Francis Scott Key was a sprinter.

In the wake of this headlong stampede, the British forces glided into the defenseless Washington City with merriment on their minds. Major General Ross was joined by Rear Admiral George Cockburn, and they ordered their men to seize the Capitol building in the name of the king. In the great hall of the House of Representatives, Cockburn took the Speaker's chair. "All in favor of setting fire to this harbor of Yankee democracy, say Aye," he cried. The vote was unanimous. A torch was applied to the drapes. Cockburn and Ross rode back down the Avenue to the President's House, where they broke into the abandoned mansion and helped themselves to James and Dolley Madison's food and drink. Another torch was applied.

About the only man in Washington who tried to stop the sacking of the city was Dr. William Thornton, architect of the Capitol and advocate of African colonization, who served as the superintendent of the Patent Office. As scores of British troops gathered ominously around his office at Seventh and G streets, Thornton feared they wanted to trash the rooms where he stored each new invention submitted for patent approval. Thornton had hundreds of models of every conceivable type of American machine: plows, buggies, ovens, and clocks, not to mention kaleidoscopes, concave mirrors, artificial limbs, unplayable musical instruments, and the odd medical device. As a man with several patents of his own, Thornton could not bear the thought of seeing his own work trashed, much less that entrusted to him by his countrymen. With the British troops closing in on his building, Thornton strode into their ranks, shouting into their faces.

"Are you then not Englishmen, but Goths and Vandals?" he yelled. "Would you rival the barbarian Turks who burned the Library at Alexandria?"

The soldiers stood back, puzzled by this strange American.

"Yonder the genius of America is housed," Thornton railed at them. "To destroy these discoveries would condemn you before all the civilized nations of the world."

A British major waved off his men, and they went in search of less-defended targets. Thornton's outburst had saved the workshop of American ingenuity.

That evening, a low black thundercloud settled over the city. A torrential rain began, then a tornado ripped through the streets, rattling windows and bringing down branches. As the British officers retired to a bawdy house for the evening, Lieutenant Key was cowering in his Georgetown home. He was a God-fearing man, and always would be. He took defeat and death as the instruments of a demanding God displeased by earthly sinners.

"Key heard the voice of God in the howling of the tempest," said one biographer. "He did not bear up as bravely under the humiliation as a godly man such as he might have done. He looked on the spectacle as a prodigious disgrace. So unnerved was he that for several days afterwards he had neither time or mind to do anything."

Francis Scott Key's immortal anthem was born in this sense of disgrace. The tale of how Key came to write the song is taught so blandly to most American schoolchildren that they invariably forget it by adulthood. Yet Key's forgotten failure was the father of his success. Seeking to redeem his battlefield failure, Key proved himself to be resilient, intrepid, and creative.

First, Key came to the rescue of a family friend, a doctor named William Beanes who lived in Upper Marlborough, Maryland, southeast of Washington City. The British forces, satisfied with their pedagogical defacement of the American capital, had withdrawn and passed through Upper Marlborough, where Beanes shouted insults and attempted to detain them. The annoyed soldiers arrested him and took him away on their march toward Baltimore. When Key got word of Dr. Beanes's arrest, he became concerned about his safety and asked President Madison for permission to contact the British forces to negotiate his release. Madison approved; Key left the next day.

Traveling by carriage, Key caught up to the British forces in Baltimore, where they were massing for an attack on Fort McHenry, the U.S. military post guarding the city's harbor. Dr. Beanes was being held on one of the British ships. When Key asked for his release, he was rudely informed that he would have to wait until after the attack but that he was welcome to visit Dr. Beanes on board.

As the British forces bombarded Fort McHenry on the morning of September 14, 1814, they proved their prowess in the spectacular and useless display of military power. The British ships, anchored outside the range of the American guns, faced no return fire. The U.S. forces inside the fort hung out a massive red, white, and blue flag and hunkered down to withstand the onslaught. They absorbed the artillery fire all night, with epic explosions from the massive British cannons lighting up the night sky. When dawn came, Key saw the British had not breached the fort's walls, and the flag was still there. The British officers, not caring to expend more ammunition, decided they had made their point and prepared to move on.

Amidst the tumult, Key had the idea of writing a patriotic song. He scrawled notes for lyrics on the back of a letter during the bombardment. Upon returning to his hotel the next day, he fitted the words to the melody of a popular English drinking club song called "To Anacreon in Heaven." Key had heard the tune (or "air") used for a popular song in the 1790s called "Adams and Liberty." Key infused the air of "Anacreon" with bold images of war to pose a patriotic question:

O say, can you see, by the dawn's early light,
What so proudly we hail'd at the twilight's last gleaming?

The end of the first stanza answered the question: the fort had held, the flag survived:

And the rockets' red glare, the bombs bursting in air,
Gave proof through the night that our flag was still there.

Then Key asked another question:

O say, does that star-spangled banner yet wave
O'er the land of the free & the home of the brave?

In the modern mind, that is where the song ends and the ballgame begins. For Key, that question was just the prelude to his next three stanzas, in which the American flag not only survives but goes on to greater glory. These stanzas, taught in American public schools for much of the twentieth century, have fallen out of favor and been forgotten, probably because by then they no longer fit with prevailing notions of patriotism. In the third verse, for example, Key's lyrics condemned the African Americans who dared to join the British cause to escape bondage, declaring, "No refuge could save the hireling and slave / From the terror of flight or the gloom of the grave." By the end of Key's fourth stanza, the defensive hopes of the first had swelled into a celebration of just war that promised America would go from near defeat to a godly conquest:

> *Then conquer we must, when our cause, it is just,*
> *And this be our motto—"In God is our Trust"*
> *And the star-spangled banner in triumph shall wave*
> *O'er the land of the free & the home of the brave!*

In 311 words, Key had captured and defined something essential and enduring in America's love of nation. His song summoned the "heav'n-rescued land" into righteous action—*conquer we must, when our cause, it is just*—the divine destiny of the land of the free.

With the end of the British siege and the release of Dr. Beanes, Key took his lyrics to the offices of the *Baltimore American* newspaper, where a printer ran off dozens of copies under the uninspired title "Defence of Fort McHenry." Jubilant to see the British invaders depart, people started to sing Key's song in the taverns and the theaters. When Key returned to his family estate in central Maryland a few days later, he barely mentioned the song to his wife and children, but he told Roger Taney about it in some detail.

The next month, a Baltimore theater advertised the performance of "a much admired New Song, written by a gentleman of Maryland, in commemoration of the GALLANT DEFENCE OF FORT M'HENRY, called, THE STAR SPANGLED BANNER." The retitled song gained in popularity as the whole nation felt a sense of pride and relief as the war with Great Britain came to a close. On the battlefields of Europe, the British had largely defeated France, their principal enemy, and no longer needed to worry about the United States. In December 1814, Great Britain and the United States negotiated a peace treaty. If the United States had not won the War of 1812, it had not lost it either.

"The Star-Spangled Banner" would not officially become the national anthem for another century. But it was already a national success. Key's humiliation at Bladensburg enabled him to compose the lyrics that exulted so proudly in the joy of survival and the prospect of righteous victories in the future. Key did not have to promote his song. Its vivid scenes, stirring melody, and triumphant climax did that for him. In December 1814, a group of political men threw a banquet at McKeowin's Hotel, located at the corner of Sixth Street and Pennsylvania Avenue. Washington really was just a village then and McKeowin's a lonely outpost of camaraderie. During the toasts after the dinner, the *Intelligencer* reported, F. S. Key's "beautiful and touching" lines were sung "with great effect by several of the guests." It was the first time "The Star-Spangled Banner" had been performed publicly in Washington City.

Seventeen years later, Francis Scott Key's patriotism was undimmed. His song was famous, matched in popularity only by "Hail Columbia," an older patriotic hymn. Key's anthem, all four stanzas, was still sung with gusto, but the city that listened had changed. The corner of Sixth and Pennsylvania now anchored a growing metropolis where democracy was ascendant but morality embattled, a national capital for General Jackson and the common man but also a place plagued with gamblers, whores, and free Negroes who presumed to act the equal of white men.

Then came word of Southampton.

9

THE TERRIBLE NEWS from Southampton reached Frank Key at Terra Rubra, the family estate to which he retreated each summer. Terra Rubra was Key's solace. He and Polly and the children came every year to the rolling hills along the Monocacy River in northern Maryland. The Pennsylvania border was just fifteen miles away. Key's estate, with its slaves and slow pace, was an outpost of the South with a view of the North.

These verdant hills had been the seat of the Key family since 1753, when Philip Key, a bachelor from England, had patented some two thousand acres of wilderness between the Monocacy River and its tributary Big Pipe Creek. Philip Key built a large home on his new property and dubbed it Terra Rubra, or Red Lands, in honor of the fertile reddish soil. Three generations of Keys, including Francis Scott, had grown up on the property.

By all accounts it was a splendid place. "The mansion was of brick, with centre and wings and long porches," said one historian. "It was situated amidst a large lawn, shaded by trees, and an extensive terraced garden adorned with shrubbery and flowers. Near by flowed Pipe Creek, through a dense wood. A copious spring of purest water where young people loved to retire and sit under the sheltering oaks in summer was at the foot of the hill. A meadow of waving grass spread out toward Catoctin Mountain, which could be seen at sunset curtained in clouds of crimson and gold."

Key delighted in his time at Terra Rubra with the children, sometimes leading them in prayer twice a day. At least six of them were there that summer, along with Roger Taney, his wife, and their brood.

Key probably first read news of the slave uprising in Southampton, Virginia, in the pages of the *Frederick Town Herald* on August 27, 1831, under the headline "Insurrection of the Blacks."

"I have a horrible, heart-rending tale to relate," the author began, "and lest even its worst features might be distorted by rumor and exaggeration I have thought it proper to give you all and the worst information that has yet reached us, through the best sources of intelligence which the nature of the case will admit."

A band of slaves had taken up arms in Southampton County in southern Virginia the previous Sunday, the dispatch reported. The rebels had murdered several whole families of white people. Most of the white men in the area had been off attending a camp meeting some miles away, the correspondent noted, "a circumstance which gave temporary security to the brigands in the perpetration of their butcheries."

The account had plenty of disturbing detail, not all of it accurate. The black insurgents, reportedly led by one or two white men, numbered some three hundred, half of them riding horses. In fact, the rebels were led by a black preacher named Nat and no white men were involved. The exploits of General Nat, as he was dubbed, fascinated even as they sickened. Nat and his men had butchered a master and mistress in their bed. They bashed a baby's head on a brick fireplace. A father, who hid himself in the bushes of a garden, watched his whole family be murdered just a few yards away. Some forty to fifty people were reported to have fallen victim to their vengeance.

Whatever comfort Key felt at his family retreat was now gone. Frederick County was swept with helpless and numbing fear and irresistible speculation. The Keys lived in a sea of black people whom they thought content, just as the masters of Southampton—now dead—must have thought. Key had to protect himself and his family. Within two weeks the news became more reassuring. Sixteen of the black rebels had been captured and hanged. But General Nat had escaped, and the governor of Virginia was offering a five-hundred-dollar reward for his capture. White people slept no easier. A nervous Polly Key decided to return to Georgetown rather than think about black phantoms in the countryside. She took the baby of the family, four-year-old Charles, with her. Key stayed behind to manage his property in people.

Thomas Jefferson and other guilty slave-owning savants had long predicted that American slavery would end in "servile war" in which the slaves would annihilate their masters or vice versa. Nonetheless, the Southampton uprising was a shock for the patriotic statesmen and respectable citizenry of the slaveholding republic.

White people started arguing among themselves. The leaders of the American Colonization Society cited the massacre to stress the urgency of expatriating Africans and organized several more expeditions to Liberia. While colonization remained the most popular solution to the problem of slavery, a growing minority of whites wanted to do more. The editors of the *Adams Sentinel* in nearby Gettysburg, Pennsylvania, used the occasion to call "for the gradual abolition of slavery throughout the land." Antislavery activists found more people willing to listen to their arguments that slavery made such crimes inevitable. In the two months after Southampton, Ben Lundy gained more than 250 new subscribers to the *Genius*. In Virginia, the two leading newspapers, the *Richmond Enquirer* and the *Richmond Whig*, both came out in favor of the gradual emancipation of the Africans.

Southampton affected Key personally. He soon agreed to manumit two of his seven adult bondsmen. Key's decision was unusual in its timing. Before August 1831, white slave owners in the Frederick County area often freed their chattel, sometimes in exchange for payment, more often in their wills. After Southampton, slave owners in the area became fearful and not a single slave was manumitted—except for the two freed by Key. On September 7, 1831, barely a week after news of the massacre, Key agreed to sell the evidently unhappy William Ridout his freedom for three hundred dollars. Ridout left, and Key said good riddance. After Southampton it might have made more sense to manumit an unruly African than let him stick around and share his admiration of General Nat with others.

The second man was Clem Johnson, a trusted forty-five-year-old slave who had worked at Terra Rubra for years. Since the death of Key's father in 1821 and the aging of Key's mother, Johnson had gradually taken over the management of the household. He was the custodian of the family recipes, superintendent of the kitchen garden, and boss of the field hands, who no doubt discussed Southampton among themselves. In early October 1831, Key and Johnson traveled north from Terra Rubra to Gettysburg, Pennsylvania, where Key gave the magistrate a handwritten deed of manumission. Clem Johnson gained his freedom for a fee of just five dollars.

Key's decision to go to Pennsylvania was also peculiar. He could have—and, from a legal point of view, should have—executed the deed in Frederick County. The problem for Key was likely that he knew the clerks, lawyers, and judges at the courthouse. And they knew him as a tireless, sometimes tiresome advocate of colonization, who had long urged his slave-owning neighbors to free their property and send them to Africa—exactly what he was *not* going to do in the case of Clem. By taking care of Johnson in Gettysburg, Key spared himself from accusations of hypocrisy in Frederick Town.

Or perhaps Gettysburg was Johnson's idea. Possessing free papers in Pennsylvania gave him a new degree of personal security. As a free resident in a state that had abolished slavery, Clem had gained rights in the eyes of the law and made himself less vulnerable to the threat of kidnapping. Whatever the calculus, Johnson obtained his freedom and shed few tears. He had successfully used the white man's panic over Southampton to secure his freedom on advantageous terms. He had no interest in going to Africa. Indeed, Johnson did not even resettle in Pennsylvania, where he was now legally a free man. The red lands of Terra Rubra were his native soil too. He had gained his freedom and the right to be paid. On those terms, he resumed running the kitchen and leading prayers at Terra Rubra and made sure none of the young black men got any stupid ideas in their heads. He was free, and the Key family could sleep easier.

But something had changed in the autumn air. When Frank Key and Clem Johnson stood outside the slaves' quarters of Terra Rubra on a clear day and looked north toward Gettysburg, they could see the blue ridge of two mountains in the distance. One was called Big Round Top, the other Little Round Top. The long struggle against slavery that would culminate in the battle of Gettysburg in those hills in 1863 had just begun.

10

IN THE BALMY dusk of a Friday evening in April 1832, three gentlemen strolled west on Pennsylvania Avenue, heading for the theater. With the curtain for the show not scheduled to go up until eight o'clock, the men took their time. The sidewalks were filled with strolling ladies, stevedores heading for grog shops, and men exiting the faro banks where gambling flourished. Horse-drawn carriages clattered by as they passed Pishey Thompson's bookstore and Mrs. Queen's boardinghouse. At the corner of Eleventh Street, three men paused to look at a pedestrian crossing from the south side of the Avenue. The flame of a streetlamp illuminated the man's face as much as the full moon rising behind them.

"Are you Mr. Stanbery?" asked the tallest of the three men.

"Yes, sir," said the pedestrian, bowing.

"Then you are a damned rascal!" the tall man shouted, raising his wooden cane and slamming it down on Stanbery's head. The man's hat went flying into the gutter as he staggered backward. The attacker clubbed Stanberry again, then grabbed his victim. "Please, sir," Stanbery squealed as his attacker tumbled him to the curb. The attacker raised his cane yet again.

"Don't strike me!" Stanbery cried, now lying on his back, feet up to ward off the blows. The big man struck him again. Stanbery rolled onto his left side and with his right hand extracted a pistol from his pocket. As the big man recoiled, Stanbery pulled the trigger. Sparks glittered amidst a little snapping sound, but no bullet discharged. Enraged all the more, the big man grabbed the gun and used it to beat Stanbery some more about his much-abused head.

William Stanbery was a forty-three-year-old congressman from central Ohio who had been elected as a supporter of General Jackson in 1828 and reelected as an opponent in 1830. His assailant was Sam Houston, the thirty-nine-year-old former governor of Tennessee who had made his name as an Indian fighter, succumbed to drinking, then threw away the bottle and returned to politics by getting himself elected to Congress as a Jackson ally. After the beating, Stanbery tottered back to his room at Mrs. Queen's boardinghouse, while Houston continued on to the theater with his two companions, both of whom happened to be members of the U.S. Senate.

Stanbery knew why Houston had assaulted him. Ten days before, Stanbery had delivered a bitter attack on the Jackson administration on the floor of the House of Representatives, alleging corruption in western road construction contracts. Stanbery said that the superintendent of construction on the Cumberland Road, a mammoth public works project, had defrauded the government, yet remained in his position—perhaps because one of the contracts involved Sam Houston.

The beating of Stanbery shocked the city and the Congress. Lawmakers in the capital had come to expect the insults, lies, deceptions, and calumnies that flourished in the struggle for power. On questions of honor, some congressmen resorted to the elaborate and often deadly ritual of dueling. But an unannounced cane to the head broke even the lax rules of the democratic game. The House went into session that afternoon. By a vote of 145 to 25, the members approved a resolution calling for Houston's arrest. The sergeant at arms took Houston into custody that night.

"MOST DARING OUTRAGE AND ASSAULT" blared the headline in the *Telegraph* on Monday morning. "What gives more importance to this transaction is the known relation which Houston bears to the President of the United States," wrote editor Duff Green. ". . . The proof that he [Houston] contemplated a fraud upon the government is conclusive yet he is still received at the executive mansion and is treated with the kindness and hospitality of an old favorite."

Francis Blair, an ally from Kentucky and editor of the newly established *Globe* newspaper, served as Jackson's chief bodyguard in the press. A homely man who wielded a wicked pen, Blair rejected Green's "vile attempt" to connect the president with the affair of Governor Houston and Mr. Stanbery. Blair's indignation was hardly necessary. Jackson believed Houston was fully justified in beating Stanbery, and Green was right that

Houston could expect hospitality at the President's House. Indeed, when Houston visited Jackson a few days later, he brought a souvenir of the encounter, Stanbery's malfunctioning gun. The president just chuckled at the sight. Jackson thought his friend needed a good attorney to fend off his petty foes, and he knew just the man for the job.

The trial of Sam Houston got under way in the hall of the House of Representatives on April 19. Houston arrived wearing a long buckskin coat with a fur collar, leaning on his habitual hickory walking stick. His counsel, Francis Scott Key, slim, handsome, and conventionally dressed in cravat and jacket, walked by his side. Appearing together they caused a stir: the alliance between the rugged frontiersman and the patriot poet was as exciting as it was unlikely. Before long, the crowd of awestruck spectators exceeded any seen in the Capitol since the Senate galleries overflowed in January 1830 for the debates between Daniel Webster and Robert Hayne over states' rights and nullification. The semicircular gallery of the House chamber grew crowded with tourists, ladies, lobbyists, editors, auditors, scriveners, messengers, clerks, and correspondents. Members flocked to their desks on the floor. "On no occasion, we believe, has the House of Representatives been so entirely filled," reported the *Intelligencer.*

In his earlier days, Francis Scott Key might have been a pious dreamer, a sensitive poet, a tranquil philanthropist. Under the influence of President Jackson, said one admirer, he had hardened into a militant warrior of galvanized conviction: "ardent, zealous, fearless." From the outset of Houston's trial, Key sought to exclude Jackson's critics. He made a motion that no member who had formed or expressed an opinion on the assault should sit in judgment. That would disqualify the majority, who had voted to arrest Houston and neatly end the proceedings before they began. Indignant representatives shouted that Mr. Key had questioned their integrity. Somewhat abashed, he withdrew the motion.

Stanbery, still bruised, gamely took the stand, testifying in detail about his investigation of irregularities in a government contract for Indian rations that was given to Houston when he was governor of Tennessee. Key scorned the charge as rhetoric based on the testimony of a drunk.

Houston, injured while fighting Indians, was incapable of attacking Stanbery with any force, he said. Talk of an "assault" was just a partisan game of the president's enemies.

So it went for a week. Key served as field marshal for Houston's allies as they waged a parliamentary war of attrition against those who sought to sanction the frontiersman in any way. For all the bombast, the stakes were real. The trial of Sam Houston was a struggle to define the norms of debate in Washington. Could a man assault a political opponent for words exchanged in legislative proceedings? Or, as Key put it, could Congress usurp its powers to rebuke a blameless man for responding to an unseemly challenge to his honor?

In his summation, Key raised the stakes.

"Sir," he said to the House Speaker as the galleries hushed, "this cause cannot fail to have consequences, for good and for evil, extending to distant days, when the accused, and all around him may be forgotten. It is thought to affect the high privileges of this great House; and it is certain that it affects the still higher privileges of a still greater House—the people of this great republic."

Francis Scott Key orated sincerely, his admirers noted. When he threw himself into a speech, said one, "his face reflected how deeply he was moved, sparkling beams upon his words as they fell from his lips. In his more impassioned moments his emotion was like lightning, charging his sentences with electrical power."

In such an electric moment, Key lauded his rough-hewn client.

"I am proud, as an American lawyer, to stand by such a man, in such a cause . . . ," he declared. "I consider this the proudest and most gratifying hour of my life."

That was quite a statement for the man who wrote "The Star-Spangled Banner," perhaps even sincerely believed. He went on to warn that the prosecution of Houston was but a pretext for creeping tyranny.

"A free Constitution can be nowhere safely written but in the heart of virtuous and vigilant people, who shall watch and restrain the first step of power or privilege that passes the limits assigned to it," Key declared. "Surely the men who framed the Constitution would have thrown their unfinished work with indignation from their hands, if they could have foreseen that a day like this was so soon to come."

Even Key's most sympathetic biographer lost patience with this performance.

"As a matter of fact, a ruffian had brutally assaulted a Congressman for words which he had spoken in debate on the floor of the House," scoffed Edward Delaplaine a century later, "and the House has the right to protect its members. Nevertheless, the ruffian's lawyer continued to ramble on for two hours, trying to make the Congressmen believe they had no jurisdiction in the matter."

Key and Houston's allies in the House forced several more days of tendentious debate. The galleries drained and the exhausted lawmakers yearned for a roll call vote. Finally, on May 11, a motion to declare Houston guilty of a breach of House privileges was put by the Speaker. The vote was 106 to 89 in favor of guilty. Then came the question of punishment: censure or reprimand? Censure would send the stronger message of disapproval to Houston and the Jackson administration. But the motion to reprimand, the milder rebuke, passed 96–84.

Thus Sam Houston departed from the Capitol claiming vindication for pummeling poor Stanbery. Thanks to Key's obfuscations and the loyalty of the Jackson faction in the House, he had obtained leniency.

The president would not forget Mr. Key's service.

Yet Frank Key had little time to savor his triumph, if that's what it was. Just a few days later, he was working in his office when he received a note from his son Frank Jr., asking to see him. Twenty-five years of age, Francis Scott Key Jr. was his father's oldest son. He lived the life of a young gentleman with his wife and two children on the West River near Annapolis. Less religious and self-sacrificing than his father, Frank Jr. was generous, impulsive, and fond of lavish entertainments. He dressed in colonial style, wearing knickerbockers, a blue coat with brass buttons, a buff vest, buckled shoes, and a powdered wig. Like Sam Houston, he walked with a stout cane.

When they met, the father thought the son looked wretched and ashamed. Frank Jr. admitted why: He had just been charged with rape. The younger man told his mortified father a convoluted story about a woman who was new to the West River area. She charged that he had used threat of force to have his way with her in someone else's house. She had gone to the local magistrate seeking his arrest.

The son expressed contrition for his sin and shame but denied he had used force with the woman.

"Acknowledge your guilt," said the wounded father. "Repent and submit to all the consequences of your sins."

Key sent his sixteen-year-old son, Daniel, to West River with a rather adult mission: to talk to a friend of Frank Jr.'s who knew the woman involved. Key did not want to believe his son was guilty of rape, but he did not flinch from the possibility. "I have thought it my duty to have every effort made to ascertain the truth," Key wrote to his son-in-law Charles Howard. "I must bear this state of suspense a few days—trusting that God, who alone can help in such extremity, will order such events to these appalling circumstances as shall ultimately be best for my poor boy + for us all."

Two days later, Daniel Key returned from Annapolis with merciful news: The charges would be dropped.

"Everybody is satisfied that our poor child has been falsely accused," Key explained to Howard. The woman was brought before the magistrate and "is proved to be a vile and infamous prostitute of the lowest character. Frank's account of the transaction is fully confirmed. It is a shameful exposure on his part but she is shown to be equally guilty."

Key's God-fearing faith survived. So did his reputation and his ambition.

After his reelection in November 1832, President Jackson was ready to pay off a standing political debt. Roger Taney had proved a welcome addition to the cabinet. As attorney general, he worked tirelessly in the four-story office building on the west side of President's Square, or from his home in Baltimore. Jackson had quickly come to trust Taney with the national government's legal policies on everything from maritime law to Indian removal. Now he wanted the same kind of efficiency and loyalty in the court of Washington City. On Tuesday, January 29, 1833, Jackson sent the clerk of the Senate a message: "I nominate Francis S. Key to be Attorney of the United States for the District of Columbia." Key, well known for his good deeds, law practice, and song, was approved by unanimous consent the same day.

The district attorney position was a hard-earned reward for Key and an easy decision for President Jackson. Key had obtained the conviction of Tobias Watkins and talked down the egregious Reverend Campbell. He had proven his acumen in showing out Berrien and bringing in Taney. And he displayed real fortitude in the grueling defense of Sam Houston. Jackson left no record of why he appointed Key, but the increasingly contentious issue of slavery in the District of Columbia probably played a role too. With northern congressmen trying to make an issue of slavery in the capital, the administration needed a district attorney certain to share the president's understanding of the white man's constitutional rights.

The district attorney job, said one Key biographer, was "not altogether to his taste because he had to prosecute and he was an unvindictive man." But Key would overcome this reticence for the sake of his vision of justice. He had no difficulty identifying the city's crime problems. Some were eternal, like fighting and thieving. Some were new, like gambling. The proliferation of gaming establishments—card parlors, faro banks, and roulette tables—had rendered the city's system of small fines ineffective. In 1830, the common council had increased the fines for gambling houses and required operators to post a bond, the latter on penalty of a stay at the workhouse. Then the council made running a gambling house a penitentiary offense, and the pastime became more discreet but no less prevalent. Not long after Key took office, the *Intelligencer* admitted, "There is no city in which gambling is carried to a greater extent than the metropolis of the country."

To combat such ills, Key had a weak constabulary. The city employed twelve magistrates who could bring criminal charges and order arrests, along with ten constables who patrolled the city's six wards. The constables received a wage of fifty dollars a year, which they supplemented with reward money for capturing runaway slaves and the illicit proceeds of kidnapping free Negroes and selling them to slave traders.

In September 1833, Key made his mark. In an effort to clear the court's backlog of cases, the new district attorney called a special early session two months before the circuit court traditionally opened. He came back early from Terra Rubra and proceeded to prosecute seventy-two assault cases and twenty-six larceny cases in just a few weeks. He stepped up prosecution of gambling houses, closing down five different establishments, most of them on Pennsylvania Avenue.

Most of all, Key went after the bawdy houses, otherwise known as houses of ill fame or whorehouses. Once ignored, these enterprises became a target of Key's constables. No longer would authorities tolerate women selling their favors to men, a trade well known to the locals. In his 1822 comic novel, *The L—— Family in Washington,* George Watterston, the writer who served as the Librarian of Congress, depicted the forthright beauties who openly trolled for customers in the galleries of the House and Senate "dressed in the extreme of fashion . . . their cheeks possessing a beautiful red and the rest of their face a most delicate white." When a newcomer expressed shock at their brazen style, his guide shrugged and said, "This is a free country, and such things must be tolerated for the sake of freedom." Watterston called the customers of these working girls the "worshippers of Venus" and observed their temples "appeared to be more devoutly and better attended in this than any other city he had seen, especially in the winter."

In the fall of 1833, Key brought charges against the proprietors of seventeen of these "temples of Venus."

The demimonde of the Washington bawdy houses, documented mostly in court records, was a world of male pleasure controlled by women. Of the thirty-one people whom Key charged with running a sex business, twenty-nine were women. White and black women participated roughly in proportion to their numbers in the city. About a third of Washington's population was black at the time. Of the seventeen bawdy houses Key sought to shut down, white women ran thirteen and black women ran four. Some of these "houses" may have consisted of no more than a room or two; others occupied whole buildings and had elaborate food and beverage service.

Key hoped to shutter them all. He indicted a white couple, George and Celia Gray, for keeping a house of ill fame on F Street, not far from the Methodist meetinghouse. He charged Mary Wertz and her daughter with entertaining customers in their boardinghouse on Pennsylvania Avenue between Second and Third streets. Matilda Thomas and Susan Webster allegedly operated bawdy houses in the First Ward. Henrietta and Harriet Jurdine were accused of the same in the Third Ward. Key went after a black couple, Eliza and Henry Butler, who were said to keep a house of ill fame on Twelfth Street. Three Irish women—Sally McDaniel, Patty Pallison, and Kell Simpson—were charged with plying the trade in a house between Pennsylvania Avenue and Tiber Creek, near Fourteenth Street.

So common were these arrests that Key had a standard indictment form printed up. Whereas most criminal indictments up until that time had been written out by hand, these documents could be run off by the dozens. The printed bill gave a feel for what Key found most abhorrent in the bawdy houses. The indictment charged the defendant—a blank space for the suspect's name—with operating "a certain common bawdy house, situated in the City of Washington . . . for filthy lucre and gain." The criminal offense was running a house that attracted "diverse & evil disposed persons . . . and whores [who] unlawfully and wickedly did receive and entertain . . . and commit whoredom and fornication." The bottom of the document identified the charging officer: "F. S. KEY, USA."

Key's campaign against the houses of ill fame exemplified his ambition to uplift the city's morals by force of law. Yet if Key took pride in this effort, he did not mention it in any writings that have survived. His various biographers would never mention it. The city's newspapers did not report on it. The very correct ladies who chronicled Washington social life in those days—Margaret Bayard Smith and Anna Maria Thornton—did not even allude to such sordid matters in writing.

Francis Scott Key had never stood higher in the estimation of President Jackson. In November 1833, Jackson pulled him temporarily from his duties as district attorney and dispatched him on another sensitive political mission: to quell a dispute between white settlers and federal authorities in Alabama. The trip confirmed the newfound force of Key's personality, fame, and power.

Jackson's policy of Indian removal across the southern states had encouraged the in-migration of white settlers looking for land. In 1832, his administration had signed a treaty with the Creek Indians to protect the pockets of land to which they had been consigned along the Georgia-Alabama border. Nonetheless, growing settlements of whites encroached on the Creek reservations in violation of the treaty. When federal troops attempted to oust the squatters on the Alabama side, the soldiers shot and killed a local postmaster. The incident escalated into a test of the national government's authority within the state. Floundering in the middle was Governor John Gayle, an ally of Jackson's under intense pressure to capitulate to the settlers by putting the federal troops on trial for murder. Gayle wrote to Washington for help, and Jackson sent Key.

The arrival of the famous author of "The Star-Spangled Banner" was an event of no small interest in Alabama, which had become a state only in 1819. Not since General Lafayette had passed through in 1825 had such an illustrious guest stopped by, and the locals were eager to greet him. When Key arrived at Fort Mitchell, he was met by an amateur band that played "The Star-Spangled Banner" over and over again. As the serenaders blasted the autumn air with the tune of the anthem, Key turned to the gentleman with him. "That is a pretty air," he said quizzically. "What is it?" Key, alas, was tone-deaf.

Politically, he proved more astute. By day, Key shuttled between Governor Gayle, the state legislators, local authorities, and the federal military commander. At night he wrote regular letters to Roger Taney seeking legal and political advice. Over the course of a month, he gradually forged an agreement that all could live by.

Along the way, Key found himself enmeshed in romance. The governor's wife, Sarah Haynesworth Gayle, was twenty-nine years of age, a high-spirited and observant woman, a loving if frustrated wife, and the doting mother of three children. Alabama's illustrious visitor intrigued her.

"He is very pleasant—intelligent, you at once perceive, and somewhat peculiar in his manners," Mrs. Gayle wrote in her diary. "He is a little, nay, a good deal absent in company, not always attending when others converse, and often breaking in with a question, though evidently unconscious of what he had done. His countenance is not remarkable when at rest, but as soon as he lifts his eyes, usually fixed upon some object near the floor, the man of sense, of fancy, and the *poet* is at once seen."

What's more he was a Christian. Religious thoughts governed Mrs. Gayle's feelings, and she admired her guest for his spiritual fidelity. When Key wrote a bit of pious verse in the autograph album of her nine-year-old daughter, Sarah, Mrs. Gayle burst into tears. In her diary that night, she wondered why "when a man of talent, of wit, of eminence, of imagination and of honor should name the name of Jesus Christ, my heart should swell with emotions impossible to define partaking of pleasure, pride, veneration and an overwhelming desire to do the same." Why? Perhaps because she had fallen in love with the man. Key, for his part, gravitated to her parlor and company.

"He has been around frequently," she noted in her diary, "and sat an hour or two last night (Mr. Gayle absent) chatting to myself and the children." Mrs. Gayle took the occasion to slip him a poem that coyly confessed her feelings: *"A timid girl may yet be bold t'admire / The Poet's fervor and the Patriot's fire."* A few days later, Key wrote out his response, a poem to her entitled "To Miss ———." In it, he marveled that his song had won her from afar. He was honored. Key, the poet, knew how to speak to a woman's heart:

And is it so?—a thousand miles apart,
Has lay [lyric] of mine e'er touched a gifted heart?
Brightened the eyes of beauty? won her smile?
Rich recompense for all the poet's toil
That fav'ring smile, that brightened eye,
That tells the heart's warm ecstasy.

This fervent exchange qualified Mr. Key and Mrs. Gayle as lovers at least in the nineteenth-century sense of the word: as romantic suitors. But they needed to act with restraint. Sarah Gayle was a passionate woman. She loved her husband and lamented in her diary that she no longer attracted his attention, or any other man's. She felt the need to guard against physical temptation. By her own admission, she had run wild in her youth. Now she was wiser. "I will set no wicked things before mine eyes," she quoted from Psalms in her diary. The potential victim of the libertine, she wrote, "must execrate the first glance of wantonness."

Key also knew the lure of temptation. In the early 1820s, he joined the Delphian Club, a group of hard-drinking poets in Baltimore for whom he composed an erotic reverie entitled *On a Young Lady's Going into a Show Bath*, which lovingly depicted a "trembling blushing maid" whose charms "would fire the frozen blood of apathy." In tracing the progress of water through the luscious landscape of the lady's naked self, Key's poetic gift for vivid, descriptive verse did not fail him:

Each drop of me should touch
should eager run
Down her fair forehead, down her blushing cheek
To taste the more inviting sweets beneath.

Key, it seems, liked to set wicked things before his eyes.

"Few men were more unfavorably circumstanced for a pious life," conceded the Reverend John T. Brooke of Maryland, who knew Key when he was a young man. "Few had stronger inward impulses to control or a thicker array of outward temptations to encounter. He was a man of ardent convictions and strong impulses; these he had to grapple with continually." Not long after his visit to Alabama, Key himself admitted thirst for admiration was a guilty weakness. "The pride of learning, the love of human applause, and the subtle acts of the great adversary of man [i.e., the devil] present powerful temptations, requiring incessant watchfulness," he said. "It is difficult to be great, and successful and applauded, and humble."

In mid-December, Key returned to Washington, his mission accomplished. "The Creek controversy which might have bathed Alabama in blood, was over, forgotten, a slight Jacksonian episode," said one biographer.

But for Sarah Gayle and Frank Key, their "heart's warm ecstasy" encounter would live on in their thoughts long after they had parted.

Roger Taney's influence continued to grow in Jackson's second term. "From the very beginning the gaunt man from Maryland was one of the most trusted advisers of the President," said one historian. Only Martin Van Buren, now the vice president, and Francis Blair of the *Globe* had as much sway as the attorney general.

Taney served Jackson faithfully, especially on issues related to slavery. Like Jackson, Taney had no patience for the notion that Negroes could have rights under law, even if legally free. He emphasized the point in May 1832. South Carolina had passed a law authorizing the imprisonment of any free black sailors who came ashore while their ships were in port. During the administration of John Quincy Adams, Attorney General William Wirt had objected to South Carolina's law, saying it was unconstitutional.

Taney declared it was not. The U.S. government did not need to respect the liberties of free black seamen, the attorney general wrote in a memo. In language foreshadowing his infamous *Dred Scott* decision twenty-five years later, Taney declared, "The African race in the United States even when free, are everywhere a degraded class, and exercise no political influence. The privileges they are allowed to enjoy are accorded to them as a matter of kindness and benevolence rather than of right." South Carolina's law was allowed to stand.

Taney also encouraged Jackson's greatest political ambition: to destroy the power of the country's largest private financial institution, the Bank of the United States. Based in Philadelphia and run by an overbearing financier named Nicholas Biddle, the bank had huge influence over the economy, financing between a quarter and a third of the nation's business. As a western landowner, Jackson had grown up mistrusting eastern bankers, whose control of capital gave them inordinate influence over the frontier economy.

The bank's charter, issued every five years by Congress, legally installed the bank as the depository institution for all the agencies of the U.S. government. The constant flow of tax and tariff revenues into the government accounts gave Biddle's bank a remarkable measure of stability and liquidity, not to mention profitability. For many in the U.S. government, it was an acceptable arrangement. In May 1832, the Ways and Means Committee of the House of Representatives approved the renewal of the bank's charter.

Jackson asked his cabinet if he should sign the legislation into law. When Secretary of the Treasury Louis McLane equivocated, Taney replied with a closely argued twenty-six-page letter that bolstered Jackson's prejudices. While the rest of the cabinet preferred to avoid a fight with the bank, Taney relished it. He followed up with another letter to Jackson—this one running to fifty-four pages—which urged the president to veto the charter. Taney's detailed proposal for a new national banking system intrigued Jackson. Taney envisioned a collection of state banks—"judiciously selected, and arranged"—that would replace the U.S. Bank at the center of the financial system. Jackson approved the idea. His critics derided it, saying the state banks would be selected for political loyalty and become the docile "pets" of the administration.

Emboldened by Taney's ideas, Jackson vetoed the legislation rechartering the bank in July 1832. Taney helped draft the president's famous veto message, which justified a much more active use of executive power than any previous president. The bank charter veto proved a formative moment in the evolution of the American presidency, and Taney did much to make it happen.

In September 1833, Jackson adopted Taney's new national banking plan.

He had appointed a new treasury secretary, William Duane, and ordered him to remove the government deposits from the bank's accounts. When Duane balked, Jackson dismissed him and replaced him with Taney, who immediately started moving the government's accounts to the pet banks.

With the U.S. Bank's profits threatened, Biddle started calling in loans. As debt-ridden businesses struggled to come up with hard currency to preserve their credit, the country was thrown into a financial panic. Biddle, in the words of a Taney biographer, made "the whole nation groan under the pressure. . . . For months there were the most fearful scenes of dismay and ruin when the paper currency was thus suddenly and violently contracted. . . . Property became unsellable. The price of produce and labor was reduced to the lowest point. Thousands and tens of thousands of laborers were thrown out of employment." The bank panic of 1833, as it was dubbed, left the country destitute.

It also ruined the Bank of Maryland, a Baltimore institution that was controlled by Thomas Ellicott, an amoral Quaker businessman and close friend of Taney's. Ellicott had been secretly speculating with bank funds and suffered massive losses. The bank's account holders, many of them working people, lost their life savings. The Bank of Maryland's failure, in turn, threatened a second bank controlled by Ellicott, the Union Bank, where Taney had served as a director. Taney, mortified that Ellicott's irresponsible dealings might discredit his new national banking policy, quietly tapped Treasury Department accounts to make good on Ellicott's losses. Taney, in the words of one economic historian, "knew he would have to bail him out or absorb a severe political setback." In modern political parlance, the Union Bank was too big to fail.

The Bank War amounted to a personal power struggle between Andrew Jackson and Nicholas Biddle. The imperious banker relished the disarray in the financial system and did not feel responsible for the suffering of those thrown out of work. He expected that desperate debtors would pressure the president to restore the bank's charter, and they did. A delegation of leading businessmen called on Jackson to describe their plight. With no currency in circulation, businesses were failing, which meant people had no money to spend, which meant that ever more businesses were becoming insolvent. Jackson erupted. "Insolvent you say?" he barked at his visitors. "What do you come to me for then? Go to Nicholas Biddle. We have no money here, gentlemen. Biddle has all the money!" Jackson intended to prevail over Biddle even if it pained the workingman and the shopkeeper in the short term.

Biddle had misread the politics of the situation. In the spring of 1834, amidst the country's worst economic contraction since 1819, Jackson won. The House of Representatives, swelled by the ranks of newly elected Jacksonian congressmen, voted against the renewal of the bank's charter. It was a death blow to Biddle's financial empire. Without the guaranteed government deposits, the U.S. Bank lost its competitive advantage and eventually went bankrupt. Biddle had been defeated. Thanks to Jackson and Taney, the country had entered into a new financial regime, more democratic and less stable.

In June 1834, Jackson felt confident enough to finally submit Taney's formal nomination to be treasury secretary. Now it was Jackson's turn to misread the politics. Taney's too-cozy friendship with the now-notorious Ellicott still rankled leading newspaper editors. Biddle retained many allies in the upper chamber of the Congress. The Senate promptly rejected Taney, the first time in the history of the United States that a cabinet nomination had been turned down. Jackson had won the Bank War but lost the battle to keep Taney in the cabinet.

Taney and Key celebrated anyway. In August 1834, they attended a political picnic on the lawn of the Frederick County Courthouse attended by more than three thousand people. The crowd sat at tables spread with hams, joints of beef, chicken, jellies, vegetables, and sweets. As the guest of honor, Taney spoke first, taking credit for slaying the monster that was the U.S. Bank. Key was toasted as a friend of the administration, "worthy of being honored wherever genius is admired or liberty cherished, as the author of 'The Star-Spangled Banner.'"

Key took the podium. He flattered the hometown audience with nostalgia.

"Never even in my boyhood had I come within view of these mountains without having my warmest affections awakened at the sight." He acknowledged the praise for his song and recalled the circumstances that impelled him to write it in September 1814. The people of Maryland inspired him, he said, a muse not previously disclosed.

"I saw the flag of my country waving over a city, the strength and pride of my native state. . . ." he declared. "I witnessed the preparations for its assaults. I saw the array of its enemies as they advanced to the attack. . . . Then did I remember that Maryland had called her sons to the defense of that flag."

Key recalled another triumph, which he said was even more glorious: the Battle of New Orleans in 1815. There, he said, General Jackson had faced "the flower of the British army" and repelled them. "Yes, even now, when he has administered the Government with unparalleled wisdom and success, we are told he is a man of no learning, of no ability as a writer or a speaker. . . . Andrew Jackson was there. He made neither proclamation nor speech; but he put a tongue in the mouths of his artillery and bade them to speak to them. There was a speech to be had in everlasting remembrance."

Key hailed this man of action who let his guns do the talking. To oppose Jackson was to abandon the country to the corrupting influence of the U.S. Bank, he said. At stake was the very soul of America as evoked in his "Star-Spangled Banner." "If forgetful of her past," he declared, "our country shall cease to be the land of the free and the home of the brave and become the purchased possession of a company of stock-jobbers and speculators."

Key walked off to a chorus of cheering and whistling. The poet turned partisan had perfected a trope that would endure in American politics: To oppose the president was unpatriotic.

A s DISTRICT ATTORNEY for the City of Washington, Key had the mission of enforcing the laws of the slave system: to protect white men from the loss of their human property. He worked with the men of the grand jury to address the problem. The jurors, white men of diverse backgrounds, met daily on the second floor of City Hall, upstairs from Key's office. In April 1833, the grand jury indicted John Prout, school-teacher and colonization critic, for helping an enslaved man named Joe Dozier and his girlfriend escape to Baltimore. When Dozier was caught, Key charged Prout on two counts: for forging a pass describing Dozier as "a free person" and a "laborer," and for enticing him to run away by arranging for another free black man, Abraham Johnson, to drive him north. Johnson was also charged with enticing a runaway.

At trial, a petit jury found Prout not guilty of forgery because the escape had not succeeded but convicted him of enticing and persuading. Johnson was also convicted. Both were fined fifty dollars. Key registered a victory for local slave masters when Prout left town.

Key stepped up his campaign against the city's antislavery subversives in November 1833 when his constables caught a printer named William Greer reading an issue of Ben Lundy's *Genius of Universal Emancipation* in which the crusading editor declared, "There is neither mercy nor justice for colored people in this district."

Lundy reported a story well known among the free people of color. A group whom Lundy described as "people of quality" decided to throw a party for themselves. They applied to a constable for a permit; he wrote one and took payment for it. "The blacks assembled, under permission as they thought, enjoying themselves in a very orderly manner, when about 11 o'clock at night, fourteen constables surrounded the house armed with guns, pistols, and clubs." The constables proceeded to rob the partygoers of all their money and watches. The next day they brought the colored men before a justice of the peace, where each was fined as much as he could pay, with the constables and the justice of the peace dividing the proceeds among themselves. Key's constables, Lundy charged, amounted to little more than a gang of thieves whose "gross imposition and cruelty" were "practiced upon unoffending colored people with impunity."

In the same issue Lundy reported another story perhaps even more damning to the district attorney. One day a "very decent, orderly looking" colored woman was crossing the Long Bridge into Washington when Constable Gilson Dove saw her. Dove tried to grab her, perhaps intending to take her to one of the Georgia pens where Negro families and laborers were sold to the South. The woman wrenched herself loose and ran across the bridge. Dove gave chase and when she had no way to escape, she fell into the river. She vanished beneath the Potomac's waters.

"No fuss or stir was made about it," Lundy noted. "She was got out of the river, and was buried, and there the matter ended."

Lundy did not just report the story, the likes of which had been ignored before. He wrote that the Congress should act if District Attorney Key would not.

"It is the duty of Congress," Lundy said, "to provide for the peace and good government of the district, and to protect the inhabitants from the depredations of unprincipled men invested with a little brief authority, by securing the just and equal administration of the laws. And if they fail to do this and permit such scenes to be acted with impunity . . . the guilt and ignominy will fall upon the whole nation."

At his desk in City Hall, Mr. Key was furious. He decided that obnoxious line "There is neither mercy nor justice for colored people in this district" constituted an insult to his associates that he could not ignore. The district attorney filed charges against both Lundy and his printer, Greer. In the handwritten indictment, Key declared Lundy's article was intended "to injure, oppress, aggrieve & vilify the good name, fame, credit & reputation of the Magistrates & constables of Washington County."

Lundy, aware the constables were looking for him, had already left town. Tired of the threats and confrontations endemic in Washington, he collected one last care package from his black friends. "The little pale thin man never departed empty-handed," said Isaac Cary. Lundy relocated his one-man paper to Philadelphia, and Key had to content himself with prosecuting Greer. In his defense, the printer called two witnesses. One was Jacob Janney, the young Quaker who sold subscriptions to the *Genius*. The other was James Thompson, a boat captain who may have seen the drowning of the colored woman. Greer presumably wanted them to corroborate the truth of Lundy's stories for the jurors.

As district attorney, Key called Gilson Dove and another constable, David Waters, as witnesses. Both men had been charged the year before with unspecified "illegal practices," probably a reference to the kidnapping of free Negroes. Presumably Key wanted their testimony to prove Lundy's article was libelous.

Both sides were heard in the City Hall courtroom, and the district attorney failed to convince. The jury found Greer not guilty. Already there were at least a dozen white people in Washington City who did not share Mr. Key's vision of justice. There would be others.

PART III

ANNA AND ARTHUR

Anna Maria Thornton, a socialite and slave owner who lived
on F Street, as depicted by Gilbert Stuart in 1804.

14

MRS. ANNA MARIA Thornton still missed William Thornton, her late husband, five years after his death. Anna and her aging mother, Ann Brodeau, and their various Negro servants lived in a fine three-story brick house on F Street, between Thirteenth and Fourteenth streets, one of the city's most prestigious addresses. F Street was a hard dirt thoroughfare that ran east-west atop a ridge that yielded a splendid view of the Potomac River. The residents were people of means. Anna's friend, former president John Quincy Adams, and his wife, Louisa, lived next door. Anna and Dr. Thornton, as she still called him, had lived there for thirty-two years before his death on March 28, 1828. During their eventful and affectionate marriage, William Thornton had designed the U.S. Capitol, saved the Patent Office from British marauders in 1814, advocated for African colonization, and done many other wise and foolish deeds. The anniversary of their wedding (October 13, 1790) had once pleased her. Since his death, the anniversary of his passing always pained her.

At fifty-six years of age Anna Thornton still had some of the beauty of her youth, particularly the bright eyes and sharp features that painter Gilbert Stuart captured in a portrait in 1804. She played chess and the piano, read history and novels, and kept a detailed diary of her daily life. In matters of business, Anna was said to be the equal of a man, which was fortunate because Dr. Thornton's passing left her in charge of his extensive household and his rather more extensive debts.

Anna knew Francis Scott Key well, regarding him as a gentleman and a friend. Key's wife, Polly, was a cousin of her dear friend Benjamin Ogle Tayloe, and she occasionally called for a social visit. Mr. Key had been a friend of her late husband and represented him in one of the many lawsuits he provoked.

Anna did not know Beverly Snow, though she often rode by the Epicurean Eating House in her carriage. After dinner, she liked to take a ride, accompanied by her mother or a friend. Sometimes her driver, a Negro man in his forties named George Plant, drove her and the other passengers up Sixteenth Street to the heights of Kalorama. Other times, they proceeded down Pennsylvania Avenue and out to the Long Bridge over the Potomac to enjoy the sights and the night air. On these evening tours, Anna almost always passed the corner of Sixth and Pennsylvania, but it is unlikely she ever dined at Beverly Snow's restaurant. Anna Thornton was no Epicurean.

Mrs. Thornton's house on F Street was not sumptuous, but it had a distinguished air. The front parlor was adorned with Gilbert Stuart's portraits of her and of her husband, a rocking chair, a bookcase, a glass bust of George Washington, and a tripod that the first president had given to Dr. Thornton. During the winter, Anna and her mother and their servant, a black woman in her thirties named Maria Bowen, slept in the back room, warmed by a fireplace. In the summer, the three women slept upstairs to catch the night breezes.

Anna Thornton was by no means wealthy. Thanks to her late husband, she owned property around Washington City from Rock Creek to the far end of Capitol Hill. But she no longer had his salary from the Patent Office. She tried to sell land to raise money, but few had reason to buy remote fields along the Eastern Branch. Even her lots on C Street near the Long Bridge did not attract much interest. Her expenses were not small. She owned a five-hundred-acre farm in Bethesda that produced potatoes and firewood but not much else. She also owned a country house up in Kalorama Heights that required maintenance.

It was Anna's slaves, her property in people, that sustained her. She owned seven people, most of whom had worked for her for many years. She owned three men—Joe, Bill, and Archy—who took care of the Bethesda farm. Archy was the oldest and the most reliable. When he was not hauling supplies into town, Anna hired him out to work at a rock quarry. He blasted the rocks, and she received seven dollars a month for his labor.

Around the F Street house, Anna relied on George Plant, her driver and jack-of-all-trades. In an arrangement not unknown at that time, Plant did not actually have to live in the household. Although Anna owned George and was entitled to the fruits of his labor, he spent evenings with his free wife and children in Georgetown. In the mornings, he showed up for work on F Street. George Plant was that peculiar Washington character: a slave who commuted.

Personally, she depended on three generations of Bowens. There was Maria Bowen's mother, Nelly Bowen, who had been her servant when she and William first came to Washington in 1795. Now elderly, she had passed the job to Maria, her daughter. Maria, in turn, had given birth to a boy, John Arthur, who by 1830 was going on fourteen years old.

Without this retinue, Anna Thornton could not have enjoyed her active social life. Maria Bowen shopped, cooked, and helped her take care of Mrs. Brodeau, who often fell ill. Nelly did sewing and cooking, and Arthur was expected to work as a servant himself, though he wasn't very good at it.

Arthur had grown up a frisky boy who loved the streets of Washington City. At an early age, he picked up on Dr. Thornton's passion for horses. "Races today + Arthur gone without leave," Anna noted dismally in her diary in 1828. When Maria Bowen finally found her son in a billiards hall the next morning, the lad explained that he had slept in the backyard, as if that set matters straight.

Arthur was soft-spoken and quick-witted. Mrs. Brodeau had taught him to read and write at an early age. He had few duties around the house and plenty of room to roam. As Arthur grew older, the memory of William Thornton grew dimmer. He had no father. No older man lived in the house. The women expected George Plant to wield a manly hand with the boy, but Plant had four children of his own. As Arthur explored the city at will, his wayward ways disrupted the household. One day Anna overheard George shouting at Maria and Nelly about Arthur. "They are violent and unreasonable when in passion," Anna wrote in her diary, "but who is not?" When the spring races came, Arthur ran away again.

Around the Fourth of July, George had a ferocious fight with Arthur. Anna had an urgent errand, requiring a trip on horseback, and George had failed to show up for work, perhaps sleeping off the effects of patriotic inebriation. Normally, she wouldn't entrust such a job to a boy, but this time she did. Arthur took the horse and somehow the animal was injured. When George finally showed up, Anna was furious at him, and George was in turn furious at Arthur, threatening to whip him for mishandling the horse. Arthur took off and did not return until night had fallen.

"Archy is dead."

Maria Bowen was speaking to Mrs. Thornton as they stood in the parlor of the house on F Street. Archy was the oldest of the male slaves, a member of the family household.

"He was killed yesterday by the blowup of a rock at the quarry," Maria said bleakly.

Anna could not believe it. Archy? Dead?

"I didn't know they blew up rocks there," Anna said, a dubious claim. She was the one who had hired Archy out to the quarry, and she was the one who received his wages. The women no doubt wept and consoled each other.

Arthur felt the loss as much as anyone. Archy had been working and living at the Bethesda farm ever since Arthur was a little boy. His death left him even more alone in a house full of women, his own father nowhere to be seen, never to be mentioned. The house was dismal. It rained for days. To cheer up Nelly and Maria, Anna gave them three dollars to buy themselves gowns.

Not long after Archy's death, Anna decided it was time to do something about Arthur. The boy knew what he could expect as an enslaved person. Just down the street at the southwest corner of Thirteenth and F streets stood Miller's Tavern, home to a notorious incident around the time Arthur was born. Like many taverns in Washington City, Miller's had a locked room where slave-owning travelers might house their bondsmen. One night, an enslaved woman, despondent that her two children had been sold to the South without her, jumped out of the window of her third-floor cell. She was badly injured but lived to tell her story to a young writer, Jesse Torrey, who made it famous with a dramatic drawing in his book on the cruelties of slavery in America. Arthur passed Miller's Tavern often, a reminder of the cruelty of the world outside the comfortable house in which he was growing up.

Anna didn't have enough work for him around the house, so she hired him out to her friend Mrs. Thompson, who agreed to pay Anna seven dollars a month for his services. Unfortunately, Arthur didn't take directions well, and Mrs. Thompson sent him home before the month was out. Anna hired him out to Mrs. Cochrane, a widow who lived a few doors down on F Street. He bickered with her servants and was fired. Anna hired him out to Mrs. Carlisle, who ran a boardinghouse on C Street. Within a few days, he came home claiming he had a sore leg. She hired him out to Mr. and Mrs. Fuller, who owned the American Hotel at 14th and Pennsylvania. Arthur came and went from that job too. He refused to obey any woman, white or colored, free or slave. Even worse, he was making new friends and drinking spirits, which worried Anna.

"It was obvious," Anna said, "that he had become dissipated and idle and addicted to occasional intoxication, though by no means a confirmed sot."

The best thing to happen to Arthur Bowen was also perhaps the worst: He met John Cook. In 1833 the onetime shoemaker from Fredericksburg had left his clerk's job at the Land Office to take over John Prout's school for colored children at Fourteenth and H streets. Cook was twenty-five years old and in full command of his powers. Arthur was now seventeen years old and still impressionable. Cook was teaching himself Latin. Arthur couldn't hold a job.

Arthur started attending meetings of the Philomathean Talking Society, where Cook led discussions with prepared remarks about slavery, temperance, and tobacco and handed out copies of forbidden newspapers like the *Genius of Universal Emancipation* and *The Liberator*. Arthur was inspired and returned to hear more. As Anna later conceded, he began keeping "the company of such free Negroes as were most actively engaged in propagating notions of general abolition, and disseminating inflammatory pamphlets from the North."

Mrs. Thornton may have owned Arthur Bowen, but she could not control him.

15

ANNA HAD OTHER worries besides Arthur. For one, there was her mother's perennial poor health. At nearly eighty years of age, Mrs. Brodeau (as everyone addressed her) suffered from glaucoma, dementia, and the effects of several strokes that had incapacitated her body and afflicted her mind. "Mama poorly" was one of the most common phrases in Anna's journal, along with its optimistic rejoinder "Mama better" and its inevitable variations "Mama unwell" and "Mama a little better."

Anna's servant Maria Bowen provided crucial help in the daunting and emotional chore of taking care of her mother. Anna depended on Maria. When Maria fell sick, Anna noted in her diary "a great inconvenience."

Fortunately, Anna liked Maria. Yes, they had a great difference in age, and yes, they bickered. Anna was annoyed when Maria wanted to go to a party with her friends. Maria was not pleased when Anna did not give her time to properly prepare for a dinner party. But together they kept the house on F Street in good running order. The rhythm of their life could be idyllic. Happy were the warm and hazy days of autumn when Maria baked a cake while George and Arthur harvested potatoes and Anna read a book.

Anna liked and depended on George Plant too. While she complained about his occasional absences, she took comfort in his presence around the house as well. When George went to visit relatives in Virginia for a week, Anna wrote in her diary, "I shall miss him very much."

Anna Thornton had sometimes found it hard to live with her late husband, Dr. Thornton, but she was finding it harder to live without him. She had never known another man as well. They had been married when she was fifteen and he was thirty-one. Her mother, then a schoolmistress in Philadelphia, had arranged the match, and it proved a good one for her daughter. With his winning design of the Capitol, Dr. Thornton took his young bride and her mother to live in the growing village of Washington, where they gave dinners and parties that constituted the first social society of the new capital.

Almost everywhere she looked in Washington City, Anna could discern Dr. Thornton's genius. When she rode out on the Avenue for her daily postdinner ride, she saw his magnificent building on Capitol Hill. When visiting friends in Georgetown, she saw Tudor House, the mansion he had designed for George Washington's kin in the Custis and Lee families. When she passed through the intersection of Eighteenth Street and New York Avenue, she saw the Octagon House, which he had designed and built for her friend Benjamin Ogle Tayloe, and where her friends Dolley and James Madison had lived after the sacking of the presidential mansion in 1814. An eight-sided Georgian home with a central circular hall, a grand staircase, and sculptured mantels, the building was perhaps Washington City's most elegant residence, a marvel of architectural ingenuity that showed the city's ambitions for splendor were not entirely unrealistic.

Dr. Thornton's handiwork had also led to one improvement that forever changed the capital's landscape. When the Thorntons first came to the newly created District of Columbia in 1794, Dr. Thornton had explored the byways and channels of the vast tidal swamp that covered its southern section. As a wandering student he had seen the great capitals of Europe, strolling along the Thames in London and the Seine in Paris. Tramping on the marshy edge of the Potomac, he imagined what this new capital city might one day become. As an experiment, he planted saplings and bushes around the periphery of about eighteen acres of tidal mud on the theory that the roots of the plants would cause it to fill up more rapidly with silt than it naturally would. In time, the swampland within the circle of trees would grow solid and could become a useful part of the adjacent city. Thornton's folly, people called it. Yet after years of scoffing, people realized Dr. Thornton was right—the ground in the pastures grew more solid and valuable, and soon a man named Kidwell claimed it as his own. What had been an impenetrable bog was now a productive pasture (and would, in the fullness of time, become home to the Reflecting Pool in front of the Lincoln Memorial on the National Mall).

He even found the time to write two full-length unpublished novels, depicting sympathetic females enduring the travails of judgmental Washington society. The first, "Julia," described the plight of an unhappily married woman who has an affair with a dishonest sea captain. The second, "Lucy," followed a likable young woman who has a child out of wedlock and has to win back the love of her ashamed family.

And he had moral courage. Who could forget Dr. Thornton's defense of the Patent Office during the British invasion of 1814? Or his rescue in 1806 of poor Mrs. Turreau, the much-abused wife of the French ambassador? She had saved the ambassador from the guillotine during the French Revolution, and he repaid the favor by beating her. When the shameless man ordered soldiers to drag her onto a boat for an unwanted return trip to France, Dr. Thornton intervened in his official capacity as the magistrate for the Second Ward.

"Mr. Thornton, you don't know zee laws of the nation," said the angry French diplomat.

"But I know the laws of humanity," Dr. Thornton replied, "and I mean to enforce them."

With the help of a small crowd, Dr. Thornton forced Mr. Turreau to cease his tyranny and let his wife choose her own departure.

Anna remembered her husband's faults too. He spent money too freely. He had all the attributes of a rich man, said a wag, save the most important one: His intelligence was not always practical. With a man named Fitch, he had devised the world's first steam-powered boat but, alas, had never perfected the idea. A cannier man named Robert Fulton swiped their design, built a fleet of steamboats, and made a fortune. Thornton filed a lawsuit against Fulton that dragged on for years without result. At the Patent Office, Thornton met, and annoyed, almost every inventor of consequence in the country. He denied more than one patent request by saying that he had actually thought of the invention long before. To those he did not like, he was quarrelsome.

He could also be vain. "He knew many things, indeed, he knew almost everything," said one bemused admirer. "And what he knew he was disposed to fully let everybody else know." He was easily distracted. He enjoyed lively company and the pleasures of the racetrack at the expense of his intellectual pursuits. "His thirst for knowledge was great, and perhaps too diffuse and general, but his views were noble and enlarged," Anna wrote after his death. ". . . Alas, he lived not to complete any of his plans but left all unfinished, tho his industry and activity were unsurpassed."

Anna's friend and neighbor John Quincy Adams was harsher. The former president wrote in his diary that he thought Thornton was a fool, "a man of some learning and much ingenuity, of quick conception and lively wit" who was also "entirely destitute of Judgment, discretion and common sense."

Yet Anna was stubborn in his posthumous defense. The former president might be condescending, yet as she looked around Washington City, she could say without fear of contradiction that her late husband had a more visible and enduring influence on the capital than the estimable Mr. Adams.

For better and worse, she had loved him. He was her first and only lover, an older man with fascinating and sometimes dubious friends. He was a compulsive inventor and ingenious architect. Well born and well read, he had a love for horses that did him no good. He had a thirst for liberty yet a weak will. He was wise about the human heart, naïve about power. Dependent on women, he was immune to their influence. A failure at fisticuffs, he had a wit that could charm. He was sensitive to slights, prone to argument, imaginative about big things, oblivious about details. He was carefree, valiant, and foolish. And he was gone.

ALL THE WHILE Anna was worrying about Arthur, Beverly Snow ran the Epicurean Eating House with ingratiating élan. With wife Julia and business partner William Walker at his side, he tended the stoves, shopped in the Centre Market, met the steamboats down at the Georgetown docks, and wrote up advertisements for the newspapers extolling what his establishment offered. "LUXURY LUXURY LUXURY!" boasted one. The Epicurean Eating House was a busy place, especially at night.

The Avenue had been paved with hard-packed stones, now spanning a width of eighty feet, with fourteen-foot-wide sidewalks on either side. All agreed the new hard surface of the boulevard was a marvel until it was noticed that the steel wheels of the carriages tended to grind the rocks' surface to a fine powder. On gusty days, tourists gaping at the Pocahontas sign above Brown's Hotel would find themselves engulfed in a passing thunderhead of powder and emerged looking like ghosts. Shopkeepers took to hosing down the Avenue in self-defense.

Familiar and distinguished faces abounded on Snow's corner. Andrew Stevenson, the Virginia congressman who served as Speaker of the House of Representatives, lived at Brown's, as did a half dozen other representatives. Every year there seemed to be more visitors from England and even the Continent. Across Sixth Street, the white and black hackmen in front of Gadsby's Hotel flicked their reins and steered their carriages out onto the Avenue, ferrying politicians, lobbyists, and ladies to the Capitol. They returned with tourists and attorneys. The shiny blue carriages of Beltzhoover & Company boarded passengers for Baltimore at four and eight thirty in the morning and at three in the afternoon. There were even larger omnibuses, seating a dozen people at a time, that took all manner of passengers to Georgetown, Alexandria, and the Capitol on the hour.

Inside the Epicurean Eating House, Beverly was offering what a future generation would call soul food and what contemporaries regarded as one of the city's finest dining experiences. Stepping down the stairs to the basement door, visitors entered a cozy, aromatic warren of dining rooms lit by candles. At a time when hotels and taverns were mostly run for men, Snow made a point of welcoming women and children. "Families furnished as usual," he declared in his advertisements.

At the busiest of times, ladies and gentlemen of the best sort filled his tables. John Withers, Beverly's landlord, partook of the food but passed on the spirits. After all, he was vice president of a temperance society. Daniel Webster, the mammoth orator from Massachusetts, was known to duck in the door. So was Harry Clay, not so disdainful of the colored man that he wouldn't sample his repast now and then. Even John Calhoun, the embittered former vice president, showed up now and again.

Diners chose from a menu specializing in, but not limited to, small game birds, offering roasted woodcocks, partridges, plovers, and pheasants. Each might be dressed with currants, guava, or jelly. The refined scent of canvasback duck competed with the sweeter aroma of the smaller birds likes ortolans and snipes. In the warmer months, he touted trout and soft-shell crabs. At one table, you might see a man eating that new French meat concoction known as "patte" with a glass of Madeira. At another, ladies sipped "champaigne."

Beverly's specialty was green turtle, served as an entire meal. In the early summer, he would go down to the docks and buy a massive terrapin right off the steamboat. These creatures, weighing up to one hundred pounds each, were brought in from distant coves and marshes along the Chesapeake Bay. Beverly would cart one, still alive, to his basement kitchen, where he probably prepared it in a manner similar to that prescribed by Mary Randolph in her popular cookbook *The Virginia Housewife*.

"Kill it at night in winter, and in the morning in summer," Randolph advised. "Hang it up by the hind fins, cut off the head, and let it bleed well.

"Separate the bottom shell from the top, with great care lest the gall bladder be broken, which must be cautiously taken out and thrown away. Put the liver in a bowl of water. Empty the guts and lay them in water. If there be eggs, put them also in water."

Beverly would have used a big knife to cut all the flesh from the bottom of the massive shell. He put the meat in a pan of water, then broke the shell in two, washed it, and put it in a big pot to boil. If he followed Mary Randolph's recipe he cleansed the guts, peeled off the inside skin, and added bacon and chopped onions, leaving the mixture to cook for three hours.

With the soup under way, Beverly then turned to the meat of the turtle. He cut out the flesh of the belly, known as the calipee and renowned as the tastiest part of the animal. Then he removed the calipash, the flesh underneath the top shell, also a delicacy. He chopped both into small pieces, sprinkled on salt, and covered them. He parboiled the fins, removing all the black skin, and put them in the oven to bake at a medium temperature. When the shell and the guts were done boiling, he would take out the bacon, scrape the shell clean, and strain out the big pieces of the guts. What was left was the pride of Beverly's kitchen: a fine green turtle soup.

To prepare the calipee in "the West Indian way," which many colored cooks did, Beverly would use a moderate seasoning of butter, mixed with chopped thyme, parsley, and young onions, as well as salt, white pepper, cayenne pepper, and a pint or more of Madeira. While the turtle meat marinated, Beverly would fry up the chopped turtle guts into a fricassee and finish baking the fins.

The results were served up as a five-course terrapin feast. Diners began with the pièce de résistance, the calipee, followed by the fricasseed guts, the soup, and the fins, served warm or cold. The calipash was eaten last.

Beverly Snow was not falsely modest about the quality of his dishes or his customers.

"Some of the most refined Epicureans, of this Epicurean city, have said the Callapash and the Pattes, were the greatest luxury of the table," he claimed in the *Intelligencer*.

For the crowds coming to the fall races, he declared his culinary credo:

HEALTH BOUGHT CHEAP
Just received from the steamboat *Potomac,* a Fine Green
Turtle, which will be served up this day, at 11 o'clock.

Beverly stressed the salubrious rarity of this delicacy, boasting, "This luxury has been recommended by some of our most eminent physicians as a restorative." Said physicians were not identified by name, but no matter. The practical message of "Health Bought Cheap" was inspired, even ahead of its time. The food at the Epicurean Eating House was not only good, it was good for you.

In 1833, Beverly made the city tax rolls for the first time, reporting three hundred dollars in personal property. Since his arrival three years before, he had saved an average of one hundred dollars a year, no small feat for a colored man who was new in town.

Beverly was by no means rich. He was not even the wealthiest Negro in Washington City. That distinction probably belonged to Poll Robinson, a madam who ran a bawdy house in the First Ward. But Beverly did well by any standard. He pocketed more money than virtually all of the Irish mechanics who helped pave the Avenue outside his restaurant. He had more money than some of the constables on the city police force. He had made a name for himself among the most distinguished white people in the capital of the country and was not shy about advertising the fact. In one ad in the *Intelligencer*, he proclaimed himself "The National Restaurateur."

If Snow's corner at Sixth and Pennsylvania was glamorous, with its daily bustle and late-night tempo, it could also be treacherous. While the ablest free men of color, like Beverly Snow and Isaac Cary, lived and worked among white people, they knew that, at night, the slave traders herded groups of chained families of black people through the city to transport them to the new cotton plantations of the South and West. Beverly did not have to pay attention to this daily crime any more than anyone else. The armed white men usually moved the coffles after curfew so that their fellow Americans would not suffer the experience of seeing enslaved people trudging past the Capitol. But Beverly had to be careful.

He was not exempt from the pressure that District Attorney Key and his constables applied to the free people of color. In June 1834, Key's constables arrested Thomas Cary, the brother of Isaac, who worked next door in the Emporium of Fashion barbershop. The charge against Thomas Cary was not entered into the record, but it must have been serious because Beverly and Isaac put their money together and posted a five-hundred-dollar bond for his release. Whatever the charge, Thomas Cary, a dedicated antislavery man, had likely defied the legal restrictions on free Negroes in Washington that Key sought to enforce. A trial was scheduled for November 1834, but before it could take place, Key seems to have dropped the charges, possibly because Thomas Cary left town.

Around this time Beverly seems to have left town as well. Perhaps his financial success combined with his association with the outspoken Cary brothers had brought him unwanted attention from the authorities. Perhaps some white men found his audacious style obnoxious to their feelings of racial superiority. Perhaps he had gone, like Benjamin Lundy, to check out the growing colony of free blacks in Canada, where slavery had just been abolished. In any case, he stopped picking up his mail for the next few months, and William Walker ran the Epicurean Eating House in his absence.

By the end of the year, Beverly had returned. Congress had reconvened with the usual talk of tariffs and Texas, contracts and audits. The bars and hotels swelled again with people engaged in the business of American government. President Jackson delivered his annual message to Congress. Mr. Key commuted daily to City Hall. Anna Thornton shopped in Centre Market and rode out on the Avenue. Beverly cooked his dishes and welcomed customers. In the capital of the slaveholding republic he had obtained a rare thing for a free man of color: respect.

"This man Snow," said Julia Seaton, "was a mulatto at the very head of the respectable colored population, keeping a restaurant much frequented by the good society of Washington."

17

THE MOOD WAS somber but brisk as the mourners hastened out of the funeral service in the hall of the House of Representatives on January 30, 1835. Congressmen and senators in their long black coats moved along with a swarm of ladies in bonnets, sailors in uniform, clerks, gentlemen, ministers, and dowdy newspaper correspondents. The deceased member from South Carolina had been duly eulogized and now Friday's business was calling.

Former president John Quincy Adams, portly and grim, exited the Capitol Rotunda as fast as his legs could move him. He wanted no contact with his successor, who lagged behind. President Jackson was walking arm in arm with Levi Woodbury, the secretary of the treasury. As the two men approached the marble pillars that framed the brass doors to the eastern exit, a thin-faced man with dark hair and whiskers stepped forward, standing still as the crowd passed him by. In his right hand, he held a pistol. He raised it.

Jackson, though frail, still had a soldier's instinct for action. He pushed off from Woodbury and started toward the gunman. The young man— "of genteel appearance and rather pleasant countenance," a bystander said—pulled the trigger. Jackson was less than nine feet away when the explosion blasted the air. The man lowered the pistol in his right hand and calmly raised his left hand, also holding a pistol. Unhurt, Jackson was advancing with his cane raised when a second shot exploded. A passing navy lieutenant named Gedney tackled the gunman, sending him sprawling to the marble floor. Pandemonium rippled through the Rotunda. Bystanders rushed to surround President Jackson, who was shouting, "Let me alone! Let me get him," and waving his cane. Kindly people tried to calm the old man.

A few feet away, the young man on the floor thrashed about as a few men held him down. When the constables arrived, he was put in handcuffs, lifted up, rushed outside, and stuffed into a carriage. It was the first attempted assassination of a U.S. president.

It was another job for Francis Scott Key.

A strange winter thunderstorm engulfed the city as the district attorney arrived at the courtroom in City Hall for the arraignment of the would-be assassin. The space was filling fast. Chief Judge William Cranch was seated on the bench. Duff Green of the *Telegraph* was prowling about. So was his bitter rival, Francis Blair of the *Globe*, who eyed the shiny pistols already laid on the evidence table. Several spectators recognized the accused man, who was seated in the defendant's dock in the middle of the courtroom. His name was Richard Lawrence. He was a house painter and said to be a good one. After Judge Cranch gaveled the hearing to order, Key rose from his seat at the government's table and called Tom Randolph, the congressional sergeant at arms, to the stand.

Under questioning from Key, Randolph testified that he had spoken to Lawrence in the carriage ride after the attack and asked him why he had fired the shots. "Because the president killed my father," Lawrence had replied.

Key called Lieutenant Gedney. The sailor testified that he had taken the pistols from Lawrence and examined them. Suddenly Frank Blair stepped to the front of the courtroom and approached the evidence table. The district attorney, who knew Blair well, did not object, nor did the three judges. The homely editor was known as the president's confidant, and his newspaper showed no mercy to anyone who stood in Jackson's way. Blair picked up one of the pistols and pulled back the trigger to expose the gun's bullet chamber. He held up the gun for inspection to the now-silent and fascinated courtroom crowd. The chamber was fully loaded. The gun, which looked new, had misfired. Jackson's life had been in real danger.

Blair's grandstanding had a point: The president had been saved by a miracle. Duff Green watched Blair's stunt with disgust. When he turned away, he noticed that Richard Lawrence was smiling for the first time, like the whole thing was a joke.

Judge Cranch set bail at fifteen hundred dollars, and Lawrence was taken, in the rain, to City Jail, a long two-story brick building on Fourth Street behind City Hall.

In the days that followed, Francis Blair and Duff Green fixed on the assassination attempt as the quintessence of the political moment. In the pages of the *Globe*, Blair insinuated that Jackson's enemies, in their desperation to bring down the man of the people, had incited Lawrence. In the *Telegraph*, Green denounced the incident as a sham designed to elicit sympathy for a failing tyrant. As people discussed the shocking event, two discernible schools of thought emerged, a division of opinion that would become familiar in American culture. Some perceived a nefarious political conspiracy, while others saw the actions of a lone maniac.

As district attorney, Key had to sort out the matter legally. The next day, he went to the dingy jail, where a guard led him to Lawrence's cell. The prisoner wore a short-sleeved shirt, impervious to the cold. When Key began his interrogation, Lawrence informed him that no one in the country could punish him, because Europe would object.

"What led you to do it?" Key asked.

"I have long been in correspondence with the powers of Europe," Lawrence replied. "My family has been wrongfully deprived of the crown of England. I'll yet live to regain it."

Frank Key rarely lacked for words, but this was one of those times. He excused himself. The man was completely unhinged.

Key's problem was that President Jackson had a very different understanding of what had happened. In the mansion on President's Square, Jackson startled guests by declaring that he was certain, absolutely certain, that Lawrence had acted at the behest of George Poindexter, a senator from Mississippi. Once an ally of Jackson, Poindexter had broken with the president over the Bank War and the distribution of patronage jobs. Poindexter was no statesman. He was rather better known as a whoremonger and wife beater.

Jackson often told the story of how Senator Poindexter had persuaded his third wife to marry him by offering her twenty thousand dollars—and repaid her affection by whipping her regularly. When Poindexter was chosen to serve temporarily as president of the Senate the year before, the *New York Evening Post* saw a new low in American governance. "This man . . . yet rank with the fumes of a low debauch, his step yet tottering and his eyes rolling with a drunken leer, this man, all filth and vermin, called probably from a brothel or gin cellar, to the Senate Chamber, this man they chose . . . to preside over the U.S. Senate."

Jackson was certain this man had sought to have him murdered.

Key had no evidence of that, putting him at odds with his political patron, an uncomfortable situation. But Jackson persisted. When Harriet Martineau, the best-selling English writer, visited with the president and mentioned the insane attempt on his life, Jackson rebuked her.

"He protested, in the presence of many strangers, that there was no insanity in the case," Martineau recalled. "I was silent, of course. He protested that there was a plot, and that the man was a tool. . . . It was painful to hear a chief ruler publicly trying to persuade foreigners that any of his constituents hated him to the death."

Jackson took satisfaction a few days later when a bricklayer who worked on the presidential mansion sent word that he had information of interest. His name was Charles Coltman. In addition to his day job, he represented the Second Ward on the city's common council. Coltman said he had two friends who wished to share what they knew about Richard Lawrence. A mechanic named David Stewart who worked on Poindexter's carriage said he had seen Lawrence talking to the senator in the Capitol lobby on the Tuesday before the assassination attempt. Mordecai Foy, who ran an ordinary near Poindexter's house on Four and a Half Street, recalled seeing Lawrence come and go at different times, including the previous Tuesday. Coltman said he had encouraged both men to give statements to a justice of the peace.

The president invited Stewart and Foy for a visit. They called on the presidential mansion on February 12, and Jackson interrupted his meeting with Congressman Dutee Pearce of Rhode Island to usher them in. As the men told their story and shared their affidavits, Congressman Pearce scanned the statements, amazed at their allegations. After the meeting, Pearce told the story of Stewart and Foy's affidavits to Sam Southworth, a Washington correspondent for a New York business newspaper, which may have been Jackson's intention all along. Pearce was an ally, and Jackson knew the story would have more credibility if it did not come out in the *Globe*. Within a day Southworth's article became the talk of the capital. *The president had proof of an assassination conspiracy!*

Senator Poindexter was outraged. He demanded the Senate address allegations "highly injurious to my moral character," and the Senate responded by creating a six-member investigative committee. On February 22, Stewart and Foy testified. Under oath, they hedged on their statements. Stewart said he had only seen Lawrence near Poindexter's house—he had never actually seen them together—and he admitted that Poindexter owed him four hundred dollars for work on a carriage. Foy could not even identify the location of the senator's house. No other witnesses came forward.

The committee issued a unanimous report that exonerated Poindexter, asserting that "not a shade of suspicion rests upon his character." The report was received with applause from the Senate gallery and unanimously approved. Down at City Hall, the board of aldermen and the common council passed two resolutions, one denouncing Coltman, the man who had encouraged the statement, and the other blasting "every individual involved," a slap at the president himself. Jackson's conspiracy theory was dead.

Some thought the Washington grand jury should indict Jackson and Coltman for subornation of perjury, but the district attorney was not interested. Key was more convinced than ever that the failed assassination proved Andrew Jackson was living under divine protection. The rest was politics.

"The whole transaction is inexpressibly base," muttered John Quincy Adams to his diary, "and approaches much too near to the President for the good of his reputation."

Frank Key had managed the situation adroitly, neither succumbing to Jackson's manipulation of witnesses nor alienating his patron. In April 1835, Key brought the failed assassin, Richard Lawrence, to trial. He told the judges and jury that Lawrence was not guilty for reasons of insanity and ought to be committed to an asylum. The court agreed. Lawrence was convicted and sent back to the fetid City Jail. He would live in confinement until his death forty years later.

WASHINGTON CITY DID not lack dangers and attractions for Arthur Bowen, a wayward young man in search of freedom in the spring of 1835. There were occasional entertainments like balloon ascents from Mason's Island, or the traveling exhibition of a rarely seen creature, the Orang Utang. There were also perennial diversions like the billiard halls, grog shops, the circus, and the Jockey Club. When the spring races opened on Meridian Hill in May 1835, Arthur attended and paid a price. The crowd was vast as usual. There were drinking and betting, cheering and arguing, girls to impress and rivals to challenge. Arthur got into a fight and did not come out the winner.

"Arthur came home this Evening (from the races) with his head cut + much hurt and bruised," Anna wrote in her diary. "Sent for Dr. Causin who came late . . . trouble-trouble-trouble."

She did not identify Arthur's assailants in her diary. Were they other Negro boys like himself, slave or free, who were not so well dressed or so well spoken? Or was it white men annoyed by his assertive ways? Maybe Arthur never told her. A week later, he was still unwell.

Eventually Arthur recovered and made his way to the next meeting of the Philomathean Talking Society, where he might well have absorbed some of John Cook's urgency. The schoolteacher had just returned from Philadelphia, where he served as secretary at the Fifth Annual National Negro Convention, the yearly gathering of free Negroes. The convention, well attended by Washington men, had spawned a national network dedicated to economic self-sufficiency and independence. Returning from this conclave, Cook breathed the gospel of freedom and reform as never before.

In the bare classroom on H Street, Cook tried to bake an audacious idea into the heads of the young black men who gathered to talk: Their cause in America was sacred. He wanted them to understand that education, temperance, and freedom were all part of the fabric of emancipation. He told them to reject the colonization scheme in favor of an American dream as voiced in the Philadelphia convention's declaration, which he had signed, and may well have drafted.

"We rejoice that we are thrown into a revolution where the contest is not for landed territory but for freedom. . . . Let no man remove from his native country, for our principles are drawn from the book of Divine Revelation, and are incorporated in the Declaration of Independence, 'that all men are born equal.'"

Cook told them white Americans and their laws sorely abused them as people of color. But oppression would not defeat them.

"We pray God . . . that our visages may be so many Bibles that shall warn this guilty nation of her injustice and cruelty to the descendants of Africa, until righteousness, justice, and truth shall rise in their might and majesty, and proclaim from the halls of legislation that the chains of the bondsman have fallen—that the soil is sacred to liberty, and that, without distinction of nation or complexion, she disseminates alike her blessings of freedom to all mankind."

Arthur yearned to join Cook's contest for freedom in all its glory. But he couldn't even hold a job. His failings were evident to all. Well born and well read, he had a love for horses that did him no good. He had a thirst for liberty yet a weak will. He was wise about the human heart but oblivious to the workings of power. Dependent on women, he was immune to their influence. A failure at fisticuffs, he had a wit that could charm. He was sensitive to slights, prone to argument, imaginative about big things, oblivious about small. He was carefree, valiant, and foolish. He resembled no one so much as the late Dr. William Thornton.

There is no proof—or even published allegation—that William Thornton was Arthur Bowen's father. But the evidence does not exclude the possibility. Arthur was often identified as mulatto, so his father was almost certainly white. His mother, Maria Bowen, had belonged to the Thorntons since she was a little girl, which meant she had never been the property of any other white man besides William Thornton. She was born around 1800 and lived in his house at the time of Arthur's conception in 1815 and his birth nine months later, and for many years thereafter.

Liaisons between white slave owners and their black chattels were common. Dr. Thornton's friend Thomas Jefferson had his colored companion of many years, the beautiful Sally Hemings. Senator Richard Mentor Johnson, nominated in May 1835 as Martin Van Buren's vice presidential running mate in the 1836 election, had at least two African consorts, Julia Chinn and Parthene, whom he treated as wives. If William Thornton had taken young Maria Bowen by rape or seduction, it would not have been unusual.

Nor would it have been out of character. Dr. Thornton displayed a friendly and knowing interest in Negro women in his unpublished novel "Lucy." The story, which sympathetically portrayed an unmarried white mother, depicted her free black servant Becky as especially perceptive about the ways of white people. "Miss," Becky tells Lucy at one point, "a colored person may have quite the genius, and his master and mistress never be the wiser."

What Anna Thornton thought is unknown. She probably recorded some reaction to Maria Bowen's pregnancy and Arthur's birth in late 1815 or early 1816. She kept her diary from 1800 to the 1850s, filling some fifteen notebooks with neatly composed recollections, but her journals for the years from 1815 to 1827 are missing. Anna (or her heirs) decided not to save her journals from the period in which Arthur Bowen was conceived, born, and grew up. Why her account of those years was lost is unknown, but the timing is suggestive. Anna Thornton, who had a keen sense of history, may not have wanted some things to be remembered. So while there is no certainty that William Thornton fathered Arthur Bowen, he is the most likely candidate.

Yet what could Dr. Thornton's paternity mean to Arthur but betrayal and mockery? William Thornton had designed the seat of government for what people said was the freest country in the world, yet Arthur remained in bondage. In his third-floor garret in the house on F Street, he felt he deserved his freedom. But what could he do if Mrs. Thornton did not care to give it to him? His predicament was intolerable yet inescapable. He had to do something. But what?

In search of answers, he returned again to the Philomathean Talking Society.

19

THE ABOLITIONIST MENACE arrived unbidden and unnoticed on the docks of Georgetown in June 1835 when a twenty-nine-year-old white man walked off a steamboat, just arrived from New York City. By the 1830s Georgetown was turning into what it would become, a residential enclave with more society and charm than Washington City. But charm is not what the arriving passenger, Dr. Reuben Crandall, sought. He was more a man of science and religion. Recipient of a medical degree from Yale College in 1828, Crandall was a doctor, a botanist, a Christian, and a temperance man. He was also deeply opposed to slavery. Not since Benjamin Lundy prowled E Street had such a courageous antislavery man decided to make the capital his home.

Reuben Crandall was looking to settle down with a teaching position. To that end, he called on Benjamin Hallowell, the headmaster of a school in Alexandria who needed a lecturer in science. Hallowell, a Quaker and leader in American scientific education, told him that he would hire him on the condition he provide two letters of reference. Reuben took a steamer back to New York, where he collected his clothes, his possessions, his papers, and his recommendations. He booked a return trip to Georgetown within a few weeks. He returned accompanied only by a large trunk.

Crandall's trunk was Frank Key's nightmare. It contained hundreds of bundled copies of abolitionist tracts such as *The Emancipator, The Liberator, The Anti-Slavery Record,* and *Human Rights.* It even had copies of *The Slave's Friend,* an antislavery book for children. Reuben's new neighbors did not know about the contents of the trunk, but they regarded him coolly. He was from New York, which was unusual enough. He also had a notorious last name. He was the brother of Prudence Crandall, the Connecticut teacher whose school for free girls of color had made national headlines in 1833 before being shut down, first by the state legislature, and then by a mob.

Reuben was more cautious than his famous sister but he did not lack conviction. Key would later claim that Reuben formally served as an agent of the American Anti-Slavery Society, which was not exactly true. He was not an agent but two of his friends worked for the society at a high level. Charles Denison, a fellow Yale man, edited *The Emancipator*, the society's flagship publication. Denison had visited Reuben in New York the year before and delivered the trunk that Reuben had now imported to the South. Reuben was also a friend of Robert C. Williams, who served as publications manager for the society.

Both Denison and Williams promoted the organization's audacious new strategy for shaking slavery's grip on the United States. Adopted at its second annual meeting in May 1835, the plan was concocted by Arthur and Lewis Tappan, brotherly prototypes of that enduring self-summoned figure in American politics, the Wall Street progressive. Raised in a Calvinist household in Massachusetts, the Tappans proved adept at making money at an early age when they moved to New York and started importing silk from China. Arthur Tappan would go on to establish the country's first financial newspaper, the *Journal of Commerce*, and the Mercantile Agency, the first credit-rating firm on Wall Street, both of which made him rich. The Tappans wanted to generate an antislavery message independent of William Lloyd Garrison, editor of *The Liberator*, whose fierce language had won him national notoriety and alienated more than a few people. Unlike Garrison, the Tappans did not want to denounce or shame those moderates who wanted to do something about slavery. They wanted to persuade them that the procrastination of colonization was pointless, and that America should simply abolish slavery and give citizenship to the blacks.

Arthur Tappan envisioned using the newest technology, powerful steam-driven cylinder printing presses imported from England that could publish ten times the output of the hand-driven presses then in use. The antislavery society could then inundate the South with their own publications and provoke the public discussion that the slave owners always sought to suppress in the newspapers, the churches, and everywhere else. The pamphlet campaign, as they called it, would take special aim at the District of Columbia. In closing their meeting, the group prepared a memorial, or petition, insisting that the U.S. Congress certainly had the power to outlaw slavery in the capital, "and it is hardly less certain that a majority of this nation desire its abolition."

Reuben Crandall did not attend that meeting, but his friends Denison and Williams did. The society had already published more than 120,000 copies of its various pamphlets. This effort, the society decided, should be vastly increased. "It is obvious to remark," said the final report of the meeting, "that a proper organization of its friends throughout the country might enable the Society to accomplish a hundred-fold more by the press."

Within weeks bags of antislavery pamphlets, each individually addressed, began reaching the post offices of Washington and other cities in the South. Before the end of 1835, the society would distribute a million copies of four different publications.

The government's spies were among the first to notice the deluge of antislavery material. In July 1835, James Kennedy, a Post Office clerk in Washington who had the job of surveilling the mails, was appalled to see a bushel basket full of copies of *The Anti-Slavery Reporter* and *The Emancipator* arrive for local delivery. Another clerk, Charles Gordon, followed the abolitionist sheets so closely he could cite their various publication schedules from memory.

"A shower of Anti-Slavery periodicals and pamphlets have . . . descended . . . chiefly through our city post office," the weekly *Mirror* reported. "*The Emancipator* and the *Anti-Slavery Record*, in particular, have been addressed to most of the gentlemen belonging to our public offices, to the President and Professors of our Colleges &c. We understand that in most instances, these firebrands have been flung back to the source from which they sprung."

By then Reuben Crandall had rented an office with lodgings in Georgetown, near the corner of First Street and High Street, the town's north-south thoroughfare (now known as Wisconsin Avenue). In the privacy of his new quarters, he opened his trunk and took out one of the bundles. Scrawled neatly on the top copy, in his own handwriting, was the injunction "Please to read and circulate."

Reuben Crandall would do just that.

B EVERLY SNOW SENSED the city's growing agitation. As the newspapers filled with reports on the influx of incendiary tracts evan-
gelizing about "abolitionism," he offered a less controversial alternative:
GREEN TURTLEISM.

His next advertisement in the *Mirror* declared that "Green Turtleism" came in four different variations: "Soup-ism," "Calipee-ism,"
"Calipash-ism," and "Patte-ism." Snow offered this menu of culinary ide-
ologies to "politicians of every denomination," saying they would go down
easier than any other "ism." As an Epicurean, he naturally held himself
aloof from public affairs. (The wise man, said the Grecian sage, "shall not
take upon him the Administration of the Commonwealth.") Snow's ad
seemed to mock the passions of both the abolitionists and their enemies
with the playful suggestion that a good meal might be as important as
their arguments. Or was he suggesting that immediate emancipation was
as natural and urgent as eating? With Beverly Snow one could only be
sure of one thing: While others boiled, he would stay cool.

Jocose irreverence hung in the air of Washington City. With the
arrival of summer the congressmen and senators had mostly gone home,
and the usual claques of lawyers and lobbyists had vanished. All the cabinet secretaries save Postmaster Amos Kendall and Treasury Secretary
Levi Woodbury had absconded to cooler climes, and the clerks in the
government office buildings on President's Square took to knocking off
work around three in the afternoon in time to catch the daily band concert at the Capitol. The slow recovery from the bank panic of 1833 had
brought pedestrians and tourists back to the Avenue and customers into

the shops. The rough-hewn slavers still moved coffles of slaves at night toward uncertain fates in the South while their free brothers and sisters could only watch helplessly. Yet the peculiar respectability of the successful free people of color in Washington City undermined the pretensions of the slave republic by refuting its presumption of white superiority. As a result, everyone was feeling more free and less safe.

New technology was changing the city's daily routines. In the print shops, the introduction of the steam-driven cylinder press had transformed the traditionally prestigious printer's job. In 1831 Francis Blair had launched the pro-Jackson *Globe* with a cylinder press that offered competitive advantage over his rivals. Whereas the traditional iron hand press could produce two hundred copies an hour, a cylinder press could run off a thousand or two thousand. The new presses required new jobs such as feeding paper and stitching pamphlets that did not require the labor of highly paid men. These new machines could be run just as well—and more cheaply—by teenage boys and girls. When Duff Green announced in May 1835 that the *Telegraph* was bypassing the city's traditional apprentice system to hire workers—male and female—to run his new steam presses, the male members of the printers' guild, the Columbia Typographical Society, denounced the new employees in print as "rats." Rival bands of printers brawled in the streets.

Obnoxious assertion prevailed among the mechanics living in hovels near the Navy Yard or in work camps along the canal. Amidst the economic slowdown, they had few women and fewer jobs, only ample opportunity to drink. Disdained by the city's ladies and gentlemen, they started to feel free to do whatever the hell they wanted, starting with mockery of the monthly civic ritual known as Muster Day. By law, all men in Washington City between the ages of eighteen and forty had to muster as a militia once a month. Forced to leave their offices and workshops, the unarmed men paraded indifferently through the streets for no useful purpose. As they lined up, various gentlemen assumed the airs and titles of commanding officers. The militia was headed by Walter Jones, a fifty-eight-year-old lawyer and friend of Anna Thornton's. General Jones, who had last served in the War of 1812, was a leader of men, but he had not heard a shot fired in anger in a long time.

In the tropical torpor of summer, Muster Day was a dismal routine, often lubricated into jollity by massive consumption of spirits in the taverns and grog shops along the Avenue. Those unsalaried men who lost a day's wages especially resented the occasion, even more so because of the free Negroes whose dark skin, for once, conferred an advantage. Since they could not be part of the militia, they were free to work. Jobless white men had to march while free black men got paid.

When Muster Day came in May 1835, one of the mechanics dared to disrupt this stale routine. As the men paraded on the Avenue, a fellow wielding an enormous sword made out of papier-mâché darted into their ranks. He had red whiskers pasted on his cheeks and, like a French toy soldier, a ridiculous pasteboard chapeau de bras on his head. This rollicking clown attracted younger boys, whooping and hallooing among the glum mechanics, who started to laugh at the farce of it all.

William Thompson, the sympathetic young editor of the weekly *Mirror*, reported on the incident. The dressed-up mechanic and his friends, he wrote, hoped to end the mandatory muster "by force of public ridicule." There seemed to be a new spirit of insubordination floating above submerged resentments, both social and racial.

Mr. Key was rather too busy to pay much attention. He was too old for mandatory militia duty, and much engaged besides. With the circuit court in session, he traversed the stairs between his office on the second floor of City Hall and the courtroom on the first a dozen times a day. At his desk, he wrote up indictments and arrest warrants, then did his correspondence. In court, he prosecuted the usual array of wrongdoers. The human propensity for assault and battery, larceny and rioting remained impressive among both whites and blacks. His campaign against the bawdy houses continued. Key brought charges against Poll Robinson, the prosperous colored courtesan. He obtained conviction of the Sifford sisters—Ann, Rachel, and Sarah—who were said to entertain men in sumptuous style. But his case against Mary Wertz and her oddly named daughter, Mary Wertz Jr., could not be sustained. As usual, Key's family relations suffered from his dedication to work, though he did not seem to worry about it.

"I did not think it would be so long before I wrote to acknowledge your last letter," he informed his daughter Ann, who was living in Maryland, "but have been so completely engaged in Court and with other affairs that I am sure you will excuse me."

In the spring of 1835 Key had decided to move to Washington City to live closer to his office. The once-idyllic house in Georgetown had lost something when the new Chesapeake & Ohio Canal was routed through his property along the banks of the Potomac. Key had protested at a community meeting on the path of the canal, but to no avail. The canal cut off the Keys' house from the river. Now the noise of progress, not the river breeze, rattled his windows.

"At present we are full of trouble about the house," Key wrote to his daughter. "The one we are in is to be sold and we have been looking out in vain . . . for another." Key soon found a new home in Washington City, a new wide brick house on C Street near the corner of Third. For a man who liked to work, the location exuded attractions. City Hall beckoned just a couple of blocks away. The hotels could be reached in minutes. He paid the builders to construct a separate entrance for a home office. Then he and Polly and the youngest children moved in, but now they were fewer. Eighteen-year-old Daniel had left home, enlisting in the navy and then shipping out to the Pacific on a frigate called the *Brandywine*.

Eight hundred miles away in Tuscaloosa, Alabama, Mrs. Sarah Gayle was thinking of Mr. Key. Governor Gayle was traveling on political business as usual, and Sarah's thoughts were drifting to her famous lover's words.

"I had a wakeful hour late last night, in which I thought over a conversation, or rather several conversations I had with Mr. Key during his visit," she wrote in her diary. The memory of their talk stirred profound emotions, which she struggled to understand and control. As she often did, Sarah Gayle expressed her feelings in poetry. Addressing Key as a "genius," she confessed a sense of guilt weighing on her soul like a heavy stone. Illicit feelings of love were not easy to harbor.

Deep is the injury done to things divine
By men unknowing how to work the mine
In which the gems of truth lie all concealed

Waiting for Learning's light, to bid them be revealed
Not Learning only gathered from the page
Of books—the gift, at once, and the relic of the sage
From high sources comes this purer light,
Which throws within, its radiance keenly bright,
And show that guilt is weighing on the soul—
That stone which Heavenly hands away must roll.

Sarah Gayle's religious faith shone in her choice of words. For her, books and sages could not expose the "gems of truth." Only "Learning's light" could do that. And only "Heavenly hands" could roll away the stone of guilt. Yet, she went on to admit, the human will is weak compared to sin's attractions:

Our nature's weak disgust will steele the heart,
And bid the influences from above, depart,
The hearer grovels on the earth again,
And Satan binds him with a stronger chain.

It was a confession of sorts. Sleepless in Tuscaloosa, Sarah felt like a sinner bound by Satan. She wanted to follow the light, yet her human weakness ("nature's weak disgust") had rationalized her dismissal of godly influences. She had succumbed by lying down, groveling on the earth. In the end, she chose not to send the poem.

For his part, Frank Key remembered her with unfeigned fondness. "I have often thought of Tuscaloosa and your family circle," he wrote to Sarah in a letter, "and could I transport myself as easily as my thoughts, I should still be a frequent visitor."

They had a bond of love.

T HE EXASPERATED FEELING among white men in the summer of 1835 was not confined to the nation's capital. On July 29, a steamboat entered the harbor of Charleston, South Carolina, carrying a regular ship-ment of mail from New York that was laden with the publications of the American Anti-Slavery Society's pamphlet campaign. The postmaster decided to confiscate the publications, and when a Charleston newspaper carried stories on the contents of the cargo the next morning, the news incited an angry mob of white people to break into the post office, seize the mailbags, and heap them onto a bonfire. Effigies of William Lloyd Garrison and Arthur Tappan were also burned.

News of a massive slave rebellion in Mississippi created more unease. The *Intelligencer* cited an uprising near the town of Clinton, ten miles west of Jackson, the state capital. The story, reprinted from the *Nashville Republican*, described "an intended insurrection of the slaves, assisted by many white men." The author of the dispatch told of joining a company of volunteers who sought to suppress the rebellion. The group seized a white man named Cotton, supposedly the ringleader, and nine blacks. All were hanged on the Fourth of July.

Two days later, the *Intelligencer* had more of the story under the head-line "HORRIBLE CONSPIRACY." Before Cotton's execution, the *Intelligencer* reported, he had confessed that he was an accomplice of "the celebrated MURREL," a notorious bandit of the Mississippi Delta. Their scheme was said to be huge and evil, embracing the whole slave region from Maryland to Louisiana, and seeking "the total destruction of the white population of all the Slave States, and the absolute conquest and dominion of the country." Moreover, they had help. "A large number of bold, enterprising and unprincipled white men are . . . engaging the aid of . . . the negro population . . . the bold, the sagacious, the desperate."

These headlines revived at a glance the sickening, soul-deadening worry felt after Southampton. Had the long-feared all-out rebellion of the Africans and their white allies against the slave owners finally begun? Suddenly the specter of "servile war" seemed all too plausible, maybe even imminent. Could a Southampton happen right there in Washington City? Who would prevent it? On the next page was a story about "the Vicksburg Tragedy" in which a Mississippi mob had hanged five gamblers, white men, without trial. Some were bewildered by the spread of lawlessness. Others welcomed it.

Edgar Snowden, the editor of the *Gazette* newspaper in Alexandria, thought a mob was just the instrument needed to stem the flood of anti-slavery publications into Washington City. In print, he invited William Lloyd Garrison and Arthur Tappan to come visit the South, all but promising they would be hanged forthwith. Lynching was a perfectly respectable business in his eyes.

"We would not have these eminent philanthropists to take the trouble to go all the way to Mississippi and especially to *Vicksburg*; but any spot south of the Potomac would answer," the editor wrote. "We can assure them they would meet with a *warm* reception. We hope they will not slight nor neglect this invitation. It is given in much sincerity, and with a perfect knowledge, from recent observation, of the state of Southern feeling."

Snowden disputed the *Boston Courier*'s charge that "the state of society in some of our southern and western States is deplorable." There were mobs in Boston and New York too, he noted. Something had gone wrong all over America.

"There is evidently a bad spirit at work over the whole of this country," he wrote, "a spirit of insubordination, misrule, fraud and violence. How is this evil spirit to be driven out of the land? Where is the exorcist that can arrest its disturbing and troubled wanderings?"

Epicurus was not in Washington City, not for long.

. . .

Anna Thornton did not know or care what Edgar Snowden was writing that day. She did not read the *Gazette,* much less care for such grand pronouncements. She read the *Intelligencer* and the *Globe* but did not concern herself much with public events, preferring to see friends in the parlor, do her household accounts, and worry about her mother.

On the evening of Tuesday, August 4, she went out for her usual twilight carriage tour of the Avenue, with George driving her past the Centre Market and the Epicurean Eating House on her way to the Capitol. On the way back, George took the carriage up Fourteenth Street and out to the racetrack on Meridian Hill. On the way home, Anna told George she wanted to call on a friend, but the friend was not home. Anna returned to the house on F Street and the company of her mother and Maria. Before retiring, Anna noted in her diary that the thermometer on her porch had not risen above seventy degrees Fahrenheit all day. It had been an unusually cool day for August.

PART IV

THE PERILOUS FIGHT

As rioting spread nationwide in August 1835, a white mob
attacked the Charleston Post Office, seeking to destroy
pamphlets mailed by the American Anti-Slavery Society.

22

ARTHUR BOWEN SPENT most of the evening of August 4, 1835, in President's Square, the park across the street from the executive mansion, quiet ever since General Jackson and his family left for their summer vacation. Gentlemen strolling home that evening hardly noticed the young Negro idling in the shade, save that he seemed to be drinking spirits from a bottle. Those who looked closer could see he was about nineteen years of age, standing five feet nine inches tall with a bushy head of hair. His face looked blistered with cuts from the fistfight at the racetrack. Another young black man, never identified, joined him in talking, sipping, and talking some more. While legally a slave owned by a white woman, Arthur was attending to his primary interests in life: avoiding work and thinking about freedom.

Arthur and his friend had just come from a meeting of John Cook's talking society at the Union Seminary schoolhouse over on H Street. Cook, and another older colored man, had talked with Arthur and his friends about slavery and how they might disenthrall themselves from bondage. This clandestine group met often to talk, read poems aloud, or study articles in the latest issue of *The Liberator*, the banned antislavery newspaper. Cook's message was, You have a right to be free. That day the young men had argued about slaves who killed their masters and slaves who betrayed those who dared to rebel. Who was right? Who was wrong? The talk got hot before the elders told them to knock it off and go home.

Arthur and his friend kept the conversation going in President's Square, a leafy redoubt in the middle of a drab city and an agreeable spot for discussion and dissipation. Growing up in the neighborhood, Arthur had seen the square change from a bumpy pasture to a landscaped park lined with vegetable vendors and fine homes. After the scheduled visit of the great General Lafayette was announced in 1824, workmen had leveled the grounds, filled the gullies, and carved out winding pathways through the trees, all in honor of the French soldier who had come to America's aid during the War for Independence. When an adoring crowd welcomed Lafayette that summer, eight-year-old Arthur Bowen might have scampered among the spectators. The square was renamed in Lafayette's honor, but the new name would not catch on for years. Anna Thornton still called it President's Square, and Arthur probably did too.

He and his pal moseyed along one dirt path through the low-hanging trees and then another, taking care to stay beyond the hearing of any white person. They talked about freedom and human rights and what they could do to escape slavery, excited by new thoughts and the whiskey that warmed their tongues. Did they dare to hope? Arthur could hardly avoid the landscape of his predicament.

On the south side of the square stood the home of President Jackson. The mansion, said one guidebook of the day, resembled "the country seat of an English nobleman in its architecture and size," except that the surrounding grounds were a mess featuring grazing sheep and mounds of dirt from the construction of a new driveway and stable.

Arthur had actually seen the inside of the President's House at least once. When he was a boy, Mrs. Thornton had assigned him to serve as a footman for her friend Benjamin Ogle Tayloe when he attended a dinner hosted by President Jackson. Arthur might have recalled the grand East Ballroom where the event took place. Now the mansion looked empty. Jackson and his family had gone for the summer to a seaside retreat in southern Virginia, accompanied by their household slaves.

President's Square, now almost chilly and lit only by a few streetlamps, turned shadowy in the dusk. A white man named Watson passed through on his way home from work and noticed Arthur Bowen was "much intoxicated." John Cook, the schoolteacher and leader of the talking society, had warned his young charges that liquor did the devil's work. "By drinking the sudden passion of the murderer is sharpened," Cook said. "The cherished revenge of the assassin is made stronger, and he is made ready to plunge the instrument of death into the bosom of the object of his hate, perhaps his own mother, father, brother, sister, wife or child." Arthur admired Mr. Cook but did not worry about this warning.

When the ten o'clock curfew came Arthur still lingered. With all the talk in the newspapers of abolitionist mischief and slave rebellion, the city's constables had become more vigilant about enforcing the law that required Negroes to get off the streets by the middle of the evening. But the constables did not look in President's Square that night. Arthur loitered until after one o'clock in the morning.

When he finally decided to go home, Arthur probably left by way of the south side of the square. The city was now silent and dark, the streets lit only by candles in windows and the galaxy of stars above. At the corner of Fifteenth Street and G Street, Arthur passed the construction site of the grand new Treasury building. At Fourteenth Street, he turned right. No carriages or horses moved on its washboard surface. Halfway down the block to F Street, Arthur turned left into the tree-lined alley and made his unsteady way down the darkened lane.

Arthur passed under the catalpa trees in the back area of Mrs. Thornton's house, an enclave lush with wisteria and azaleas. A stairway rose up to the back porch. He stepped down to the rear basement door, which, as usual, had been left unlocked by his mother. She wanted him to come in at night without disturbing the sleep of the women of the house. Arthur groped his way through the blackness to the wooden steps and stumbled up to the first floor. At the top of the stairs, he touched the axe, used for chopping firewood, which was stored in its accustomed place inside the doorway. He picked it up and put its polished handle, headed by a four-inch steel blade, in the crook of his arm. He eased his way into the main hallway of the house.

In Arthur's inebriated mind, the house was tilting like a steamship on the Potomac, not that the feeling was unpleasant. Arthur loved steamships. Up the dimly lit passage one way, he saw the beveled glass door at the front of the house. Down the other way, the stout back door blocked the way to the porch and the garden. Arthur blinked, his eyes getting used to the darkness.

To his immediate left, the main stairway curled around and up to the second floor, and then to his garret on the third. Directly in front of him,

Arthur faced a choice of two doors. One led to the dining room and parlor in the front of the house. The other led to Mrs. Thornton's bedroom in the back.

Did Arthur think he was already on the upper floor about to enter his own room? Or did he have something to say to Mrs. Thornton?

Arthur undid the catch of the lock and entered the room where the three women slept, the axe still hanging on his elbow.

23

THE ORANGE GLOW of a single lamp illuminated the contours of the room. To Arthur's right lay the tiny figure of Mrs. Brodeau barely visible under her covers. To his left, Anna Thornton slept. His mother's bed lined the opposite wall.

The noise of the opening door wakened Anna Thornton and Maria Bowen at almost the same time. Mistress and servant registered the same extraordinary and terrifying sight: Arthur in the dim light of the doorway, an axe on his arm. *An axe.* Anna was not dreaming. This might have been how it began at Southampton four years ago. This is probably how it began in Mississippi the month before. As Maria stirred in the far bed, Anna extracted herself swiftly from her own covers. While keeping her eyes on the boy, she skirted fast around the small table that stood in the center of the room, bolted past Maria's bed, and ran to a door on the opposite side of the room.

Meanwhile, Maria was climbing out of her bed. Younger than Anna, she was quicker and stronger too. She rushed straight at her son and pushed him back through the doorway as Anna escaped into the front parlor, then through the front door. Bursting onto F Street, Anna screamed, "Dr. Huntt! General Gibson!"

Her friends Henry Huntt and George Gibson lived in the next house. The street was deserted and the windows up and down the block were mostly dark. The sky was clear, the moon almost full. Anna, still dressed in her nightgown, ran to Dr. Huntt's door.

"She's killed!" she cried. "She's killed!"

There was no answer.

"Dr. Huntt, come now," she called up to the windows. "Don't put on your clothes. Come directly. General Gibson, come! She's killed."

Dr. Huntt soon emerged. At fifty-three years of age, he was a well-known physician, doctor to President Jackson, and a member of the city's board of health. He was followed by the panting figure of his friend Gibson, a retired general who boarded in his house. The two men ran to Mrs. Thornton's door with Anna following close behind. Inside they found Maria in the front hall, comforting Anna's mother, who had not been killed and indeed did not know what the commotion was about. Arthur was nowhere to be seen.

"I've got him out," gasped Maria, still in her night shift, pointing to the back door. "He's crazy."

Dr. Huntt and General Gibson hurried down the darkened hallway toward the back door that led outside. From the other side came shouts and thumps, almost wailing. Arthur was outside, pounding on the door.

"He's crazy," Maria said.

General Gibson knew Arthur from his visits to the Thorntons' house.

"Be quiet, boy," he said through the door. "Quiet."

"Damn you to hell," called Arthur from the other side. "I'll have the heart's blood of y'all."

General Gibson gaped at Dr. Huntt. *What did he say?*

"Let's go out there," said Gibson, an old soldier too ready to charge into battle. "We can overawe him."

The pounding continued.

"He's got an axe," Dr. Huntt observed, "and we are unarmed."

Gibson gulped, now glad to be inside the locked door. Maria Bowen felt weak with relief that she had gotten him out. Anna Thornton's mind was still awhirl in disbelief at what was happening in her own home.

"I will have my freedom," Arthur was shouting now from the other side of the door. "I'll have my freedom, you hear me? I have as much right to freedom as you do."

Anna and Maria listened and were mortified. The boy was mad drunk!

"If Philo Parker and the others hadn't been put in jail, he would've made 'em all smell hell," he was shouting. "We'd have been free by now."

Anna, Maria, and the two men did not recognize the name "Philo Parker," but it sounded like he was a slave who had tried to rebel and almost succeeded, someone like Gabriel Prosser, the blacksmith who planned a massive slave rebellion in Richmond, Virginia, in 1800. Prosser was arrested and executed after an informant betrayed the rebels, but his story lived on.

As her panic subsided Anna heard the incoherent ravings of a spoiled boy mad at being turned out. Perhaps she felt a sense of failure or anger. Arthur had fallen, first to drink, now to the fiendish ideas of the so-called abolitionists. She had not been able to control him since Dr. Thornton's death, and he could not control himself.

A crowd of people had gathered on F Street. Neighbors entered the house cautiously, calling out to Mrs. Thornton, inquiring after her safety. Then two constables arrived. One of them was Madison Jeffers, a long-time constable and slave trader who was especially worried about the prospect of a slave rebellion. Jeffers went to the still-locked back door and addressed it on the assumption Arthur was outside. They were going to arrest him, Jeffers yelled. Silence.

Jeffers pushed the door open and the men peered out into the back area. Nothing moved in the blackness of the garden. Someone pointed at his feet. There was a wooden scrub brush on the porch, the implement that Arthur had used to pound on the door. Arthur was gone and the alley was silent. Anna felt a sense of dread and knew the feeling must be worse for Maria Bowen. Her son's life was forfeit. He would soon be hanged, shot like a dog, or in some manner struck down.

The men in the room had a different thought, and they didn't have to say the words: *Runaway nigger with an axe.*

"A DREADFUL NIGHT WAS last night—never to be forgotten," Anna wrote in her diary the following day. She was sitting at the writing desk in the parlor. The weather outside was cloudy and cool with rain. She dipped her pen in the black ink.

"Arthur entered the room at ½ after one o'clock with an axe, with the intention we suppose to murder us. His mother (Maria) sleeping in the rooms with us, & being fortunately awake, seized him & got him out, while I ran next door to alarm Dr. Huntt & got help—Oh what a horrid night."

Anna did not leave the house all day, declining an invitation to attend a musical party in Kalorama. "I have not spirits for such parties now," she said. Maria Bowen was even more miserable. Anna was grateful to her for shoving Arthur out of the room. At the same time, she pitied her for her child's fate. Anna asked Maria if she could find out where Arthur had gone.

"It could save his life," she said.

Maria knew something of Arthur's favorite haunts: the racetrack, the billiards room, the talking society. She probably knew John Cook, or knew of him. The Union Seminary schoolhouse was located just two blocks away. Heeding Anna's advice, Maria set out to find her son.

To Anna's way of thinking they had to sell Arthur as soon as possible to someone who would take him far away. She had never intended to sell him, but now she had no choice. Bayard Smith, the twenty-five-year-old son of her friend Margaret Smith, stopped by the house and agreed to help. A graduate of Princeton who was friendly with Arthur, Bayard came to sleep at the house to make everyone feel safer. He said he would look for "a Negro buyer"—polite society's term for a slave trader—who might be willing to cooperate in whisking Arthur away for a price.

The story of Arthur's intrusion spread quickly thanks to Madison Jeffers and Dr. Huntt and took on lurid overtones as it was repeated. A black slave. A white woman. An axe. In the offices of the *Intelligencer* at Ninth and E streets, editors Seaton and Gales thought it best that they not report the matter, lest it encourage other mischief among the blacks. When Thursday morning brought no sign or word of Arthur, Anna wrote out an advertisement and sent George to take it over to the *Intelligencer*. The ad appeared in Friday's paper.

$100 REWARD

Ran away from the subscriber on the night 4th instant, her mulatto boy named John Arthur Bowen, aged about nineteen years. He is about five feet nine or ten inches high, straight and well made; one side of his face is scarred by recent blisters, and the mark of a wound on the back of one hand. He has a bushy head of hair, and speaks civilly and softly in general. He went off without shoes, hat, or jacket. The above reward will be given for his apprehension out of the District of Columbia and delivery in the city of Washington, together with all reasonable expenses incurred for keeping him. If taken within the District a reward of fifty dollars will be given.

AM THORNTON.

When Anna looked for the advertisement, she discovered Seaton and Gales had decided to report on the rampant rumor after all. A headline at the top of the page, more prominent than her notice, declared

FIRST FRUIT

A circumstance of a shocking character, which was within a second of time of resulting in the perpetration of a most bloody tragedy, occurred in this city two nights ago.

This event, Anna read with a sinking feeling, was "one of the immediate fruits of the incendiary publications with which this city and the whole slave-holding portion of the country have been lately inundated."

The article was about Arthur.

> On Tuesday night last, an attempt was made on the life of
> Mrs. Thornton, of this city, (the much respected widow of
> the late Dr. Thornton, superintendent of the patent office)
> by a young negro man, her slave, which, from the expres-
> sions he used was evidently induced by reading the inflam-
> matory publications referred to above.

This was not what Anna wanted, not at all. Helpless, she read on.

> About half past 1 o'clock, in the dead of night, Mrs. T.'s
> chamber in which slept herself, her aged mother, and a
> woman servant, was entered by the negro, who had obtained
> access to it by forcing the outer door. He approached the bed
> of Mrs. T. with uplifted axe.

Anna was shocked. How could the newspaper say such things? That
was not what happened. Arthur had not forced the door. He had not
raised the axe. He had not rushed at her. The boy was drunk. But she had
to admit some of it was true.

> During the whole time that he was endeavoring to force a
> second entrance into the house, he was venting the most
> ferocious threats, and uttering a tissue of jargon, much of
> which was a literal repetition of the language addressed to
> the negroes by the incendiary publications.

Anna's parlor thickened with friends coming to call and servants bearing cards of anxious inquiry from other acquaintances. Anna tried to
explain what had happened, but she could not talk to everyone who heard
or read the story. Worse yet, Duff Green had reprinted the *Intelligencer*'s account, word for word, in the afternoon edition of the *Telegraph*. In
Georgetown, the *Metropolitan* embellished the story with a more alarming
headline: "Desperate Attempt at Murder, by a Negro in Washington." The only difference between the *Metropolitan* and the *Intelligencer*

lay in their assessment of Arthur's motive. "We believe the negro was incited to this foul deed by the hope of plundering a large quantity of valuable plate belonging to the Lady," said the editors of the Georgetown sheet, "and not, as some would represent it, by the effect of any incendiary publication or language whatever."

That was reassuring but wrong. Arthur did not want Anna's silver. He could have taken her plates and cutlery from their drawers at any time. He wanted his freedom.

The regulars loitering down at Linthicum's drugstore in Georgetown did not believe Arthur Bowen was a thief either. Instead, they wondered if he might have known their new neighbor, Dr. Reuben Crandall. Henry King, a doctor who had an office at First and High streets, had paid a call on his fellow physician earlier in the summer and noticed that Crandall kept an antislavery newspaper lying about openly in his room. King had mentioned this brazen behavior to a friend. Another man, William Robinson, had borrowed a copy of an abolitionist tract from Crandall. Well aware of these incidents, George Oyster, a butter maker who owned the house where Reuben rented his rooms, confronted his tenant in the backyard of the house.

"Did you hear the news?" Oyster asked.

"No," said Reuben.

A slave boy tried to murder Mrs. Thornton, Oyster said. He failed but he got away. "We got nobody to blame but the New Yorkers and their aide-de-camps," Oyster added pointedly. "They say the boy had been excited by these New York publications."

"I do not approve of putting them into circulation," Reuben said, turning away. "The excitement is too high already."

George Oyster was more suspicious than ever. *Who was talking about putting them into circulation?*

On the third day, John Arthur Bowen reappeared. Maria brought him in. He was alive, bushy hair and all. He had not been caught but had returned on his own volition, or that of his mother. If Anna was surprised or angry with him, she did not record her feelings. As time went on, she believed ever more confidently that he had not intended to harm her when he stumbled into the room that night. She did not fear his presence in the house. As for the obvious questions—Why did he do it? Where had he gone?—Anna did not ask, much less answer them, at least not in her diary. Arthur said he remembered nothing.

But there was no time to talk. Anna told Maria that Bayard Smith had found a Negro buyer, a gentleman willing to take Arthur away. He would come at six o'clock in the morning.

25

Down at the Epicurean Eating House, Beverly Snow heard the rumors and read the newspapers. Some people were saying Arthur Bowen's attack was the first blow in a slave insurrection, that there was a plot among the colored people. Some people even said that the authorities had intercepted a letter to Snow that contained details about the uprising. He hastened up Sixth Street to see his friend William Bradley, the banker who had been elected mayor the year before. At City Hall, Beverly offered his services, pledging to discourage any talk of rebellion among the blacks. Bradley said he appreciated the gesture.

The free people of color in Washington City had reason to be uneasy. No one seemed to be in charge. President Jackson had gone for his usual summer vacation at Rip Raps, a U.S. Army–built island in the middle of Hampton Bay on the Virginia shore. White men were demanding someone take action, and colored men knew what that meant. The boy did not have long to live, that much was sure. Would others be blamed too? Among the Negroes, the many often paid for the sins of one.

Beverly hoped not. He could see the emotions of the white people in his restaurant and on the Avenue: the shock, surprise, fear, and anger. He could see the same in the faces of the colored. In his own mind, he thought as an Epicurean. He walked over to the offices of the *Mirror* on Louisiana Avenue and handed over a dollar and the text for another advertisement, which appeared the next morning:

Look at This!

A FINE GREEN TURTLE will be served up this day at the EPICUREAN EATING HOUSE, in all the various modes of cookery: together with a very fine SHEEP'S HEAD, and every other luxury of the season, to be prepared and ready to be served up at eleven o'clock A.M.

SNOW & WALKER

The sentiments were familiar but the ad was unusual. Beverly had never advertised in the summer season, the slowest time of the year. But with feeling running high about abolitionism, he wanted people to know he still offered the balm of Green Turtleism. What the people of the National Metropolis needed, he thought, was a good meal.

Saturday morning dawned cool and pleasant on the F Street ridge. Anna and Maria woke up early to meet the gentleman who said he would buy Arthur. But they were soon disappointed. The man took one look at Arthur's blistered face and backed out of the transaction.

"I'm afraid of trusting his future good behavior," he said, excusing himself. Not long after, Bayard Smith arrived with alarming news: People on the street had learned Arthur was back in the house.

"There might be a mob raised," Bayard warned. "People are much incensed against him."

Someone knocked on the front door. It was Constable Madison Jeffers, accompanied by his partner, Henry Robertson, asking if the runaway, John Arthur Bowen, was present in the house. Anna and Maria had no choice but to surrender him. Mrs. Thornton agreed with Jeffers that Arthur must be taken to the jail for his own safekeeping and assured Arthur it was for the best. Before he could register any reaction, the constables had escorted him out the front door and pushed him into a waiting carriage.

Arthur sat between the two white men as the carriage rolled down F Street.

"What possessed you to attack your mistress?" Jeffers wanted to know.

Arthur, now sober, considered his answer.

"I have a right to be free," he said finally, "and if it hadn't been for the law, we would all be free."

Jeffers and Robertson were not expecting such a saucy reply.

"We *ought* to be free," Arthur went on coolly, "and we *will* be free.

And if we are not, there is going to be such confusion and bloodshed as to astonish the world."

Stunned by this insolence, the white men rode on in silence.

When they reached the City Jail at Fourth and F streets, the constables pulled Arthur out of the carriage, passing by the "whipping machine" as they entered the jail. Inside, the guards took Arthur to the second floor, where the Negro prisoners were kept, and locked him in a cell.

On F Street, Anna, Maria, and Bayard still hoped they might sell Arthur and get him away. But it was not to be. Not long after the constables took Arthur, a messenger arrived with a writ from the magistrate. Based on what Dr. Huntt and General Gibson said, one of the magistrates for the Second Ward had filed charges. Arthur had been committed for trial—for attempted murder.

"Oh this is dreadful," Anna wrote in her diary that evening. "His poor mother how I pity her. The people are incensed against him as he is thought to be one of a party instigated by some white friends to raise an insurrection."

26

JOHN QUINCY ADAMS learned, via letter, of Anna Thornton's ordeal while summering in his hometown of Quincy, Massachusetts. Adams was mortified. The former president came across as a chilly man to many, but he had warm feelings for his neighbor on F Street. He adored Anna Thornton. For Adams, a lonely statesman, brilliant and besieged, a friendship of swelling bosoms and faithful hearts with a beautiful woman like Anna Thornton provided welcome respite from the political wars he waged daily. Alas, when Adams heard that Arthur had attempted to murder his friend, he was more analytical than romantic. In his diary, he explained the politics of the moment with his usual concision.

"The theory of the rights of man," he wrote, "has taken deep root in the soil of civil society. It has allied itself with the feelings of humanity and the precepts of Christian benevolence. It has armed itself with the strength of organized association. It has linked itself with religious doctrines and religious fervor. Antislavery organizations are formed in this Country and in England. . . . They have raised funds to support and circulate inflammatory newspapers and pamphlets, and they send multitudes of them into the Southern Country into the midst of the swarms of slaves."

Adams noted there was a call for a town meeting in Boston to put down the antislavery men, but he didn't think it would do any good. "The disease is deeper than can be healed by town-meeting resolutions."

Nowhere was the former president's mordant analysis more accurate than in the nation's capital.

As Adams wrote, a spontaneous assembly was taking place around the jail behind City Hall. Angry white men streamed into the square from every direction—from the Navy Yard and Capitol Hill, from George-town, Alexandria, and Greenleaf's Point. By nightfall there were scores of mechanics crowding the jail's locked doors and shouting their own resolutions, which, shorn of profanity, amounted to "Give us Arthur Bowen so that we can enforce the law." The contempt for colored people, the waning influence of gentlemen, the anxieties generated by new machinery, the fear of another Southampton, and the resentments of the poor had combined into a combustible rage. The gathering crowd argued with the city's marshal, Henry Ashton, who was in charge of the jail, about how best to punish the black villain. At one point, Ashton was shoved to the ground. The men were incredulous. Why wouldn't the authorities turn him over? Why were they protecting the nigger from justice?

The clamor forced the reticent Francis Scott Key to leave his office in City Hall. With Mayor Bradley he went outside to address the mob intent on snatching the prisoner. Key too had heard the talk of a slave insurrection, but he served as officer of the court, a man of the law, and an official with duties. If he turned over Arthur Bowen to the mob, he would forfeit his position and self-respect. He recognized the weakness of his position. He, the mayor, and the marshal had only ten constables at their disposal, and some of them would prove more loyal to the mob than to the law. He had to resist and as he did, his predicament deepened. How could he appease the angry white men who crowded around him? These men, their ranks swelled by inebriated mechanics and filthy street urchins, spat contempt at all authority. The Mobocracy that had manhandled the Vicksburg gamblers had now turned on public servants like himself. Amidst the angry throng, Key and Bradley pleaded for order without effect.

Inside the jail, Arthur could hear the shouting and the cursing, the lusty threats to kill and maim him. Through the bars of the second-floor windows, he could see the angry men swirling around the entrance below.

"They said their object was to get Mrs. Thornton's mulatto man out and hang him without Judge or juror," wrote Michael Shiner, a black carpenter who was watching from a safe distance. Shiner was a bondsman who had been hired out by his owner to work at the Navy Yard. Uniquely among Washington's blacks, Shiner kept a journal of the events of the summer of 1835. His spelling was uncertain, but he had a knack for showing up at big events. Mr. Key and Mayor Bradley, he reported, made "every effort to preserve peace and harmony among those men. But all of it appeared to be in vain."

As the furor grew, someone notified Secretary of the Navy Mahlon Dickerson, who sent a message to the Navy Yard calling for troops. Soon a detachment of blue-uniformed Marines armed with blunderbusses came marching down Pennsylvania Avenue into the square around City Hall and established a perimeter around the jail. The irate mechanics turned sullen and stood back from this display of force. Shiner wrote that the Marines "done their duty without faction or favor." The thwarted crowd eventually dispersed into the night. Key's authority had survived, if barely. Arthur Bowen was safe, at least for the moment.

On Monday, Anna sent Bayard Smith to see Mr. Key at City Hall and ask about the possibility of selling Arthur off before his trial. Bayard returned with discouraging news. Mr. Key had said, "Nothing can be done but to let him stay and take his trial."

Anna wanted the district attorney to speak with her lawyer, Walter Jones, before making a decision. Jones, a good friend of her late husband, was one of the leading attorneys in Washington, as well as the head of the militia. He had also been a friend and colleague of Key's for many years. The general, however, was not in the office; he had been summoned to Baltimore to defend the former officers of the failed Bank of Maryland, who faced another mob, this one consisting of working-class white people who had lost all hope of recovering their savings.

There was another knock on the door. A constable said that Maria Bowen was wanted at City Hall to answer questions "about some suspected persons." With misgivings, Maria went. When she did not return within a few hours, Anna became worried, and she sent George with the carriage to pick her up. Back in the house Maria recounted the urgency of her interrogators. The grand jury was looking for some free black men and suspecting the worst, she said.

"Great excitement with thinking there is some plot among the Negroes," Anna wrote in her diary that night.

. . .

At City Hall, Key was determined to choke off the incendiary publications that had apparently provoked Arthur. He called in some former neighbors who had been keeping an eye on Reuben Crandall in Georgetown. The district attorney wanted the grand jury to hear what they knew. William Robinson, a gentleman of means, told Key he had seen a pamphlet of "the most incendiary and insurrectionary character" inscribed with the words "read and circulate." Robinson had compared the notation to Crandall's handwritten prospectus for a botany lecture and concluded they were written by the same person.

That sufficed for the grand jury. By the afternoon, Key had issued an order for Constables Jeffers and Robertson, commanding them to bring in Reuben Crandall "to answer to the charge of exhibiting and circulating dangerous and insurrectionary writings and thereby attempting to excite an insurrection." Key also authorized the constables to search Crandall's residence.

As the constables descended the steps in front of City Hall with the warrant in hand, they found the crowd of last night had reassembled and grown. There were now hundreds of mechanics clamoring for the head of Arthur Bowen, but the Marines had not budged. Hoping to do something that might appease the rage of the crowd, Jeffers and Robertson climbed into a carriage and set off to Georgetown in search of Reuben Crandall.

Reuben Crandall resided on a respectable block at the north end of High Street, a hard-packed dirt road that passed between tree-lined rows of brick buildings and wood-frame houses. His neighbors included a music master and a portrait painter, as well as a bricklayer, a currier of leather goods, a clerk, and a butcher. There was nothing to distinguish Crandall's quarters from his neighbors', no sign of his business in the windows.

After Jeffers rapped on the door and received no answer, Henry Robertson struck up a conversation with George Oyster, Reuben's landlord. Oyster was sitting on his porch, not surprised that the constables were hunting for the New Yorker. It was about time, he thought. Soon enough James Gettys, a magistrate for the city of Georgetown, came out of his office and asked Jeffers the nature of his business. It didn't take long for the word to get around. It was late afternoon when Crandall finally came striding down High Street. As he entered his office the two constables stepped up to him.

"Are you Crandall?" Robertson asked.

The rapid approach of two strangers did not unduly ruffle Crandall. He acknowledged that he was. Robertson showed him the warrant, and Crandall bade the men enter his office. Jeffers locked the door behind them.

"Where's the printing press?" Robertson asked, looking about the messy office. There was a desk, several wooden boxes, and a table covered with dried plants and newspapers.

"I don't understand," Crandall said. "Can you explain?"

He was playing for time. He knew what had happened to Ben Lundy and William Lloyd Garrison when they tried to raise the flag of liberty in the National Metropolis. The fact that a local jury had acquitted Lundy's printer, William Greer, was small cause for comfort. He might have also heard of the charges against Thomas Cary and John Prout.

"Where are the pamphlets?" Jeffers demanded.

"What pamphlets?"

"The abolition pamphlets," said Robertson. "We want all of them."

"Look and see," Crandall said. "I will give you any satisfaction in my power."

The constables began to paw through the newspapers on the table. There were a number of *Telegraph*s, as well as papers from Baltimore, New York, and Boston. In the pile, Jeffers found a copy of *The Emancipator*. Crandall knew it well. His friend Charles Denison edited it, but he did not say that.

Jeffers showed the sheet to Robertson, who stuffed it in his pocket. Jeffers pulled a box away from the wall. It was open at the back, filled with a bundle of copies of *The Anti-Slavery Reporter*, all the same issue.

"How did you come by these?" Jeffers asked.

"They were sent around," Crandall said, shrugging.

Robertson bundled them up.

"Can we go up to your lodgings?" Jeffers said, growing more confident that he had bagged his prey. "Do you have more there?"

"A few," Crandall acknowledged.

They went up the stairs to his room. There was the big trunk he had brought from New York. Jeffers nodded at it, and Crandall opened it. There were more bundles of a sheet called *Human Rights*. The constables riffled through them. The copies appeared quite new.

"Where did you get these?"

Crandall knew what they were thinking. He had read the stories about the Anti-Slavery Society's pamphlet campaign that was disturbing the city and the South.

"I did not get them in the mail," he assured them.

"You are charged with distributing this material," Robertson reminded him.

"I haven't distributed any," Crandall objected, pointing to a copy of *Human Rights*. "I was taking *The Emancipator*, but they had stopped it and sent this instead."

Outside on High Street, the sun was setting. The constables could not see in the dimming light of the room, so Jeffers left to get a torch. Outside he was besieged by people who wanted to know what he had found.

"More than I expected," Jeffers said, as he headed for Linthicum's store. "We found a hundred fifty, maybe a hundred and sixty pamphlets."

The men lounging around the counter at Linthicum's gasped in excitement as those numbers made the rounds. Torch in hand, Jeffers went back up the street and pushed his way through the crowd around Crandall's office. He reentered the building and locked the door again.

He and Robertson finished searching the room by torchlight as the clamor of voices outside mounted.

"We can take you to a magistrate here in Georgetown," Jeffers said to Crandall, "or go to the jail."

"Let's leave these people here," Crandall said. "The jail is fine."

When the three men stepped out of the front door, a chorus of oaths, insults, and imprecations greeted them. The constables, carrying the bundles of pamphlets, pushed their way through the crowd.

"We ought to take the damned rascal and hang him up on one of those trees," someone shouted.

Inside the carriage, Robertson said he did not want to risk taking the main streets. The choice proved wise, as Robertson later learned that a gang of men had stationed themselves on the main road and would have waylaid the carriage and killed Crandall on the spot.

Like Arthur Bowen two days before, Crandall sat between Jeffers and Robertson. The bundles of publications rode on the seat beside them.

"What were you doing with so many of them, all of the same number?" Jeffers asked.

"I got them for information monthly," Crandall replied.

"Why did you want so many of the same number?" Jeffers persisted.

Crandall would not be intimidated.

"I don't mean to deny my principles," he said. "I'm an anti-slavery man."

"Would not colonization be the better plan?" Jeffers demanded.

"No," Crandall said. "I'm in favor of the immediate emancipation."

Jeffers was appalled.

"Don't you think it very dangerous, at the present time, to set all the slaves free?"

"I'm in favor of it," Crandall said with a shrug. "The slaves ought to be all free. They have as much right to be free as we do."

The constables were aghast. This New Yorker sounded just like the Bowen boy the other day. One says, I have a right to be free, and the other says, They have as much right to be free as we do. Why did they incriminate themselves?

"Don't say too much or speak too freely," Robertson warned him. "We might be witnesses against you."

When the carriage arrived at the jail in Judiciary Square, night had fallen. The constables handed Crandall off to the guards. They led him down the dark central corridor of the jail's first floor and locked him into an eight-foot-square cell.

Nine blocks to the east on the F Street ridge, Anna Thornton and Maria Bowen had no comfort either. Walter Jones had just returned from Baltimore, saying he had consulted with Mr. Key but "nothing can be done at present but to keep quiet and wait til time of trial." Anna was dismayed. The circuit court's fall session would not begin for three months.

"O my God," she wrote in her diary that night. "I hope some method may be found in the time come (November) to release him."

O N WEDNESDAY, AUGUST 12, 1835, Washington City went crazy, or at least a good portion of it did. As a result, not many people of color were seen on the streets. The bondsmen sat tight in the company of their owners. The free Negroes went to visit kin in the country. The president was on vacation, and the white man was running wild.

The crowd in Judiciary Square was now immense, numbering three thousand people in one estimate and united in its determination to see both Arthur Bowen and Reuben Crandall hanged. Inside City Hall, Frank Key had assembled a group of witnesses in his office. But there was no way to bring Crandall over from the jail without endangering his life.

"An alarming crisis," one visitor to Washington wrote to a friend. ". . . The public indignation is rising high, and the general impression is the culprit will not go unpunished. It is seriously feared he will meet the same fate as those in Mississippi."

The jeering assemblage only grew jollier when drenched by a passing rainstorm. Perhaps the loudest voice in the tumult belonged to a young man named Andrew Laub, not thirty years old. Laub proclaimed himself leader of the mob and demanded the authorities hand over Bowen and Crandall. Laub scorned appeals for peace and calm.

Not everyone agreed. "Our hearts grew sick within us when we hear the determination to 'Lynch him' ferociously expressed and applauded by the crowd," wrote eyewitness John O'Sullivan, editor of the *Metropolitan*, the Georgetown newspaper.

Andrew Laub represented that sizable segment of the white population who were not rich and not gentlemen. The son of John Laub, a career clerk in the First Comptroller's Office of the Treasury Department, he was married with three children and owned two female slaves. Roger Taney certainly knew Laub's father and might have even known him. The younger Laub had also worked as a clerk at the Treasury Department but did not last. In the wake of the fire that destroyed the department's offices in 1833, authorities suspected him of financial irregularities, of which he was eventually cleared. He then found work as a groundskeeper on Mason's Island in the middle of the Potomac River; he sold tickets when a balloon ascent was held there in the summer of 1834. Yet Laub was short of money. He had owned two lots of property on New York Avenue near Fourteenth Street but had recently lost them for failure to pay taxes. Laub was not poor, but he was on a losing streak.

With coy malevolence, he roused the crowd against Arthur Bowen. The correspondent for the *Richmond Enquirer* was probably referring to Laub when he reported that "one of the men who seemed most anxious and resolute in raising the mob said they only intended to cut off both his ears and give him a good coat of tar," adding, "I don't think anything short of his life will satisfy them."

For the most part poor, the men and the boys clamoring in the streets found support from respectable gentlemen around town. Moore Galway, an editor at the *Telegraph* who was running the paper in the absence of the traveling Duff Green, had no objection to the lynching. "There was a great disposition manifested to exercise summary justice on him, which would have been by far the best course," he editorialized. "It would have put a stop to the matter."

At noon the cloudy skies dropped more torrential rain, unaccompanied by lightning or thunder. The cascade, one of the severest in memory, drenched the men crowding the square but did not drive them away. The water ran downhill toward Pennsylvania Avenue. The whole of Sixth Street between Gadsby's Hotel and the Epicurean Eating House resembled a broad river.

Beverly Snow was nowhere to be seen.

After the rain stopped, Mr. Key and his witnesses pushed their way through the crowd around the jailhouse door and gathered in Reuben

Crandall's cell. The scene inside the jail scarcely improved on the scene outside. In 1825, a congressional committee had condemned the jail's "gloomy dominions" as unfit for the safekeeping of the unfortunates within its walls. A decade of neglect had just made things worse. Below the rotting beams in the ceiling, Key began the examination of the prisoner.

Reuben Crandall felt panicky. The noise of the mob, the heat of the jail, and the arrival of his interrogators oppressed him. One witness described Crandall as "greatly agitated" by "the great collection outside the jail, which naturally caused a great excitement within." With good reason Crandall feared he might soon go the way of a Vicksburg gambler.

Two magistrates listened as the district attorney presented his witnesses. Dr. King of Georgetown said that he had seen a pamphlet endorsed with the words "please to read and circulate" in Crandall's office. William King, a flour merchant, confirmed the story.

Crandall struggled to keep his composure. When Key grilled him about the pamphlets, he answered evasively. At several points, he choked up in fear. Key felt that the magistrates had heard enough to charge the prisoner and completed the examination. The men left his cell.

As Crandall collapsed, Key rallied. He exited the jail to address the infuriated and soggy crowd outside.

"Crandall will be punished if you let the trial progress," he declared to the throng. The crowd now occupied most of the plaza between Fourth and Sixth streets. Key knew how to project his voice without straining himself. He strove to be calm. He told the men that he sympathized with their anger and asked for their patience in letting the law take its course. The district attorney's appeal, along with that of Mayor Bradley, finally succeeded in restoring quiet. The mechanics began to disperse into the night, still angry and resentful. Key walked to his house on C Street.

Once again Key found himself at the center of a cataclysm. In 1814 he had faced the overwhelming British force at Bladensburg. Now he faced the unruly mobs of mechanics without adequate defenses. Mayor Bradley knew the city could not expect more U.S. government soldiers. All available troops were tied down in Baltimore, where the mobs had destroyed the homes of two leading bankers before order was restored. As backup, Bradley contacted Walter Jones, nominal leader of the city's much-ridiculed militia. Bradley asked Jones to organize a force to restrain the crowds, protect public buildings, and preserve the peace. Expecting trouble, Bradley arranged for the Ordnance Office of the army to supply Jones's men with fifty-five carbines, as many pistols, and fifteen hundred rounds of ball cartridges.

29

THE NEXT MORNING, the mob had a new target: Beverly Snow. The Epicurean Eating House was now surrounded by a crowd of mechanics led by the outspoken Andrew Laub, who shared a shocking rumor about the colored restaurateur: that he had dared to speak coarsely about white women. No one agreed on exactly what he had said. By one account, Snow had visited a butcher's stall in the Centre Market and made "a remark derogatory to the character of the ladies of Washington."

The story gained detail as it spread. "Snow was reported to have made some very gross reflections on the mechanics of the city, as also on their wives and daughters," the *Telegraph* reported.

"He had used very indecent and disrespectful language concerning the wives and daughter of Mechanics," reported the *Mirror*, adding he made an "infamous boast . . . in speaking of a respectable white woman."

Snow's enemies may have invented the story with malicious intent. Beverly was a hospitable man by nature who had not cultivated a prosperous white clientele for his restaurant by dispensing coarse insults. No butcher, or any other man, white or colored, ever came forward to say he had heard Snow utter such sentiments, not even when there was great advantage to be gained from doing so. As for Washington society, Julia Seaton said she knew no one who believed the accusation. Michael Shiner, probably the best-informed black man about town, was less certain. "God knows whether he said those things or not," he wrote.

Given Beverly's wit, it is possible the rumor had some basis in truth. He might have tossed off a cutting remark about the mob then running rampant in the streets. Many white people were appalled by the disorder too. Perhaps Snow was shopping for venison when his butcher mentioned the mob. The amiable chef might have responded by joking that while the mechanics waited around the jail to lynch poor Crandall, their wives and the daughters might be getting lonely at home. Such barroom banter would have been in keeping with Beverly's irreverent character without intending to offend.

After all, it was not Beverly's literal words that disturbed white people. It was his example, his Epicurean style, and his evident success. John O'Sullivan of the *Metropolitan* said Beverly's "insolent and overbearing effrontery had long rendered him obnoxious in this city." But what made Snow obnoxious to some white people endeared him to others, including white women, who perhaps noticed that the proprietor of the Epicurean Eating House treated them rather better than other hotel keepers. As a free man of color, Snow had proven he could mix and compete with any white man in Washington City. The popularity of his dining rooms gave lie to Francis Scott Key's conventional wisdom that the Negro was inherently inferior. Snow disproved that daily, showing that white and black people could break bread together in peace and pleasure. Not to mention that Snow dressed better, spoke better, and carried more money than Andrew Laub and the mechanics now squalling in the streets. As a married man and good Epicurean, Snow no doubt guarded himself against "the charms of love," but if there was any black man in town capable of having a white woman, via seduction or payment, it was Snow.

Whatever Beverly's innuendo, it was not appreciated.

"A number of persons assembled at his door, with a determination to inflict punishment on him," the *Telegraph* reported.

The crowd soon numbered in the hundreds and swelled to block the carriage traffic on the Avenue. Beverly was not caught by surprise; he had arranged for some white friends to come to his defense. "All the gentlemen of the city protected Snow so far as they could, not believing him guilty," said Julia Seaton. Even Mayor Bradley favored his escape, complained Anne Royall.

The mechanics overwhelmed Beverly's friends with sheer numbers, pouring down the stairs and into the dining rooms of the restaurant and through the kitchen. There was no sign of the voluble cook, and Beverly's friends denied any knowledge of his whereabouts, reminding the milling crowd not to damage the furniture as it belonged to a white man, John Withers.

The mechanics asked more questions of the gentlemen defending Snow and did not believe the answers. Much to the disgust of the *Telegraph,* the restaurateur's friends had "kept the people amused while Snow made his escape." He took refuge, the paper reported, in the block of buildings behind his restaurant.

Snow was already in motion. The rear of the Epicurean Eating House opened on the yard of Brown's Hotel, where supplies and servants moved constantly. There were likely Negroes, enslaved or free, working there who would have helped Snow escape. He made his way down the alley and out to Seventh Street. When the mechanics realized that Snow was gone, one gang of men set out to find him. They "started a hunt for him, carrying ropes, pistols and other weapons," one constable later recalled, "and it is safe to say that had he been overtaken, 'Judge Lynch' would have made short work of him."

The men left behind trashed the Epicurean Eating House. Over the objections of the outnumbered William Walker, the white men pulled down the "Refectory: Snow & Walker's" sign on the wall over the outside door. They started bringing out and smashing the furniture. They helped themselves to the bottles of whiskey and champagne they could not afford to buy. They handed out drinks for themselves and poured the rest out on the street. Then they destroyed the apparatus of Beverly's extensive kitchen. The ubiquitous Michael Shiner said mechanics of all classes "gathered in Snow's restaurant and broke him up root and branch."

The story of Beverly's boast spread across the city.

"Today the mob are parading the streets in search of a negro by the name of Snow who keeps an oyster house," one resident wrote to a friend. "He is reported to have said he could get any mechanic's wife or daughter he pleased, and the mob are determined to be revenged upon him, if he is caught."

Even those who had no use for Beverly Snow were appalled.

"The Mob-mania," said the *Metropolitan,* "has become beyond control."

Beverly had a head start. He made his way to Tenth Street, running north. At that time, there was a runoff creek called the Sluice that meandered from a spring at Thirteenth and K streets down through the city to the Tiber Canal. As the armed gang of mechanics came up the street in pursuit, he sped north toward the bridge that crossed over the Sluice with the white men closing in on him. The chase continued north of F Street and beyond, but the gang could not catch up. They eventually lost his trail and headed back to the Avenue in search of new sport.

In fact, Snow had ducked into a sewer under the bridge. The mob thundered overhead and continued up Tenth Street chasing a phantom. When they were gone, Snow moved on, unnoticed in the warm night.

By early evening City Hall swarmed with people. As the excitement and fear grew—Would Crandall be hanged? Would the slaves rebel?—the city council met in emergency session. Its members had no love for a rebellious slave or a New York abolitionist, but they were appalled at the chaos in the streets. Working quickly, they approved a proclamation authorizing Mayor Bradley to "adopt such measures as may appear to him best calculated to allay the excitement now existing among a portion of the population of this City, and for the preservation of peace and public order."

Bradley then took the podium. He deputized General Jones's volunteers, who were still gathering. He ordered Jones and his men to take "utmost vigilance" in "preventing any assemblage of meeting of colored persons, bond or free," as if the black people of the city were interested in starting any kind of trouble.

Jones, in turn, called on "the friends of Order and of the Laws" to join him outside on the steps of City Hall. Before long, sixty men had gathered, many carrying rifles or muskets with fixed bayonets. Others took the carbines requisitioned from the War Department. They were ready to take back their city from the mechanics.

Frank Key made his own arrangements. He took a carriage to Georgetown, where he asked for a reinforcement of constables to come guard his house on C Street. Then he went home for the night.

Two blocks south of City Hall, at the corner of Sixth and Pennsylvania, a herd of three or four hundred men, led by Andrew Laub, still occupied the ruins of the Epicurean Eating House. As they drank Beverly's liquor and cursed his name, the appearance of General Jones's militia up the street "excited great indignation on the part of the mechanics." They felt the mayor's militia was coming to protect Beverly Snow and his property. Laub and others emerged from the basement restaurant to shout at General Jones and the militia that they must go away, or they would be driven away. Laub and friends claimed, according to the *Telegraph,* that they "had no intention to injure any property, or do any mischief, except chastise Snow." They refused to disperse as long as the militia remained in arms. After some negotiation between the two parties, the militia retreated to the defense of City Hall while a group of constables kept an eye on the most unruly mechanics and later arrested Laub and five others, who were charged with rioting.

When General Jones and his volunteers retired to City Hall to sleep for the night, they effectively surrendered the streets of Washington City to the whims of the mob. The mechanics, now lubricated by Beverly's bar, realized they were free to indulge their instincts to administer justice wherever they pleased. They started to disperse across the city in squads of tens and twenties in search of new targets and new victims.

The constables could not have stopped them if they had wanted to, which they did not.

Like many residents of Washington City that night, Anna Thornton could not sleep. With Arthur in jail and mobs rampaging, she felt close to collapse.

"I feel unwell & nervous," she wrote in her diary. "I never expected to have any cause for grief after my beloved husband's death . . . but I find there are other griefs besides death. Oh Lord strengthen me for this trial is overcoming my spirits."

30

THE EVENTS OF August 1835 would soon be dubbed the "Snow Riot" or the "Snow-Storm" in recognition of the central role that Beverly Snow's singular personality played in igniting popular passion. But the breakdown in order was not simply a loss of control, as implied by the word "riot," nor a natural phenomenon, as implied by "storm." The mobs of Washington City chose their targets, discerning observers noticed. Margaret Bayard Smith, Anna Thornton's good friend and chronicler of Washington society, noted that the anger of whites could be traced to events several days *before* Snow allegedly made his salacious jape. The disturbances, she wrote, originated during the hunt for Arthur Bowen.

"The constable in seeking him made some discoveries among the colored people that alarmed the public and gave rise to the disturbances that ensued," she wrote. "Four [men], who were objects of greatest indignation, have fled the city." Smith did not identify the four offenders but noted they posed no threat to public safety, only to white people's feelings of superiority.

"No insurrection against the whites was seriously apprehended," she wrote, "but insolence, insubordination and contempt had been exhibited that were certainly sufficient to excite the indignation that existed and called for punishment, though every one regrets that a mob should assume the right of inflicting it."

The constable who did the discovering of "insolence, insubordination and contempt" was Madison Jeffers, the man who had arrested Arthur Bowen on Saturday, and then Reuben Crandall on Monday. It was Jeffers who incited the crowd against Crandall by telling them about the pamphlets. Many a white man shared his indignation.

Beverly Snow, who had offered to help quell any talk of insurrection among the blacks, was now a target of the whites. So was John Cook, perhaps the most educated black man in the city. One mob marched up the Avenue to Fourteenth Street and then north to H Street, where his school was located. Cook too had expected trouble and made himself scarce. He mounted his horse, stabled at the house of a white friend, and sped north in the night, heading for Pennsylvania. The mechanics engulfed his schoolhouse, destroying all the books and furniture. They had started to tear down the building itself when they were challenged by Edward Dyer, a white man and auctioneer who also served as alderman for the Second Ward. Dyer planted himself between the mob and the house and the attackers moved on.

Another gang of white men invaded the boardinghouse room of a free man of color named James Hutton. Ironically, Francis Scott Key had helped Hutton win his freedom a decade before with a clever legal argument. At the time Hutton was a servant owned by a naval officer named Bell. Hutton had served Bell on a navy ship during an overseas tour of duty, but since official regulations forbade the use of slaves on navy ships, Hutton was paid for his work. Upon their return to the United States, Hutton filed suit for his freedom, saying the fact he had been paid meant he was no longer a slave. Key, in his self-appointed role as "the Black's lawyer," submitted a letter to the court saying that Hutton's paid tour of duty amounted to "implied manumission." The court ruled in his favor, and Hutton became a free man in 1825. Ten years later, the rampaging mob ransacked his room and found a copy of *The Emancipator,* one of the sheets that Reuben Crandall had brought to town. A constable accompanying the mob took this as proof that Hutton was in league with Crandall and hustled him off to jail amidst cries that he be lynched too.

Another mob went after William Wormley, the livery stable owner who had been friends with William Lloyd Garrison when the abolitionist editor lived in Washington. Wormley's sister Mary had run another school for Negro children on Vermont Avenue before falling ill and passing away a few months before. A teacher friend of the Wormleys named William Thomas Lee had taken over the school. The mob came for Wormley and Lee and they fled the city. Wormley's schoolhouse was trashed as well.

Another target was William Jackson, who worked as a messenger at the Post Office and supported abolition. "It seems there was some danger of the mob getting hold of him," a colleague recounted. "He had been a great patron of the abolition journals and used to get a leave of absence every summer to attend the negro Congress at Philadelphia." Jackson too had to clear out.

The only Negro school spared was Louise Parke Costin's academy on A Street on Capitol Hill, and it wasn't hard to figure out why. Her father was William Costin, the most respected free Negro in town. He was close to the family of Martha Washington, avoided involvement in abolitionist activities, and worked as a porter for rich men at the Bank of Washington. Costin's friendships with leading white men gave him a degree of protection, and the mob recognized it by staying away from his daughter's school.

The pattern of the disorder indicates that the white mob tormenting Washington City in August 1835 was not out of control and not solely concerned with Beverly Snow. The mechanics did not attack all free blacks or all schools. They pursued the small group of black men who were doing the most to undermine the slave system in the seat of the American government. The Snow-Storm was not just a riot. It was also a manhunt.

The carnage continued into the night, a display of ferocity that was directed at free blacks but also meant to send a message to all the people of the city. The mechanics would be heard. In the words of the *Metropolitan*, "The populace of Washington, once elevated into the dignity of a sovereign mob, seemed resolved not to separate without giving the remaining inhabitants convincing proof of their power and letting them feel the blessings of their sway." The mob would teach the city, and its leaders, a lesson.

Key himself was targeted. One gang gathered around his house on C Street and noisily reviled him as an abolitionist, which he most certainly was not. The crowd might have sacked the home had it not been for the presence of armed guards. Mercifully, Polly and the younger children were safe at Terra Rubra.

Other marauders wandered around town taking their pleasure.

"The property of every colored person who rendered themselves obnoxious to them was devoted to destruction," said the *Metropolitan*.

"The African churches and schools shared a similar fate and then the insurrectionary and violent spirit which was prevalent singled out other objects on which to wreak its fury."

The *Intelligencer* noted the mob had burned a house of ill fame in the First Ward that was frequented by blacks. The *Globe* chastely reported that they had set fire to a "hut," whose proprietor was "an old negro woman" and a "regular conjurer of the blacks of this city," a veiled way of saying she was a madam.

The assailants' goal—their pleasure—was to annihilate the black man's playground. They dragged the beds and the chairs of the bawdy house out into the open. They smashed these cradles of paid love into kindling, and then they piled it high and torched the whole building. The result was a gigantic bonfire that could be seen a mile and a half away at City Hall.

When the sentries for the militia saw the light of the flames in the western sky, Mayor Bradley and General Jones led a patrol to investigate. The armed men went out onto the Avenue, past the darkened presidential mansion, and into the First Ward (in the area now known as Foggy Bottom) and found the site of the blaze. The fire had burnt down to cinders. The house of ill fame was no more. The whores, their customers, and the arsonists had all vanished. Even the conjurer was gone.

COME MORNING, THE mood in Washington City was desolate. Not since Ross and Cockburn led the British troops in burning the Capitol and the President's House in August 1814 had the capital seen such widespread lawlessness and destruction of property. And this rampage had been inflicted not by foreigners, but by Americans. Seaton and Gales described the civic humiliation in a lead editorial for the *Intelligencer*: "THE STATE OF THE CITY."

"We could not have believed it possible that we should live to see the Public Offices garrisoned by the Clerks with United States troops posted to their doors, and their windows barricaded to defend themselves against citizens of Washington," they wrote.

"It is certainly mortifying as well as disreputable," they went on, "that a handful of People, some of them, and the most active amongst them, not residents even of the city, and a large portion of them boys, should have the power and have been permitted to commit any depredations with impunity, and keep the whole population of a large town in a state of anxiety for twenty-four hours."

In the pages of the *Globe*, Francis Blair expressed "extreme regret that we have to state that our wide-spread and hitherto peaceful City, has been the scene of riotous excitement. . . . We hope and believe that its peace will not be again disturbed."

In the *Telegraph* Duff Green displayed a previously unknown reservoir of moderation. As for "the excitement in our city," he acknowledged he would have felt no pity if Crandall had been hanged but said he preferred that a jury, not a mob, hand down the sentence. He lauded the arrest of Andrew Laub and the disorderly mechanics. He saluted General Jones for "his persevering exertions in restoring the wonted peace and harmony of the Metropolis."

The misdeeds of abolitionists and the free Negroes were no excuse for rioting, said the *Metropolitan*. The editor, John O'Sullivan, execrated Beverly Snow as "a scoundrel scarce removed from slavery." He also said the free-floating violence was unacceptable.

"We now hope there is an end to this kind of work. All parties have become disgusted with it," he wrote. "Whatever circumstances and under whatever provocation, any tardiness of a certain justice is infinitely better than the destructive and irresponsible legislation of a mob."

Yet the sense of disorder had not dissipated. Over the next few nights, gangs of young white men and boys reassembled around town, looking for trouble. One mob demolished the Sabbath schoolhouse of the AME church on South Capitol Street, just a block from where the U.S. Congress met.

The authorities remained vigilant. The city of Alexandria sent two companies of volunteers, who took over the guarding of the jail. The U.S. troops continued to fortify the government offices. And the volunteers from Georgetown continued to guard Mr. Key's home.

Anna Thornton, cooped up in her house on F Street, had to take care of her clueless mama and the terrified Maria Bowen and could not sleep.

"Noises in the street that alarmed me very much," she wrote in her diary. "As soon as I began to doze something awoke me in affright & I had a nightmare."

On C Street, Francis Scott Key could take little consolation. Yes, he had acted swiftly to detain Reuben Crandall and talked down the mob around the jail. His constables had brought charges against two dozen rioters. He did not care about the attack on Snow's restaurant, but he was determined to punish destruction of property. He still had a chance to redeem himself. In his view, the capital had fallen victim to the abolitionists' pamphlet campaign, a serious attack from wily and well-funded white men who acted in the name of so-called human rights. If the city's excitement was unfortunate, the struggle was not yet over. Francis Scott Key would go to court to defend the legal system of slavery in Washington City.

· · ·

Washington was not unique in its chaos. During the month of August 1835, cities and towns across the Upper South rallied to meet the threat of the pamphlet campaign. Postmasters in many towns had received the bundles of tracts, individually addressed, from New York. The claims of these publications—about the beatings, the mutilations, the rapes, and the robberies endemic to the slave system—libeled the southern way of life, they said. Torchlight parades, protest meetings, and outraged rhetoric greeted the arrival of the pamphlets in every major city and many smaller ones. Citizens formed vigilance committees to patrol areas where free Negroes lived and to track down rumors of "Tappan's emissaries" moving about in the countryside. The mob was everywhere.

"The state of society is awful," wrote Hezekiah Niles, editor of *Niles' Weekly Register*, a national newsweekly based in Baltimore. Niles accepted slavery as a political reality but not lawlessness. "Brute force has superseded the law, at many places, and violence become the '*order* of the day.' The time predicted seems rapidly approaching when the mob shall rule . . . ," he wrote. "The time was when every citizen of the United States, would 'rally round the standard of the law, and unite in common efforts for the common good'—when a person, armed only with a small piece of paper, could proceed a thousand miles through the country, and bring the strongest man to answer to the law, for the law was honored. But is it so now? Alas, no!"

The rule of law was buckling under the realities of a slaveholding democracy. The need to defend the slave system overwhelmed the protections written into the Bill of Rights.

"There is something extraordinary in the present condition of parties throughout the Union," wrote John Quincy Adams in his diary. "Slavery and democracy, especially the democracy founded, as ours is, upon the rights of man, would seem to be incompatible with each other. And yet at this time, the democracy of the country is supported chiefly, if not entirely by slavery."

The former president feared for his country.

"The elements of an exterminating war seem to be in vehement fermentation, and one can scarcely foresee to what it will lead."

Francis Scott Key could not foresee it either.

THE FOLLOWING MONDAY, August 17, President Jackson returned to Washington City on the steamboat *Columbia*. While basking in the breezes off the Chesapeake Bay, Jackson had frolicked with nieces and nephews and read the newspaper reports on how the American Anti-Slavery Society's pamphlet campaign had inflamed popular feeling. He loathed the abolitionists for stirring up the blacks and thought they should pay for such insolence. He had approved Postmaster Amos Kendall's proposal to give local post offices the right to refuse to deliver antislavery literature. But the president was none too pleased to hear of rioting against the free people of color in Washington City. "This spirit of mob-law is becoming too common and must be checked or, ere long, it will become as great an evil as servile war, and the innocent will be much exposed," he wrote to Kendall.

The day Jackson returned was warm with a light breeze. He disembarked at the dock on the Potomac with his niece Emily Donelson and her husband, Andrew, who served as his private secretary. The president climbed into his carriage and headed for the big house on Pennsylvania Avenue. It was time to get back to work.

That same day a group of mechanics sent the president a message. They resented the fact that the ladies and gentlemen of the city blamed workingmen for the breakdown of public order. With the help of Duff Green and the *Telegraph*, they called for a public meeting at City Hall, open to all the mechanics "and other citizens friendly to the labouring classes." By three o'clock, fifteen hundred men had gathered. It was, said the organizers, "one of the largest and most respectable meetings which ever assembled in this city." These men felt insulted that they were considered part of the drunken rabble that had rampaged. They chafed at the reality that many white people attributed the mob's destruction to them. They were mechanics and they had nothing to do with the mob. They formed a committee to draft a series of resolutions for public approval.

"We have viewed with feelings of deep regret, the excitement and riotous proceedings that have prevailed for some days past in this city," the committee declared.

Their first resolution asserted that the mechanics, "having a large stake in the advancement and peace of this city, . . . view the late excitement and riotous proceedings as highly detrimental to our prosperity and well-being."

But the truth was that no small portion of the white workingmen felt the rioting was a justifiable response to the murderous Arthur Bowen, the treacherous Reuben Crandall, and the obnoxious Beverly Snow. The problem, these men believed, was not the rioters but those who sought to suppress them. A man in the crowed named James Haliday rose to offer a substitute resolution that spoke more directly to why the mechanics were so angry: because the combined forces of General Jones's irregulars and the U.S. Marines had restored order at gunpoint—as if the mechanics had been doing something wrong in chastising the free Negroes. President Jackson should order the U.S. troops to return to their barracks, Haliday said, "their presence evincing a want of confidence in the freemen of this Metropolis to protect public and private property." The meeting, he went on, should "highly reprobate the conduct of all those who have been in any way instrumental in ordering [the troops] here."

This sally, directed at Mayor Bradley and General Jones, went over well. The organizers of the meeting said Haliday's substitute resolution was adopted "by a large majority," although one mechanic later protested that at least half of the crowd did not understand what they were approving. Haliday sat down satisfied.

The next resolution was less controversial: that the mechanics were "ready and disposed, at all times, to risk our lives in the protection of [public and private property] from a foreign or domestic enemy." But the crowd's patience had run out. The assembled men hooted down three more resolutions before the meeting broke up.

Jackson got word of the mechanics' meeting later that afternoon. Michael Shiner, always close to the center of action, said the president "sent a message to those gentlemen mechanics to know what was the matter with them and if there was any thing he could do for them, in any way to promote their happiness, he would do it."

A meeting was arranged for the next day. A delegation of mechanics went to the President's House. In Shiner's account, they told Jackson "that the Negroes had made different threats." The president's response was blunt. He expected justice to be served by the legal system.

"By the eternal god in this City there is a Jail and a court and if those negroes had violated any law whatever they shall be tried by the court and punished severely," Jackson roared. According to Shiner, the president expressed sympathy for the mechanics' anger, going so far as to suggest he might join in their cause the next time. "Gentlemen," he said, "if you have in any disposition to rebellion to let me know it, and I will lend you a hand."

But for all his bluster, Jackson rejected the primary demand of his visitors: the removal of the federal troops from the streets of Washington. On that question, editor Edgar Snowden reported that Jackson gave them "a preemptory answer in the negative." Jackson may have sympathized with the mechanics, but he was not taking any chances on the return of Mobocracy.

With the restoration of calm, the recriminations began.

"What causes have produced the declension in American character and the present supremacy of Mobocracy?" asked the *Richmond Whig*, one of the most widely read newspapers in the country. In an editorial headlined "CAUSES OF THE PUBLIC DISORDERS," the rival *Richmond Enquirer* replied that President Jackson and "the policy of the ruling dynasty and its demagogue adherents" were to blame.

In the view of editor Thomas Ritchie, the source of the problem was not the free Negroes, who constituted a small portion of the population, or the antislavery agitators who had little public support. The problem was Jackson's appeal to the common man and his supporters' hostility to traditional elites.

"In pursuit of a majority to sustain their power, they have classified the rich and intelligent and denounced them as aristocrats," Ritchie wrote.

"They have caressed, soothed and flattered the heavy class of the poor and ignorant, because they held the power which they wanted."

"The Republic," Ritchie famously declared, "has degenerated into a Democracy."

Rubbish, replied Francis Blair in the *Globe*. The Washington disturbances, he insisted, should be blamed on antislavery financier Arthur Tappan, "the arch enemy of the Jackson administration." Arthur Bowen's attack on Mrs. Thornton had been instigated by Tappan's pamphlet campaign, which had "stimulated the servant, cherished in the bosom of families, to immolate those who have protected and reared him from infancy." Tappan's incitements had forced white men to act in their own self-defense, prompting "the father, the husband and master to rush beyond the laws to destroy the instigators of a servile war, to save himself and the hapless inmates of his household from its horrible consequences." The mob, he insisted, was an expression of American self-defense.

The violent summer of 1835 had diverse and subtle causes, but one stood out. Amidst the disorder, it was clear that the burgeoning antislavery movement had forced Americans to consider its core message: that democracy could not coexist with the right to property in people. The northern abolitionists insisted that American slavery and the democratic government of the United States, based in Washington, were intertwined, mutually reinforcing, and ultimately incompatible.

That was a radical and disconcerting thought in the capital city. The emancipationist alternative proposed that Negroes should be free to become citizens, equal to whites before the law. The white men of Washington responded violently because they had seen the results of partial emancipation. Some black men like Beverly Snow wound up with more money and prestige than the average white man. That was the problem, and Mobocracy was the answer.

Francis Scott Key continued to seek justice through the law. On August 24, he told Anna Thornton of a scheduled hearing for Arthur. "You need not come," he said. "The object is to commit him for trial." Perhaps the district attorney wanted to spare Anna the need to relive the night of the incident. Perhaps he did not want to hear her view, which she had already conveyed to him through Bayard Smith and General Jones, that she did not want to see the boy punished. More likely, he did not think her view was relevant. In any case, Anna did not attend the hearing. It was a pleasant day and she chose to read a novel instead.

Arthur was led from the jail to the courtroom in City Hall. He was not entirely alone. Anna had retained General Jones to serve as his attorney, and his mother, Maria, was there as well. As three justices of the peace listened, Key called his witnesses: Dr. Huntt, General Gibson, and the constables, Madison Jeffers and Henry Robertson. Maria Bowen was allowed to testify, but the court did not hear Anna Thornton's account of what happened on the night of August 4, just as the district attorney intended. He wanted no obstacles to justice. He wanted a trial date and he got one.

"The desperate fellow who attempted the life of Mrs. Thornton was reexamined on Thursday last," the *Mirror* reported. ". . . The prisoner was fully committed for trial at the Circuit Court in November next."

33

THE MOST WANTED man in Washington was ambling his way down the Virginia turnpike. Beverly Snow rode one horse and held the reins to a second. He was headed for Fredericksburg. How he had managed to escape the city is not known. Mostly likely he found refuge with friends, then waited for an opportunity to head south with his two steeds.

Beverly reached Fredericksburg around one o'clock on the afternoon of Monday, August 17, at the very hour President Jackson returned to his desk and the mechanics gathered in City Hall. Beverly's arrival was not entirely unexpected. He had colored acquaintances in the town, and when people heard he was the cause of the excitement in Washington, they figured he might show up seeking shelter. The Mechanics Association of Fredericksburg, a dues-paying group that provided training to white workingmen, held a meeting and resolved there would be no mob in Fredericksburg. Beverly, it seems, had some friends among the white men of the town.

No sooner had Beverly appeared than a friendly crowd surrounded him. He explained to his well-wishers that he wanted to see the sheriff, and the people escorted him to the jail. He told the sheriff he wanted to voluntarily commit himself for his own safety, pending the allegations against him in Washington City. He asked the sheriff to contact Mayor Bradley to learn if there were any charges against him in the capital. The sheriff agreed.

"BEVERLY SNOW TAKEN!" shouted the headline in the Lynchburg *Daily Virginian* the next day.

In Washington, the *Intelligencer* reported, "Snow, the obnoxious free mulatto who fled from this city last week, was arrested there [Fredericksburg] on Monday and committed to prison." According to the article,

Snow had been charged with circulating incendiary pamphlets and would be sent to Washington within a day or two—neither of which was true. In Alexandria the *Gazette* said Snow was "taken and lodged in Jail to be delivered when demanded." That was wrong too.

Some expected Snow would be hanged shortly.

"We think it probable," said the *Fredericksburg Arena*, that "he may ultimately suffer at the tribunal of Judge Lynch."

In fact, Snow had not been taken, arrested, or charged with anything. He avoided most of the perils his enemies hoped or imagined had befallen him. The disarming strategy of turning himself in served to give him the initiative on the question of his freedom, which he would never lose. Snow had friends in Fredericksburg. Newspaper editor William Blackford described them as free Negroes "who have by a proper demeanor gained the confidence of all who know them." That was probably an allusion to Fredericksburg's wealthiest free men of color, Thomas Cary Sr. and Benjamin DeBaptist. Thomas Cary was the father of Beverly's friends Isaac Cary and Thomas Cary Jr. He had owned property in the Fredericksburg area since 1808. DeBaptist came from a black family that had been free for generations and owned his own slaves. If necessary, free men of color like Cary and DeBaptist could credibly vouch to white authorities about Beverly's good character.

Still, it took nerve for Snow to consign himself voluntarily to the Fredericksburg jail. He was probably remanded to "the dungeon," a basement cell secured with an iron gate, wooden door, and strong locks. Unlike the jail in Washington City, there was little chance of getting a dram of liquor there, but there was also little chance of getting hanged. Snow would just have to wait for word from his friend Mayor Bradley. As he passed the time in his voluntary cell, he might have taken solace from a maxim favored by Epicurus:

> "The Wisest of Men is not sheltered from Injustice and Envy. He may be Calumniated, tis true, but it shall not work upon him because he knows his own Probity and Virtue; and Malice, whose current he cannot stem, is not capable of discomposing his Tranquility."

If Beverly was calm, white people were agitated. The arrival of the notorious Beverly Snow, and the story of his supposedly shocking comments about white women, prompted much talk of the proverbial Judge Lynch in Fredericksburg, nowhere more than at the Mechanics Association. With Snow now in custody, the mechanics called another meeting to make clear to the gentlemen of the town and to one another that they would not tolerate abolitionists or lawlessness. The shame of Washington City would not be Fredericksburg's. At a public meeting, the mechanics adopted a resolution indignantly rejecting reports that they were organizing search committees "or endeavoring in any manner to promote or get up a Mob." They vowed, in writing, that if the civil authorities would not guard Beverly Snow in jail, they would "protect him from the populace until the authorities of Washington City demand him."

Then word came from Mayor Bradley in Washington. He told the sheriff there was no charge against Snow for the distribution of incendiary pamphlets or anything else. In the dungeon, Snow put pen to paper. He addressed his letter to William Seaton and Joseph Gales at the *Intelligencer*, two men who knew him well. They had published an article that attributed coarse comments about white women to him.

"Gentlemen," he began. "Listen to the voice of the innocent which cries aloud for justice." The *Intelligencer*'s story, he wrote, "struck a death blow to all that I held dear to me in this world, my character and my liberty."

Snow had tired of this persecution. "What is life without character?" he asked. "It is worth nothing; it's a burden to me."

He considered the whitewashed walls, the locked wooden door.

"Sirs, so thick are those dangers that I have voluntarily retired to prison for my safety, and shall remain in prison until every mind is satisfied of my innocence."

He wanted to be very clear.

"Dear Sirs, I am innocent of the charges preferred against me," he wrote. "I do swear before my God, this Sabbath day, within the solemn walls of this prison that I am as innocent as the child unborn of having excited any White man, or men, against me."

Snow requested an investigation of himself, daring his accusers to identify themselves.

"I would ask if there is a White man of any sort or kind, in any population, who is so divested of feeling and resentment, as to have brooked so great an insult. Sirs, I will answer the question myself: I do not believe there is such a White man to be found anywhere."

That was bold, but it also implied that any white man who came forward to impugn Snow would be humiliating himself for having not spoken up earlier. And that preemptive strike was followed by a reminder that Snow had associated with many a white man who never complained about his cooking or his conduct.

"Sirs, the most diligent research has been made by my enemies and friends, and no other but this untrue charge can be found . . . ," he complained. "Sirs, do me the honor to look back at my past conduct, as a citizen, for the last six or seven years. If anything can be produced against me, let the world know it. If within your own knowledge you can say any thing for me in justice, you would oblige your humble servant."

The *Intelligencer* published the letter two days later with an editor's note, stating, "We cannot better serve the ends of justice than by publishing this individual's plea in his own words."

No one came forward to corroborate the rumor that Snow had spoken improperly of white women. Within a few days, the white men of the Fredericksburg Mechanics Association held yet another meeting and resolved that Snow should be permitted to depart in peace. The editors of the *Virginia Herald* held him blameless. "The sufferings of the poor fellow, in mind, body, and property, we think, have been sufficient to allay any excitement on the part of our citizens," they wrote.

In Washington, Snow got less consideration, at least from the newspapers.

"He had better stay where he is," warned John O'Sullivan in the *Metropolitan*, "for as the old adage says, 'he may go farther and fare worse.'"

"The public has had enough of this epicurean mulatto," said one anonymous letter writer in the *Intelligencer*. "Let him not flatter himself that any disclaimers will enable him to shine in Washington."

Beverly had lost everything he had built up over the last five years, so he probably did not flatter himself about much. The truth was that he had believed too much: too much in his own ability to live within the slave system and prosper on his own terms; too much in the benevolence of the average white man; too much in the hospitality of Washington City; and too much in the possibilities of the United States of America. It must have been a bitter reckoning, but it was not one that would destroy him. Beverly left the Fredericksburg jail at a time of his choosing in pursuit of a destination unknown. He would treat the unfriendly advice of white men who warned him not to come back to Washington City with characteristic tact. He would ignore it.

PART V

THE TRIALS OF ARTHUR BOWEN

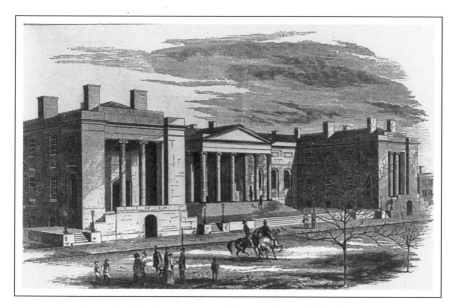

City Hall in Washington's Judiciary Square, where Francis
Scott Key prosecuted Arthur Bowen for the attempted
murder of Anna Maria Thornton in November 1835.

34

Francis Scott Key retreated to Terra Rubra that fall for a welcome vacation. He probably brooded over the breakdown of order in Washington at the same time he pondered a sad news story in the *Intelligencer*. His dear friend Sarah Gayle was no more. The newspaper reported that the wife of the governor of Alabama had died suddenly and painfully of lockjaw over the summer. She was thirty-one years old. Key never took death well. He sank into melancholy for months after the passing of his close friend John Randolph in 1833. Now his soul mate in poetry was gone. What a delight she was, as hostess, friend, and mother. As always, Key consoled himself with his enduring belief that God's way, while sometimes mysterious and painful, was best.

Likewise, the mood and morale of Washington took a while to recover from the trauma of the Snow-Storm. Even the return of President Jackson did not prevent violence from flaring several more times in the last indolent days of summer. A mob of white men attacked the AME church on Capitol Hill again, leaving the worship space in ruins. A Negro schoolhouse near the Navy Yard was attacked. So was a bawdy house on G Street between Sixth and Seventh. Ever since the rioting, hostility toward the free people of color had taken on a new vehemence. In the words of historian Constance McLaughlin Green, "The white men's shame over the lawless violence of the Snow-Storm intensified rather than lessened their resentment at the mere presence of free blacks in Washington."

Black people found themselves facing a new wave of legal harassment and social ostracism. "We have already too many free negroes and mulattoes in this city," said an anonymous letter writer in the *Intelligencer*. "The policy of our corporate authorities should tend to the diminution of this insolent class. A motion is now before the Common Council for prohibiting shop-licenses henceforth to this class of people. If they wish to live here, let them become subordinates and laborers, as nature has designed." The common council passed the new ordinance barring blacks from shop licenses.

It was a time for the leaders of the blacks to lie low. Beverly Snow came back to town briefly to dissolve his partnership with William Walker. William Wormley and William Thomas Lee returned to the city only after a personal assurance of safety from President Jackson. John Cook did not return from Pennsylvania at all. The philosophically inclined school-teacher had no taste for physical confrontation. He had taken refuge in the town of Columbia, where he taught at the school of a friend.

The pamphlet campaign of the American Anti-Slavery Society had achieved its goal of forcing public discussion everywhere. The society reaped sympathy and money, just as the entrepreneurial mind of Arthur Tappan had anticipated. But the price was high. *Niles' Weekly Register* reported that the United States had experienced fifty-three riots in 1835, more than double the year before, and more than thirteen times the four that were reported in 1833. Most of these riots involved attacks on anti-slavery speakers and free blacks. But the popularity of the antislavery message only grew. Robert Williams, publications manager for the society and a friend of Reuben Crandall, reported picking up fifteen thousand new subscribers in less than a year.

The South's violent reaction, said the society's director, Elizur Wright, "has done more than could have been done by the arguments of a thousand lecturers to convince the sober and disinterested, that slavery is a crime." The rationalization of lawlessness brought home to northerners how Negro slavery posed a threat to their own democracy. As the South demanded the northern states suppress abolitionist speech, publications, and petitions, northerners rejected the idea. "The despotism of [the] laws would . . . far exceed any in Russia or Turkey," declared the delegates to a meeting in Utica, New York.

The violence of the summer of 1835 forged a new notion in American life: that defending the republic required opposing the slave masters. Across the northern tier of the country from Michigan to Maine, people rushed to support the cause of abolishing slavery. At the beginning of the year, there were 200 antislavery societies around the United States. At the end of the year, there were 527. By 1837, there would be a thousand. The abolitionists were still a minority in the nation and the Congress, but no one could doubt their ranks were growing.

South of the Potomac, the results of the pamphlet campaign were very different. The idea of human rights had not taken root in the civil society of the South. The educated middle class was small and culturally weak, especially compared to the slave-owning elite. Those Virginians who had spoken up against slavery after Southampton had not achieved any legislative results. With the white man's property rights now under siege from the North, there would be no more tolerance of antislavery opinion in the South. Southerners who spoke out against slavery had to shut up or leave.

Anna Thornton could not stop thinking of Arthur in his jail cell. Her conviction that he had not meant to harm had hardened into a personal truth that others would find hard to believe. She did not think him guilty of anything other than inebriation. But it was the worst possible time for a white woman to be seeking leniency for a Negro accused of a capital crime. All of Washington City believed a black man attacked her in her bedroom, and she was defending him, minimizing his actions. It was almost unthinkable, but to the disbelief of her friends, she persisted.

Hoping for ideas about how to free Arthur, she invited General Jones for dinner, "but he has put me quite out of Spirits again," she wrote. She stayed that way for weeks. She made the rounds of her lady friends and shopped in the market with Maria. She read her books and played chess. Nothing helped, not even the spectacle of Halley's Comet, seen only once every seventy-six years. "I am in very bad spirits," she wrote in her diary.

In October, Anna wrote a letter to President Jackson begging him to let Arthur be released. She would sell him to someone who would take him away from Washington, she said. Jackson's response was disappointing. He told her that he did not know if he had the power (or right) to do what she wanted and said he needed "authority from the Court."

Anna went to Judge Cranch's home on Delaware Avenue to ask him what could be done. He too disappointed.

"He says the judges cannot take cognizance of the affair til brought before them judicially," Anna wrote in her diary. "And then the matter rests entirely with the President to pardon him if he pleases."

Anna wrote a note to presidential secretary Andrew Donelson asking for a meeting. He sent back word that Jackson would not honor her request. Anna realized she had to stop; she was making a pest of herself. But then she wrote another letter to Jackson. He did not respond.

As Anna's spirits waned, a new season in Washington was beginning up on Meridian Hill. The Jockey Club's fall races, said the *Intelligencer,* "will surpass in interest and brilliancy any meeting for many years past." Opening day attendance was "unusually large," the newspaper reported. "There are more strangers in the city at present—drawn hither by the races and other causes—than have ever assembled here before, except during the sessions of Congress or at an Inauguration."

When the circuit court opened in November 1835, Anna received a summons to appear before the grand jury, and she felt sick at the prospect. But when the day came, she went to City Hall and discovered she could talk about the horrid night of August 4.

"I answered as favorably towards Arthur as I possibly could and got thro' very well," she said proudly. "Anticipation is often more awful than reality."

Maria Bowen was also summoned to testify, only to be humiliated by the white men of the grand jury, who had her wait outside the jury room all day without being called. She had to go again the next day. Anna missed her help about the house and felt her sorrow when she returned home. As the fall season began, Anna withdrew from her usual rounds of social calls.

The hotels and the boardinghouses and the restaurants along the Avenue were starting to fill up, as congressmen and senators arrived for the opening of the Twenty-Fourth Congress. The next day, President Jackson delivered his annual message to Congress. In his long letter, written with the help of Francis Blair, he boasted of the country's recovery from the panic of 1833 and 1834. Jackson extolled "the unexampled growth and prosperity of our country. . . . Every branch of labor we see crowned with the most abundant rewards. In every element of national resources and

Beverly Snow opened his basement refectory on the busy corner of Sixth Street and Pennsylvania Avenue in the winter of 1832. Snow's elegant tables and excellent menu were soon popular with the high society of the American capital.

Beverly Snow's restaurant stood next to Jesse Brown's mammoth Indian Queen Hotel. Home to politicians, lobbyists, and slave traders, Brown's establishment was a social and political hub of the burgeoning capital city.

An itinerant editor from West Virginia, Benjamin Lundy started publishing in Washington City in 1831. With the help of friends among the free blacks, his antislavery publication provoked hope, arguments, and a grand jury indictment.

Lundy's newspaper, the *Genius of Universal Emancipation*, not only catalogued the crimes of the slave traders, but also needled District Attorney Francis Scott Key for overlooking them. Key responded with criminal charges.

As Lundy's assistant in Washington, William Lloyd Garrison learned the art of waging journalistic war on the American slave system. Lundy would die in obscurity while Garrison would go on to become one of the most influential journalists of the nineteenth century.

A shoemaker by trade, John Francis Cook took over a school for colored children on H Street in 1834 and named it the Union Seminary. He organized a secret talking society for young African American men seeking to escape slavery.

While the ranks of the free people were swelling in Washington City, the trafficking in humans was also booming, as slave traders sold black families "down the river" to work on the burgeoning cotton plantations in the South and West. Buying and selling people was a respectable business in Jacksonian America.

As the architect of the U.S. Capitol, William Thornton was a close friend of George Washington and Thomas Jefferson. A cranky genius, he was also an inventor, a horseman, and a bon vivant. After he died in 1828, his widow, Anna Maria, struggled to pay off his debts.

The Thorntons lived on F Street between Thirteenth and Fourteenth streets, one of the finest blocks in the capital. Arthur Bowen, nineteen years old and enslaved, lived in a garret on the top floor in 1835.

After Arthur Bowen's drunken intrusion and escape, Anna Thornton advertised a reward for his capture in the *National Intelligencer*.

A headline in the Lynchburg *Daily Virginian* announced the news that the flamboyant colored restaurateur had been arrested. The sensational story spread quickly.

The editors of the *National Intelligencer* blamed the antislavery men for provoking Arthur Bowen with their "incendiary" publications.

WASHINGTON.

" Liberty and Union, now and forever, one and inseparable.»

FRIDAY, AUGUST 7, 1835.

The first fruit.—A circumstance of a shocking character, and what was within a second of time of resulting in the perpetration of a most bloody tragedy, occurred in this city two nights ago, which, viewing it as one of the effects of the fanatical spirit of the day, and one of the immediate fruits of the incendiary publications with which this city and the whole slave-holding portion of the country have been lately inundated, we have concluded it to be our duty to make public. On Tuesday night last, an attempt was made on the life of Mrs. THORNTON, of this city, (the much respected widow of the late Dr. THORNTON, Superintendent of the Patent Office,) by a young Negro man, her slave, which, from the expressions he used, was evidently induced by reading the inflammatory publications referred to above. About half past one o'clock, in the dead of the night, Mrs. T's chamber, in which slept herself, her aged mother, and a woman servant, was entered by the Negro, who had obtained access to it by forcing the outer door. He approached the bed of Mrs. T. with an uplifted axe. She was, fortunately, wakened by his step, and still more fortunately the negro woman, the mother of the man, was also awake. As he approached the bed of her mistress, the latter sprung up, seized and held him, while Mrs. T. escaped from the room, rushed to the door of the next house, the residence of Dr. HUNTT, whom she roused by her cries. On reaching the entry of Mrs. T's. house, Dr. H. found that the mother of the Negro had succeeded in forcing him out at the back-door and locking it. Finding, however, that but one person had come to the assistance of the family, he endeavored again to force an entrance with his axe, and furiously continued his efforts, notwithstanding the party had been strengthened by the presence of a gentleman, who resided with Dr. HUNTT, and who had also been roused by Mrs. T's. cries for help ; and it was not until after the arrival of two constables, and hearing their voices as they entered the passage in front, that he desisted and fled. Had they approached the house by the rear, the Negro would have been arrested ; but, as it was, he escaped and has not yet been apprehended. During the whole time that he was endeavoring to force a second entrance into the house, he was venting the most ferocious threats, and uttering a tissue of jargon, much of which was a literal repetition of the language addressed to the Negroes by the incendiary publications above referred to. Believing that his bloody purpose was in part at least, if not altogether, the effect of those publications, and that such deeds must be the natural consequence of their dissemination, we have concluded, not, however, without some hesitation, to make the occurrence public, as well for the information of our northern fellow-citizens at large, as for that of the Fanatics them-

Famous for writing "The Star-Spangled Banner" in 1814, Francis Scott Key went on to a hectic and lucrative career in law and politics, including eight years as the district attorney for the unruly and amoral city of Washington.

Key helped his brother-in-law and close friend Roger Taney achieve one of the most remarkable careers in American politics. In the Jackson administration, Taney served as attorney general, secretary of the treasury, and the chief justice of the U.S. Supreme Court, where his 1857 *Dred Scott* decision hastened the coming of civil war.

Nearing the end of his second term in 1835, President Andrew Jackson relied on Key to advance his administration's agenda. Jackson was frail, conspiratorial, and determined to protect the slave system.

In the case of accused slave Arthur Bowen, the passionate intervention of Anna Thornton persuaded the president to pardon a young African American sentenced to be hanged.

Escaping the contradictions of Washington, Beverly Snow moved to Toronto, a mecca for Africans in America, and opened a succession of saloons and restaurants along King Street in the 1840s and '50s.

Washington's expatriate restaurateur, Beverly Randolph Snow, died free and prosperous at age fifty-seven. He is buried at left in the Toronto Necropolis.

wealth and of individual comfort we witness the most rapid and solid improvements." There were no domestic problems, he suggested, that which "would not yield to the spirit of harmony and good will that so strikingly pervades the mass of the people in every quarter."

Jackson acknowledged "the painful excitement produced in the South by attempts to circulate through the mails inflammatory appeals addressed to the passions of the slave, in prints and various sorts of publications, calculated to stimulate them to insurrection and produce all the horrors of a servile war."

The antislavery-cause activity would not be tolerated, he stated.

"Our happiness and prosperity essentially depend upon peace within our borders—and peace depends on the maintenance of good faith of those compromises of the constitution upon which the Union is founded. It is fortunate for the country that the good sense, the generous feeling, and deep-rooted attachment of the people of the non-slaveholding States to the Union and to their fellow-citizens of the same blood in the South, have given so strong and impressive a tone to the sentiments entertained against the proceedings of the misguided persons who have engaged in those unconstitutional and wicked attempts, and especially against the emissaries from foreign parts who have dared to interfere in the matter. . . .

"But if these expressions of the public will shall not be sufficient to effect so desirable a result," Jackson went on, "not a doubt can be entertained that the non-slaveholding States, so far from countenancing the slightest interference with the constitutional rights of the South, will be prompt to exercise their authority in suppressing, so far as in them lies, whatever is calculated to produce this evil."

The president urged Congress "to take such measures as will prevent the Post-Office Department, which was designed to foster an amicable intercourse and correspondence between all the members of the Confederacy, from being used as an instrument of an opposite character. I would therefore call the special attention of Congress to the subject and respectfully suggest the propriety of passing such a law as will prohibit under severe penalties, the circulation in the Southern States, through the mail, of incendiary publications intended to instigate the slaves to insurrection."

It was a radical proposal. The refusal of the Post Office to deliver abolitionist material to the South, said historian Daniel Walker Howe, "may well have been the largest peacetime violation of civil liberty in U.S. history." President Jackson wanted to write it into law. (The legislation eventually died in the Senate because southerners thought it infringed on states' rights. Local postmasters continued to rely on Amos Kendall's directive granting them the power to block delivery of antislavery publications.)

That week Anna was reading in the *Intelligencer* about Jackson's message to Congress when Maria brought in a note from General Jones. It contained the disagreeable news that Arthur's trial would begin the day after tomorrow.

35

A NNA ASKED HER friend Margaret Smith to accompany her to Arthur's trial and Margaret agreed. Smith was a loyal friend and a tireless storyteller who did not let any Washington drama go unobserved. George Plant drove them down to City Hall in the carriage. The weather was mild and Anna felt sick again, as if she could not bring herself to testify about Arthur.

The courtroom filled slowly. Anna, Margaret, and General Jones were joined by Maria Bowen and a colored friend of hers named Mary. John Cook was there. He had risked the long trip down from Pennsylvania just to testify. William Costin, the bank porter, was also there. They had insisted on testifying as to Arthur's intelligence and good character. Mr. Key sat at the government's table. On the bench, Judge Cranch sat with his longtime associates James S. Morsell and Buckner Thruston. The judges were a diverse bunch. Cranch was an independent thinker, Morsell bland, and Thruston eccentric. In the words of John Quincy Adams, Thruston was "partially insane but knows it and avows it."

Arthur sat in the dock, the prisoner's box behind the spectators, wearing a fine suit, which made an impression. He was "extremely well-dressed," noted the *Metropolitan*. Margaret Smith thought he "looked quite like a young gentleman." Having had three months in jail to think about this day, Arthur had his feelings under control. Margaret Smith studied his face "but could discern no trace of strong emotion."

Anna, seated next to her, choked up with fear.

"To me it was simply a very interesting scene," Smith wrote, almost surprised, "but to Mrs. Thornton a very affecting one. She could hardly stand it."

The district attorney rose to address the men of the jury, most of whom he knew in one way or another. Joel Brown was a gentleman from Georgetown; Richard Kerr came from one of the wealthiest landowning families in the district. Richard Jones was a blacksmith and wheelwright in Georgetown. Archibald Cheshire was a wood measurer. Samuel Wimsatt, a coal measurer. Adam Lindsey, who lived near the Navy Yard, represented the Sixth Ward on the common council. Some of these men owned slaves, some did not.

"It will be proved that the prisoner made a deliberate attempt upon the life of his mistress, under the influence of excitement of a certain kind that will be described by the witnesses," Key said without drama. "I will contend that if the prisoner had entered into his mistress's room to make the attempt charged in the indictment, it would amount to burglary, even though he was an inmate in the family, and had not forced the outer door. . . ."

"As for being drunk at the time he committed the outrage," he said, "I submit there is no legal excuse for the offense."

Key called Anna Thornton. She came to the stand, the eyes of the rapt spectators focusing on her plain dress, alert eyes, and worried look. Mr. Key, her old friend turned haughty public servant, was waiting for her. He asked her about the night of August 4.

"I was awakened by the opening of the chamber door," Anna began. "I saw the boy approaching me with an axe in his hand."

What was position of the axe?

"I couldn't tell," Anna replied. "I could not say it was uplifted. I don't think he knew where he was going. He appeared to be"—she wanted to emphasize the point—"*much* intoxicated."

What do you recall about the room before you left it?

"When I left the room," Anna said, "his mother was rushing up toward him."

From the gallery, Maria Bowen was watching her mistress; no doubt her boy's life depended on every word.

What happened next?

"When I returned he was making a great noise at the back door. He seemed to be intoxicated. He was not much used to drinking."

The district attorney yielded to General Jones. Anna's attorney was, as one friend described him, "a small spare man of insignificant appearance with plain features" except his eyes, which showed "piercing intelligence and shrewdness of expression." Jones's voice was thin and high-pitched, his questions gentle.

Do you think that the prisoner intended to harm you that night?

"I do not believe he had any malice toward me," Anna said.

Did he say anything when he came in the room?

"I did not hear him speak a word."

Jones sought to plant some doubt about the district attorney's witnesses.

When you returned to the house with Dr. Huntt, what did you see?

"When Dr. Huntt arrived, the prisoner's mother had gotten him out of the room, and out of the house."

Jones stopped. He wanted to leave the jury with this fact: Dr. Huntt didn't get there until it was all over. He had no firsthand knowledge of Arthur's actions inside the room.

Key countered by calling Dr. Huntt.

"I was lying at home in bed on the fourth of August when I was, at about one o'clock in the morning, awakened and alarmed by the screams of a female voice," he began. "It was Mrs. Thornton, crying, 'Don't put on your clothes—come directly—she's killed.'"

With a glance, the district attorney begged for explanation.

"I took her meaning to be that Mrs. Thornton's mother, who was left in the house, was killed," Huntt explained. "I ran to the mother's room. The prisoner's mother—an old woman living with Mrs. Thornton—had got him out of the house. She said, 'I've got him out, he's crazy. He came with an uplifted axe.'"

Key hoped the jury would absorb the witness's point. Dr. Huntt was saying that Maria Bowen had said her son came into the room with an uplifted axe.

"The prisoner was quite violent after he was got out," Huntt went on. "He struck the door with the axe repeatedly crying out, 'I'll have the hearts' blood of you all.'"

Did he threaten you?

"I must say that he did not use any threat towards me or any particular individual," the doctor allowed. "It was a general threat. 'He would be free, he would have his freedom.' He made use of some such expression as this. He said that 'if Philo Parker and some others had not been put in jail, he would have made them all smell hell.'"

That satisfied the district attorney, who sat down. General Jones immediately asked Anna to return to the stand.

Do you recall the prisoner's mother saying that the axe was uplifted?

Anna was in a difficult position. She did not want to question the veracity of her friend Dr. Huntt. But the fact was that Maria had never said anything about an uplifted axe. Thinking quickly, Anna took responsibility for the phrase, the better to refute it.

"I'm not certain whether I said it was an uplifted axe," Anna said. "I do not think that *I* saw it uplifted. I believe he blundered into our room, not knowing where he was going, that he was intoxicated."

Nevertheless, the damage was done. By attributing the uplifted axe to Maria Bowen, Dr. Huntt made his version of events unquestionable. Only Maria could corroborate Anna's story that the boy had not raised the axe against her. Key knew what Maria Bowen would say if called. She had told her story to the grand jury several times. General Jones wanted her to testify at the trial of her son, and her name appeared on the witness list for *U.S. v. John Arthur Bowen.*

Yet Maria Bowen was never called. By law an enslaved person could testify in cases involving other slaves or free colored people but not in cases involving whites. By attributing the uplifted axe comment to Maria, not Mrs. Thornton, Dr. Huntt ensured that Maria could not testify lest she impeach a white man's testimony. Instead, he attributed to her words that condemned her son. His testimony was central to Key's effort to overcome Anna's insistence that Arthur had never raised the axe.

Key built his case by calling General Gibson. He told the story of being awakened in the middle of the night and going to the house where Arthur "was on the outside thundering at the door, and using very threatening language. I felt glad I was inside the house."

Key called Madison Jeffers, who was even more hostile to Arthur.

Did you ever speak with the prisoner?

"As I was conducting him to jail in the hack," Jeffers replied, "I asked him what could have possessed him to make the desperate attack upon Mrs. Thornton. He said he had a right to be free, and until the colored people were free, there would be so much confusion and bloodshed as would astonish the whole earth."

Key let that idea hang in the air for the jurors.

Anything else?

"He seemed quite sober then," Jeffers said.

Against this onslaught, General Jones called William Costin, one of the most respected colored men in Washington City.

Did you see the prisoner on the night of August fourth?

"He was present that evening at a meeting of a debating society," said Costin. "He talked very strongly on that occasion."

Key wanted to know more: *Whose debating society was that?*

"He belonged to John Cook's debating society," Costin replied.

General Jones called Cook. Blacks could, and often did, testify in court cases—if the defendant was also black. The schoolteacher had taken a big chance coming back from Pennsylvania to speak for Arthur, a risk he was willing to take for the sake of explaining his efforts to educate the boy.

What was the purpose of your Philomathean debating society?

"It was a debating society," Cook said. "He was a member and I was a member."

Cook probably knew better than to talk about the Philomathean, the abolition of slavery, or the rights of man in this venue. The white jurors would probably not appreciate hearing a colored man explain to them that "Philomathean" meant "love of learning" in Latin. Cook probably said more, but the only newspaper account of the trial did not record it.

There were no more questions. All that remained was the instruction of the jury.

The district attorney spoke first. Key asked Judge Cranch to instruct the jury that "if they believe from the evidence that the Prisoner took the axe, and entered with it, into his mistress's room with the intent to murder her, and was prevented by the awakening of his mistress and her servant and by the noise, and his being seized, and forced out of the room, from executing his intention, then the prisoner is guilty.

"Second," Key went on, "if the jury believes, from the evidence, that the prisoner was drunk when he formed and attempted to execute the above intention, it does not excuse the prisoner."

When it was Jones's turn to speak, he countered by asking that the intoxication of the prisoner be "considered by the Jury as *accounting* for his misconduct and *inferring* the absence of malicious and felonious interest."

"Refused," said Judge Cranch.

"The intoxication of the prisoner is proper to be considered by the jury," Cranch ruled. It should inform "their opinion as to the intent with which the prisoner took the axe and entered his mistress' chamber."

Key had outwitted Jones and ended the trial on a note favorable to his case.

The jurors filed out of the courtroom and went upstairs to the jury room. Anna was still sitting in the gallery. She ached that Maria had not been allowed to testify. The courtroom fell quiet. The spectators contemplated the awesome silence of justice. Arthur waited, Maria waited. Anna went outside. Fifteen minutes later, the foreman returned to say the jury had reached a verdict. The jurors returned and the spectators stilled themselves.

"We find the prisoner guilty," announced the foreman.

Conversations started everywhere save the dock, where Arthur sat alone and condemned.

"Your Honor," General Jones shouted to Judge Cranch over the din, "I hereby give notice of my intention to move for a new trial."

36

"A VERDICT OF GUILTY has been returned in the Washington Circuit
Court against Bowen (negro) for attempting the life of his mistress
Mrs. Thornton, widow of the late Wm. Thornton of the Patent Office,"
Edgar Snowden reported in the *Alexandria Gazette* that week. "It will be
recollected that he entered her bed room at night with an axe, and was
prevented from committing the murder by his mother."

This was the essence of what people knew about Anna Maria Thornton and Arthur Bowen, thanks to the newspapers. The jury's verdict
obscured Anna's account of what had actually happened. Not that everyone was interested. Francis Blair at the *Globe* did not carry the news of
Arthur Bowen's conviction. Nor did Seaton and Gales at the *Intelligencer*.
Duff Green never mentioned it in the *Telegraph*. They presumably did not
want to give inspiration to other black rebels or remind whites that they
might be vulnerable to attack. So the real story of August 4—that Arthur
had stumbled into her room, not to kill her, but because he was drunk—
spread more by word of mouth.

Satisfied that justice had been done, Key turned his attention to prosecuting the rioters of the Snow-Storm. He sympathized with their anger
about the infamies of Bowen and Crandall. He was prepared to show leniency. The abolitionist provocations threatened the safety of all white people. But he also thought it important to uphold the rule of law. Twenty-six
men had been charged during the August disorder. In the court's winter
session, Key resolved the cases of nineteen. He obtained convictions of
ten, usually resulting in fines of up to fifty dollars but no jail time. The
most important Snow-Storm case, *U.S. v. Fenwick et al.*, which involved
Andrew Laub and six other leaders of the mob outside the Epicurean Eating House, was postponed until the court's spring term.

Key's prosecution of Arthur Bowen and the rioters served him well in the councils of the Jackson administration. Months before, when President Jackson was considering appointing Roger Taney to fill an opening on the Supreme Court, Key had the foresight to help his brother-in-law's cause by coaxing an endorsement from his longtime friend Chief Justice John Marshall, who was living out his life as the most venerated judge in the new republic. After Marshall died in July 1835, Jackson decided to nominate Taney to succeed him, and on December 28, 1835, he announced the appointment publicly. It had been less than five years since Key had helped lift Taney from Maryland state politics to the presidential cabinet.

In that short span of time Taney had transformed himself. From small-town lawyer in Frederick, where he felt inferior to the more gifted Key, Taney now stood atop the American legal profession. The former treasury secretary who championed the Bank War was a provocative but unsurprising choice for Jackson. In the words of historian Page Smith, Taney shared the president's "democratic aspirations and sometimes misplaced faith in the people." He was sympathetic to "the rights of states and suspicious of the moneyed interests," meaning his legal thinking defended the southern slave masters and mistrusted eastern banks and corporations. According to biographer Victor Weybright, Key worked "day and night" to secure approval for Taney's ascension to the high court.

Arthur Bowen, of course, had not gone anywhere. He sat in his cell on the second floor of the City Jail with nothing to think about except whether he would die. People urged him to repent, but how could he repent for something he did not remember? He could only blame his deed on what he called "the madness of intoxication." He swore to visitors that he had not intended to harm Mrs. Thornton. "He persists, as he has uniformly done, in denying it," said John O'Sullivan in the *Metropolitan*, "and expresses kind feelings towards his mistress, and gratitude for her exertions in his behalf."

Newspapers then circulated in the jail, so Arthur probably knew what was happening up on Capitol Hill. Indeed, if Arthur's cell sat on the east side of the building, then he could see Dr. Thornton's most famous building from his window. The issue of slavery was disrupting the work of the Congress. The pamphlet campaign, which had stoked the fears of whites and somehow instigated the Snow-Storm in Washington and anti-abolitionist riots elsewhere, had also pricked the American conscience. The issue was slavery and could not be suppressed. The aftermath of rioting inspired tens of thousands to sign petitions calling for the abolition of slavery in the District of Columbia. Arthur's neighbor on F Street, John Quincy Adams, and other northern congressmen were introducing new antislavery petitions almost every day on the floor of the House of Representatives while enraged southern congressmen shouted objections. As historian William Lee Miller has noted, the congressional debate that erupted in December 1835 proved to be "the first explicit and extended struggle" over slavery, which forced "a national fork-in-the-road choice between inherited despotism and developing democracy." For the first time, the question of the abolition of slavery dominated the deliberations of the U.S. Congress.

Not that it would do Arthur Bowen any good.

One floor below, in another dank brick-lined eight-by-eight-foot cell, Reuben Crandall sat on the bench writing a letter to his father. Like Arthur, Reuben had lived in the confines of the City Jail since August. Key had not held a bond hearing or even filed charges. From his room in the jail, Crandall too might have been able to see the Capitol as well. He certainly kept track of the fierce debate growing in Congress, where the angry southerners demanded a gag rule to prevent the northerners from even raising the issue of slavery in the District. The passions in Congress were affecting his case.

After Rueben's arrest his family had retained Richard Coxe, a respected attorney, to defend him. The son of a congressman from New Jersey, Coxe had argued both in the local courts and in the U.S. Supreme Court and knew Francis Scott Key quite well. Coxe brought on as co-counsel a thirty-four-year-old lawyer named Joseph Bradley, a cousin of Mayor William Bradley. Coxe and Bradley had originally demanded Mr. Key charge Crandall or release him. As the angry debate in Congress continued in the winter of 1835 with insults and death threats abounding, they changed their minds. They asked for a delay, fearing popular passions might inflame a jury.

"The debate in Congress on the abolition question has kept up the prejudice against me so much that it was thought unsafe to go to trial at this term," Crandall wrote to his father.

When the district attorney finally charged Reuben in early January 1836, the tone of the five-count indictment was harsh. Crandall, Key wrote, was "a malicious, seditious and evil disposed person disaffected to the law and government of the United States." He had "most unlawfully, mischievously and seditiously" contrived "to traduce, vilify and bring into hatred and contempt among the good Citizens of the United States, the laws and government of the United States . . . and to . . . excite the good people of the United States to resist and oppose and disregard the laws and government . . . and the rights of the said proprietors of slaves . . . and to inflame and incite to violence against the said proprietors of said Slaves."

Key asked for a bond of fifteen thousand dollars for Crandall's pretrial release, a sum that was triple the president's annual salary. Judge Cranch reduced the bond to five thousand dollars, still far more than the Crandall family could afford.

Reuben remained in his eight-foot cell. The place smelled awful, and the smoke from the fireplaces could not entirely dispel it. Sitting here day after day, with only an occasional walk outside, was the price Reuben had to pay for believing in immediate emancipation. He waxed bitter about the district attorney in another letter to his father.

"Mr. Key takes very unwarrantable grounds against me for nothing, only to bully the people into the belief that he is with them in this affair, hook and line," he wrote. "He is very distrustful of the people, as well as they of him. He had once been a preacher of the gospel, and then turned politician and lawyer."

Crandall alluded to Key's faded reputation as a humanitarian.

"He has been called heretofore, 'the Blacks Lawyer,' as he took up their cases for them when they sued for their freedom. . . . By his former conduct the people are distrustful of his honesty of motive."

Crandall cut off the thought as if he did not wish to complain. He had to be patient, to endure this trial with Christian stoicism.

"Please remember me to all our old neighbors," he said in closing to his father. "I should be delighted to be there among you if it were possible."

Arthur's conviction left the house on F Street gloomy. As the days dragged on, Anna Thornton all but collapsed into catatonic misery. She could think of nothing but Arthur's fate. On Christmas Day, Anna opened a note from her friend Margaret Smith, who understood her misery. Margaret told Anna that she was not going to bother wishing her a Merry Christmas. "I do not consider merriment & happiness as synonymous," she said.

Instead, Margaret said she wished that Anna would stop thinking about Arthur.

"It is your positive duty to take care of your <u>own</u> health on which so entirely depends your ability to support the declining days of your mother," she wrote. Margaret insisted that Anna take "more exercise to divert your thoughts from the painful object on which they are continually fixed."

"I repeat," she wrote, "do not <u>think</u> so much of one subject."

They were going to kill Arthur. Anna tried to stem the thought. She sought cheer by attending Margaret's annual New Year's Eve party at her house on Fifteenth Street and wound up feeling worse than ever. In her diary, Anna welcomed the end of "a most disagreeable and painful year."

She also wrote a note to Mr. Key beseeching him to drop the charges. She would sell Arthur away. Key did not respond.

Anna was not alone in her troubles. As Arthur awaited sentencing, her mother, Mrs. Brodeau, started to succumb to fits of nervous hysteria. To Anna, it seemed like her mother had been cursed, and perhaps she had. Like her daughter, Mrs. Brodeau had a family secret, and as Arthur awaited sentencing, her memory was stirred.

The secret was Anna's father. Years before, Mrs. Brodeau had admitted to Dr. Thornton, her son-in-law, that there was no Mr. Brodeau. Anna's father was actually the Reverend William Dodd, a name William Thornton would have recognized. Dodd had gained notoriety in London in the 1770s as a clergyman who preached in some of London's poshest parishes while rescuing young maidens from the clutches of prostitution in the slums. Dodd's fondness for fine carriages, silk clothes, and the company of young women delighted the scandalmongers of the London press, who dubbed him "the Macaroni parson" and catalogued his hypocrisies with circulation-boosting glee. As a young woman, Ann Brodeau had succumbed to Reverend Dodd's spiritual appeals and become his lover. After she became pregnant with his child, she moved from London to Philadelphia to start a new life, with her baby girl, Anna. Aided by a recommendation from Benjamin Franklin, a friend of Reverend Dodd's, she opened a boarding school for girls.

In one scholar's account Reverend Dodd promised to follow his mistress to America to start a new life. To fund his escape, he forged a letter from an acquaintance, the wealthy earl of Chesterfield, to secure a bond for more than four thousand pounds, a small fortune. Because of the accident of an inkblot, the bond was shown to the earl, who repudiated it. Dodd confessed right away and returned the money. He was charged with forgery nonetheless. Under England's savage criminal code at that time, the only penalty for forgery was death. Indeed, two forgers had been hanged the year before. Dodd admitted his guilt and begged the court for mercy. He was sentenced to hang. The plight of Reverend Dodd became a cause célèbre among the London intelligentsia, and thousands signed petitions calling for a pardon, all to no avail. On June 27, 1777, Reverend Dodd was hanged before a vast crowd outside London. Ann read about the death of her lover in the newspaper.

The revelation of Mrs. Brodeau's past did not seem to disturb Dr. Thornton. But the memory perhaps stirred Mrs. Brodeau in her dementia. She might have recalled something of the clamor and the crowds that engulfed her lover in London and sent her fleeing to America. The father of her only child had gone to the gallows, and she came to America to leave that dreadful life behind. Now, decades later, John Arthur, the little boy whom she had educated and adored, would die the same way as Anna's father: on the gallows.

On January 23, 1836, Anna Thornton was startled to learn that Judge Cranch would sentence Arthur that day. General Jones, it seems, had never filed his motion for a new trial. Once more, Arthur was brought in chains from the jail to the courtroom. He was losing hope. Anna was not in attendance.

"Have you anything to say why this court should not now proceed to pass sentence of death upon you for that offense?" Judge Cranch asked him when he was in the dock.

"I have nothing to say, sir," Arthur said.

"In preparing you for the awful sentence which it is my painful duty to pronounce," Judge Cranch went on, "I shall not attempt to call your recollection to the reckless fury with which you entered the bed chamber of your confiding unsuspecting mistress in the dead hour of the night with the uplifted axe ready to strike the fatal blow, which was only prevented by the sudden and spirited resistance of her faithful servant, your mother. Nor will I harrow up your conscience with awful forebodings. It is now a month since you were found guilty by the jury and you have had time to reflect upon the past and anticipate the future. You have had time to begin the work of repentance."

Arthur had heard that before.

"The remorse of a guilty conscience—the worm that never dies, and which may be one of the principal means of punishment in the world to come—may have already begun its work to prepare you for that dream tribunal before which we must all appear, to answer not only for the *works* done in the body but for every evil imagination and every unexecuted wish—where no discrimination will be made between the act and the intention, and where he who had intended to murder will be adjudged a murderer."

The words rang in Arthur's ears.

"If this divine agent has already begun to operate upon your heart, I beseech you not to resist its holy efforts. It wounds to cure, and you may yet attain that state of unfeigned repentance which may save you from the torments of another state of being. By all your hopes, therefore, of obtaining the favor the Almighty, by all your fears of the unutterable anguish of the future state of the wicked, I beseech you to devote the short remnant of your life to prayer and repentance.

"It only remains for me now to pronounce the awful sentence which the law has affixed to your crime."

"The judgment of the Court is, that you be taken hence from the place from whence you came and from thence to the place of public execution, and that you be there hanged by the neck until you are dead. And may God Almighty bless your soul!"

Judge Cranch directed the marshal to carry out the sentence on February 26, between the hours of one and four o'clock in the afternoon.

The guards took Arthur back to his cell, where they fastened on the heavy leg irons awarded to prisoners facing capital punishment. Now Arthur knew how long he had to live: thirty-four days.

37

In a grassy field adjoining the jail, workmen began to construct a wooden platform that resembled a gallows. The stench of a neighborhood pigsty lingered. Inside the jail, on the second floor, Arthur was now almost anchored to floor of his cell by the massive leg irons locked around his feet. If he moved, the steel clasps tight around his ankles would cut his legs, lacerating the skin. It was better to sit still.

The newspapermen and the slave owners may have wanted to ignore Arthur Bowen's imminent execution but the people of Washington, black and white, discussed it constantly. Mrs. Thornton's story, discounted by Mr. Key and unmentioned in the newspapers, had gotten around. Arthur had never tried to hit her with an axe. He had never even raised it. There was no "murderous assault." Yes, he had held an axe, but he was drunk. He was not in his right mind. A lot of people agreed the boy should not die for that, even if he was a slave. Capital punishment was quite rare in Washington and by no means popular. It had been eight years since the last execution in the District of Columbia, and that had not been carried out in Washington City. In 1828, a white man who murdered a neighbor whose son had stolen some blackberries from his garden was sentenced to die by Judge Cranch and was hanged in Alexandria.

Yet Anna could tell that among the people who mattered, no one cared to defend Arthur. General Jones was in Annapolis and did not respond to her notes. Mr. Key did not answer her last letter. She appealed to Judge Cranch again but "could not prevail on him to recommend the Boy to Mercy!" she told her diary incredulously. The law had been applied correctly, the judge explained. It was not his place to do more.

In almost physical panic, Anna roused herself from her stupefied misery and set out to act. There was only one hope. She drew up a petition to President Jackson and enlisted signatories to "most early and sincerely recommend . . . the pardon of her Slave Arthur." A total of thirty-five people signed, including loyal friends such as Margaret Smith and Benjamin Tayloe, influential editors such as Joseph Gales of the *Intelligencer* and Francis Blair of the *Globe*, and even neighbors General Gibson and Dr. Huntt, who had testified so damagingly about the "uplifted axe."

Even as Anna attracted support, she endured hard looks and turned faces. Seeking a pardon for an enslaved mulatto convicted of a violent crime tested the tolerance of some of her neighbors. People had to think about their own slaves and what conclusions they might draw if the authorities treated Arthur with leniency. When Anna asked one neighbor on F Street to take her petition around to neighbors, he came back with only one signature and a warning: her petition might well "induce a counter-petition to be got up."

There was talk among white people that Arthur Bowen was blithe about his actions, even reckless in the face of death. Madison Jeffers's testimony at the trial had not been forgotten. *He said he had a right to be free, and until the colored people were free, there would be so much confusion and bloodshed as would astonish the whole earth.* But John O'Sullivan, editor of the *Metropolitan,* visited with Arthur and thought it "more than doubtful" whether Arthur's act was "connected with any abolition excitement." In any case, it didn't matter, O'Sullivan said. That an intelligent young man would have strong feelings about his condition in slavery, O'Sullivan said, "was to be expected."

Anna and Maria began to hope they might prevail on the president. In one of her visits to the jail, Maria told her son of all that Anna had been doing, and he took hope too. He felt like he was going to live. And if he lived he could repent. Said O'Sullivan: "He does not at all realize the awful truth of his actual position."

Anna Thornton realized that awful truth. She had no other thought. When Arthur's execution was little more than a week away, she sent a note to President Jackson requesting a meeting. Then she sat down to write, as precisely as she could, what exactly had happened on the night of August 4. She wanted to go back to the beginning, to explain who John Arthur Bowen was and what had happened. Before she stopped writing, Anna had composed eighteen pages.

On the morning of Friday, February 19, George drove Anna to the President's House. It was a cold, dry, and dusky day, with the thermometer reaching only twenty degrees by nine in the morning. There was snow in the air. Anna entered through the north portico and went up to President Jackson's office on the second floor.

Her arrival did not catch Jackson by surprise. He liked Anna Thornton, liked her willpower and her indifference to what the ladies in society were saying behind her back. Jackson ushered her in and helped her to a seat. He took her letter but did not read it, then scanned her petition.

Jackson was a man attuned to strong women, especially those wronged by respectable society. He still wore a miniature of his late wife, Rachel, and would never forgive Adams and the others for traducing her name. Jackson had staked his whole cabinet on Margaret Eaton's honor, against the biddies of Washington.

He was not opposed to mercy for the boy, he told Anna. He just wanted to be sure all concerned agreed, particularly Mr. Key. Jackson handed the petition back to her.

"Get the recommendation of the judge and District Attorney," he said.

Anna was crushed. Of course she had tried and failed to do just that. Mr. Key was unrelenting, silent, merciless. She left the President's House with more work to do and no better prospects for saving Arthur.

Undeterred, on Sunday—five days before the execution—she wrote a note to Vice President Van Buren. He was President Jackson's heir apparent, already nominated as the Democratic Republican Party's candidate for president in the November election.

"I write to ask and entreat you to use a little of your good influence with the President to pardon my poor Slave Arthur," she said. "I think he appears inclined to do so and you can considerably strengthen this inclination by seconding it. The time is now."

She would shame the man if she had to.

"There are a great many alleviating circumstances which are not generally known—his mother's worth + goodness ought to be considered too," she wrote, underlining her words.

"The 26th is the fatal day," she reminded him. Van Buren did not respond.

While Anna wrote more notes, Maria Bowen's hopes vanished. Maria had grown up in the Thornton household and lived all her life thinking good conduct and the reputation of William and Anna provided protection to her and her son. It did not. Her persecutors were beyond belief. Mr. Key had no feeling. The president was known for his brutality to his property in people, known for inflicting a hundred lashes on a runaway. And, what was worse, she had played a part. By bringing her son in to face justice last August, she had done exactly what the law and Mrs. Thornton required. If Arthur had been white, his drunken folly would have been laughed off. Instead, he was going to die for it.

On Monday, Maria left the house on F Street without a word and was gone all day, not that Anna complained. "She is miserable," Anna wrote in her diary. "Poor soul."

Arthur would be executed on Friday.

38

I N HIS CELL, Arthur Bowen searched for a way to quell the fear of death. He hoped for a pardon from the president, but he had to be ready if it did not happen. He had to admit the truth of what John Cook had said all along. Yes, he had a right to be free, and, yes, liquor would destroy that freedom. Arthur's protestations that he never intended to harm Mrs. Thornton suddenly failed to persuade even himself. Of course, he had no intention. The drink gave him that intention, unleashed the sinner within.

"By drinking the sudden passion of the murderer is sharpened," John Cook had intoned. "He is made ready to plunge the instrument of death into the bosom of the object of his hate, perhaps his own mother, father."

Arthur had condemned himself and for that he had to take responsibility. He decided to write a poem about this feeling of repentance that he had so long resisted. Or perhaps one of his sympathetic visitors—John Cook or John O'Sullivan—encouraged him to write something, not in his own defense, but to dispel what some people were saying about him—and perhaps to justify a presidential pardon.

With pen and paper in hand, Arthur sat in the dim light, thinking of his friends from the racetrack and President's Square. Like William Thornton, he had some talent for writing:

Farewell, farewell my young friends dear;
Oh! View my dreadful state,
Each flying moment brings me near
Unto my awful fate.

He made a curious reference to his family:

Brought up I was by parents nice
Whose commands I would not obey
But plunged ahead foremost into vice
And into temptation's dreadful way.

He admitted his folly in scorning the teachings of his elders:

Nothing did I ever drink
But liquor very strong
Alas I never used to think
That I was doing wrong.

To me was read the awful sentence
Oh dreadful in my ears it rang
They gave me time for my repentance
And then I must be hanged.

Good bye, good bye, my friends so dear
May God Almighty please you all
Do, if you please, shed but a tear
At Arthur Bowen's unhappy fall.

Copies of Arthur's poem soon circulated. The *Intelligencer* published it. *Metropolitan* editor John O'Sullivan pronounced it "very creditable." Everyone in Washington City seemed to know that Mrs. Thornton's personal petition for clemency for Arthur had been presented to President Jackson. It asked him to exercise "that mercy which is in his power alone."

The people awaited Jackson's response, said O'Sullivan, "with the deepest anxiety."

In his office, the president read Anna Thornton's letter, all eighteen pages of it.

"Your Petitioner hopes to be excused for asking your attention to such facts as were and are within her own knowledge," Anna began, "and which she is about to recapitulate, under all the moral sanctions of the remembered oath upon which she testified in court."

Jackson was impressed. In precise unfailing handwriting, Anna recounted Arthur's "good and docile disposition" as a child. He was "brought up in the family with all the care and tenderness compatible with his condition and perhaps much overindulged," she wrote. As a young man, she admitted he had fallen in with free people of color advocating abolition of slavery. "In the ardor and inexperience of youth," she said, "he had his mind a good deal inflamed by such notions."

Anna wanted to put the president there in the room on August 4 so that he might understand what she saw when she awoke to see Arthur entering the doorway.

"Nothing was easier than for him, if he had come with any settled purpose of murder, to have reached her by a single step . . . but he stood motionless." He was insensibly drunk, not murderous, not in the least. After searching her memory "to the utmost," Anna said she was certain she did not see "anything of an uplifted axe."

Anna declared the hanging of Arthur would punish both her and her mother. They were "deeply imbued in their utmost consciences with an unqualified belief in the boy's innocence," she wrote. They were both "overwhelmed with the thought of his execution, and can never behold it but with grief and horror unutterable."

She begged Jackson to act before Friday.

"The execution itself," she said, "would be more horrible than the offense."

The president was almost convinced. He asked for the advice of his attorney general, a trusted New York lawyer (and future Union Army general) named Benjamin Butler. What exactly did presidential power of pardon allow him to do, the president wanted to know. Could he commute Arthur Bowen's death sentence to something milder? Butler replied he would get back to him in the morning.

In the jail, Arthur told visitors he was resolved "to meet my fate with resignation and fortitude." His words echoed what the *Intelligencer* had said about Dr. William Thornton's final days in March 1828. Back then Arthur was a twelve-year-old boy who was watching the only father figure he ever knew slowly expire from consumption. The eccentric genius was said to have met the approach of death "with unruffled resignation."

Arthur would try to do the same.

39

THE TWENTY-FIFTH OF February was a cold cloudy day with temperatures falling despite occasional sunshine. Anna, sitting at the writing table in her parlor on F Street, felt doomed. She discounted a prediction from Judge Thruston that Arthur would get a respite. She no longer believed any of the many people involved. "They have brought it to the dreadful Day," she wrote in her diary. "Oh how much we can bear when we cannot help it."

She could only think of friends who had endured the premature deaths of their children. She recalled the story of a friend whose eldest daughter died on a steamboat the day before she was to join her parents. She thought of the son of another acquaintance who drowned in the Ohio River while returning from a family visit. It was as if Arthur were her child. In two days, he would be hanged with the approval of respectable white men whom she and Dr. Thornton had regarded as friends.

Attorney General Butler delivered a four-page memo to President Jackson in his office on Thursday morning. The president's pardon power was absolute, not conditional, Butler explained. The president could remove Arthur Bowen's death penalty, but he could not modify it. Butler suggested the president could delay the sentence of execution by a series of reprieves and then issue a pardon. Jackson decided to do just that. This course would gratify Mrs. Thornton, whom he had come to admire for her candor and her courage. And it would not alienate those who wanted firmness in dealing with the Negroes. He reached for his pen.

"Let the execution of the sentence in the case of Negro John Arthur

Bowen be respited to the first Friday in June next," he wrote on the court papers.

A messenger took the package from the President's House to City Hall, where it was delivered to the marshal. Preparing to serve as hangman in less than twenty-four hours, the marshal was more than relieved to receive Jackson's order. ("Almost as grateful as the prisoner himself," quipped John O'Sullivan.) Around three o'clock on Thursday afternoon, with the preparations of the gallows well under way, the marshal went to Arthur's cell on the second floor to read the president's order. One can imagine Arthur's joy at being spared and the reaction of his fellow inmates. Even the reticent Reuben Crandall might have smiled at Arthur's good fortune.

At around ten o'clock that night big dry flakes of snow started falling from a cold sky and did not stop until dawn. By daylight, ten inches of snow covered the city of Washington. The carriages plowed through white dunes on the Avenue, but the sidewalks were deserted. On F Street Anna read about the respite in the *Globe*.

The next day Arthur Bowen, warmed by the fireplace in his jail cell and the simple fact that he was alive, wrote a letter to Mrs. Thornton. If his language was extravagant, his emotions were too.

"Respected Mistress," he began. "It is with unspeakable gratitude that I embrace this opportunity of tending you my heartfelt, unfeigned thanks for your zealous noble deportment in my unfortunate case." He wrote that he had heard that Mrs. Brodeau was indisposed and wished her good health. He asked Mrs. Thornton to "tender his obligation" to General Gibson and her other friends who had taken up his cause. He thanked her for believing him when he said he would never hurt her.

"The idea is preposterous," he wrote, "that I, in my right mind, would attempt to perpetrate . . . [the] murderous deed on you, my generous, noble-hearted, benefactor and mistress. . . . No indeed, it was the diabolical consequences of brutal intemperance, that infernal demon who is the provocateur and author of every villainous deed done by the unfortunate Sons of Man," he said, sounding more than a little like John Cook. "This is my plea in extenuation of my implied transgression."

When Anna read the letter she was impressed. "Well written and worded," she said. Indeed, the sophistication of Arthur's heartfelt letter raises unprovable suspicions that someone else might have had a role in its composition, someone who knew the ways of Washington, how to combine candor and calculation. Or maybe Arthur just had some of the blitheness of Dr. Thornton. Would a young enslaved African American in 1836 presume to flatter the president of the United States? Arthur Bowen did.

"Be kind enough, Respected Mistress," he wrote to Anna, "to tend to President Jackson the homage of my grateful heart for his truly philanthropic deportment in my case. And I hope that he will yet live many years, an honor and boast as he is of the American nation."

What Francis Scott Key thought of Jackson's respite for Arthur Bowen he kept to himself. He was not one to second-guess the general in the presidential mansion. Mr. Key might have recognized too that capital punishment was not popular in Washington and that, in this case, it no longer enjoyed the favor of public feeling, if it ever did.

Mrs. Thornton had not only saved Arthur Bowen's life. She had, with her own stubborn love, changed the mood of the city by changing how they saw Arthur. Said the *Metropolitan*, "This tempering of justice with mercy will, we are well assured, be highly grateful to the whole community of the District."

Part VI

A Dark and Mysterious Providence

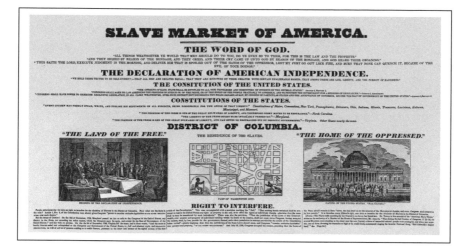

"Slave Market of America," a popular 1836 broadside about the capital's
role in the slave system, published by the American Anti-Slavery
Society, needled District Attorney Francis Scott Key with its caustic
headline: LAND OF THE FREE . . . HOME OF THE OPPRESSED.

40

AT THE CORNER of Sixth and Pennsylvania, the Epicurean Eating House was no more. Beverly Snow had not been seen in months. But his landlord, John Withers, refused to be chased off by hooligans. He and William Walker cleaned up the premises, and Walker opened a new restaurant in the same space, which he called the National Eating House.

Walker sought to emulate Beverly's style but not quite so provocatively. Like his former partner, Walker sought out the freshest in fish and fowl. Like Snow, he extolled his finds with hyperbole. "Oysters from Deep Creek, rich and plump," he boasted in one newspaper announcement. "None like them have been seen nor will any more like them be seen until I advertise them again." Walker was a good businessman. In time he would become the wealthiest black man in Washington City. But in the kitchen, William Walker was no Beverly.

Nearby in his house on C Street, Francis Scott Key did not express any regret at the attack on the colored restaurateur or his restaurant. His vision of justice remained intact, his political ambitions large, though not for himself. When not fulfilling his duties as district attorney, he dedicated himself to securing the Senate approval of his brother-in-law Roger Taney as chief justice of the Supreme Court.

In the effort to achieve confirmation, Key acted as Taney's campaign manager. The problem was Taney's actions around the Baltimore bank riots. That spring Taney had come out in favor of a bill in the Maryland legislature to indemnify two prominent Baltimore bankers—both friends of his—whose houses had been destroyed by the rioters. Taney felt bound to support them because their banks had failed as a result of the irresponsible speculations of his friend Thomas Ellicott.

In an effort to divide Taney and Jackson, his opponents in the Senate floated the story that the president opposed the indemnity bill. That seemed plausible. In his war with Nicholas Biddle and the Bank of the United States, Jackson had often justified his controversial actions by invoking the interests of the common man against the depredations of bankers. To many Americans it hardly seemed fair that the working-class depositors had lost their savings because of the bank's failure, while the bankers responsible for the failure were made whole.

That's not how Taney and Key saw it. On the morning of March 14, 1836, Key went to the President's House on behalf of Taney and put the question to Jackson in person: Did he oppose the indemnity bill for the Baltimore bankers?

"No! Positively no!" Jackson barked. "Those whose homes were destroyed ought to be paid in full."

That was the answer Key and Taney were hoping for. Key wrote a note to Taney telling him the president's views. He added that the Senate would vote on Taney's nomination the next day.

On March 15, 1836, the Senate approved Taney as the fifth chief justice of the U.S. Supreme Court. When Taney received the news in Baltimore, he wrote to Jackson, expressing thanks for the position, "the only one under the government that I have wished to obtain."

Two weeks later, on a mild spring day in Baltimore, he was sworn in. Key's brother-in-law would serve as the nation's senior judicial magistrate for the next twenty-eight years as the struggle for universal emancipation evolved toward civil war.

When the Washington circuit court opened for its spring term at the end of March 1836, Key resumed his busy life as prosecutor. He was living in the big house on C Street with Polly and the children and walking up Four and a Half Street daily to the courthouse. In his second-floor office, he worked long hours, punctuated by regular visits to Judge Cranch's courtroom downstairs.

In one of the season's first cases, he won a guilty verdict against Poll Robinson, the most successful of the city's black madams. It was a rare victory in his now-dwindling campaign against the bawdy houses. As

Robinson was led away to serve a one-month sentence, Key moved to his next case, *U.S. v. Fenwick et al.* These were the charges of rioting brought against Andrew Laub and six of his friends who led the mob during the Snow-Storm.

For the district attorney, this case was about sending a message to the disaffected white men of the city. In Key's view, the offense of Laub and his friends was in no way as serious as those of Arthur Bowen or Reuben Crandall, but still the law had to be upheld. Key didn't give a damn that Snow's place had been trashed and the obnoxious mulatto run off. He wanted to send a clear message to Laub and company and to the people of the city: Rioting was not permissible.

After hearing a day of testimony and arguments about the events of the previous August, the jury returned a split verdict, finding Laub and four friends guilty as charged, while acquitting two others. The jurors recommended the guilty men to the mercy of the court, a sign of their sympathies. Key shared that compassion and had no objection.

The jury's decision gave Judge Cranch considerable leeway in sentencing.

Cranch, who had served as Washington's chief jurist for close to three decades, had already thought the matter through. He had come to the city as a young man, married into a prominent family, and become a judge at an early age. He had lived in the District for nearly forty years. He remembered August 1814, when the British ran riot. He remembered last August and the incredible sight of the city's ladies and gentlemen cowering before a drunken rabble that ravaged public buildings, schools, and houses of worship.

Cranch spoke without notes from the bench, as Laub and his confederates listened in the dock.

"No voluntary association of individuals, unknown to the constitution, has a right to make or execute the laws, or to judge, condemn, or punish those whom they may deem to be offenders . . . however pure or holy may be their motive," he said.

If the jurors thought Judge Cranch would be lenient because the defendants felt provoked by the deeds of Arthur Bowen or the flamboyance of Beverly Snow, they were unfamiliar with Judge Cranch's rule of law.

"When a mob is once raised," he said, "no one can tell where it will end, and all who assisted in raising it are guilty of all the consequences."

Cranch considered the young white men whose fate he was deciding. These were not mere mechanics on a drunken bender. They were Andrew Laub, the son of a senior clerk at the Treasury Department; Alexander Beedle, a former constable; and John Clarke, who had served as a justice of the peace.

"The more respectable the persons engaged in it, and the more desirable the end to be obtained, the more dangerous is the example," Cranch emphasized. "If good men may use unlawful means to accomplish a good end, how can wicked men be restrained from using like means for an unlawful end?"

Cranch let the convicted men ponder that question before passing his final judgment. "All good ends must be pursued by lawful means," he said. "The supremacy of the law is the only security for life, liberty, and property."

Cranch sentenced the five men to the maximum possible punishment under law: six months in the penitentiary. He also ordered each to pay a fine of fifty dollars. That was certainly not the mercy that the defendants or the jurors or the district attorney had expected. There was rather less tolerance for the Mobocracy in Washington City than they had imagined.

T HE LONG-AWAITED MATTER of *U.S. v. Reuben Crandall* began on a cloudy Friday morning, April 15, 1836. The setting was Judiciary Square. City Hall was thronged with spectators filing into the courtroom, with congressmen jockeying for seats along with national newspaper correspondents and many other people never seen before in the circuit court. Not since the House of Representatives tried Sam Houston for the clubbing of Congressman Stanbery back in April 1832 had so many people flocked to see the workings of justice in Washington City. And they came for much the same reason: to witness a legal struggle to define the nature of democracy in the nation's capital.

Once again Mr. Key's reputation was at stake. People wanted to hear Key's response to the challenge posed by the rise of the American Anti-Slavery Society and the abolitionist movement. He would not compromise. Just as the slaveholders' representatives on Capitol Hill sought a gag rule to prevent debate over slavery on the floor of Congress, so did Key seek to silence those who would agitate for freedom on the streets of Washington City. In the trial of Reuben Crandall, he hoped to defeat the antislavery men in the court of public opinion.

The district attorney arrived in the courtroom and, with an assistant, took his place at the government's table. The defendant, dressed simply in a black suit and white shirt, sat with his lawyers Coxe and Bradley. Coxe was a temperance man, thin and precise. Bradley was young and good-looking, almost brash. Rueben Crandall looked "quite pale," reported the *Metropolitan*, "owing to long confinement in our close and noisome prison."

When Judge Cranch asked Reuben how he pleaded to the five-count indictment, Reuben said quietly, "Not guilty."

Key rose at once and addressed the jurors. He read the five counts of the indictment, stressing that the first three were the most important. He said that Crandall had "published" various libels—meaning that he had made them available to others—including statements like this: "Then we are not to meddle with the subject of slavery in any manner; neither by appeals to the patriotism, by exhortation to humanity, by application of truth to the conscience."

This, said the district attorney, unlawfully challenged the right of white men to own property in black people.

A second charge said Crandall had "published" another libelous passage, which Key read: "Our plan of emancipation is simply this—to promulgate the doctrine of human rights in high places and low places, and all places where there are human beings—to whisper it in chimney corners, and to proclaim it from the housetops." For the district attorney such sentiments were patently illegal.

A third count charged Crandall with possession of a dozen copies of publications that exhibited "disgusting prints and pictures of white men in the act of inflicting, with whips, cruel and inhuman beatings and stripes upon young and helpless and unresisting black children." Such pictures, Key said, sought to incite slaves to attack their masters.

There was no issue of freedom of speech, he added.

"Such publications are always indictable," he insisted. The publications that Crandall possessed in his Georgetown office were intended "to produce excitement, tumult, and insurrection among slaves, and among the free colored people; and among those white men who differ with most of us . . . upon the question of slavery."

There were three threats to the city, in Key's view. The first was the enslaved Negroes of the city, like Arthur Bowen, whose alleged murderousness had been encouraged by these pamphlets. The second was the free people of color like Beverly Snow and Isaac Cary and John Cook, who deluded themselves with dreams of citizenship; and the third was their fanatical white friends like Ben Lundy and Reuben Crandall, who sought to impose their northern philosophies on the South. This was what Key wanted the white men of the jury to understand: They were the city's first line of defense against this triple danger.

"There is *nothing*," he emphasized, "more calculated to excite sedition and insurrection in a community situated as ours is, than publications of such a character. It will be my duty to read some of these publications; and there can be but one opinion about their character."

Richard Coxe rose before Key's words could settle. Coxe was forty-three years old and far less eloquent than his opponent. But twenty-three years of practicing law gave him an understated style that was easy to underestimate.

"I differ from the District Attorney, in supposing that the fact that the prisoner had such papers in his possession is conclusive . . . evidence of a criminal intent," Coxe said. The publications might be very dangerous, he said, "yet the individual may have them in his possession with perfect innocence; because he is criminal only according *to the use he makes of them*."

Coxe offered a homely metaphor.

"Consider poisons, such as arsenic or sulfur, which may be dangerous in the hands of some persons," he said. "In others, such as apothecaries, physicians and discreet heads of families, it is harmless and innocent.

"Gunpowder," Coxe went on. "In improper hands, it might destroy a whole city. Properly kept, under necessary restrictions, [it] may be perfectly harmless and innocent. . . .

"My object, principally," he concluded, "is to announce to the gentleman"—a nod to his friend the district attorney—"that evidence to show merely that the prisoner had such papers as he describes in his possession, is not competent evidence of the malicious intent charged in the indictment. I will oppose the admission of any such testimony."

With that warning, the trial began.

Mr. Key called his witnesses. He summoned to the stand Reuben's neighbors in Georgetown, Dr. King and Mr. Robinson, who testified that they had each borrowed a copy of *The Anti-Slavery Reporter* from Reuben.

Coxe objected to letting the jury see it; Judge Cranch overruled him.

The constables Madison Jeffers and Henry Robertson came on to testify about their search of Reuben's quarters in Georgetown and what they found. Coxe objected. Until the district attorney proved malicious intent, he told the three judges, the publications did not constitute evidence of anything. Exasperated, Key replied that the jurors had to decide the question of intent. Judge Cranch overrode Coxe's objection. The defense attorney's mild-mannered obstructionism was draining the drama from the courtroom and from Key's efforts to portray Reuben as a fiend. The questions droned on.

The high windows of the ramshackle City Hall failed to ventilate and the chamber grew steamy. The congressmen were first to flee, pleading business on the Hill. The newspaper correspondents ducked out to visit the outhouse or an ordinary. In the dock, jurors saw Reuben Crandall, the alleged abolitionist, looking placid. If found guilty of sedition, Reuben might be hanged. Yet the *Metropolitan* observed that "he listens to the discussion with patience, and betrays no particular anxiety of countenance, gesture or manner. There is no appearance of fear as to the result of the trial."

Crandall's courage impressed even those who disliked his politics. His landlord George Oyster, openly hostile to Reuben's New York ways, had to acknowledge he was "a correct man in all his habits . . . a very steady man in every respect."

Before long, Key was floundering. The district attorney could produce only one solid piece of evidence that Reuben ever intended to distribute the pamphlets in Washington: the inscription "please to read and circulate" scrawled on one of the copies.

Coxe denied the words proved anything. In the chaos of his jailhouse arraignment, Reuben had said he wrote those words long ago and that he merely used the antislavery pamphlets to wrap his plants. But Key did not pursue the point. Crandall could not be compelled to testify, and, in any case, Key did not want to give him a platform to denounce slavery. The district attorney did not call any of the free people of color, like Isaac Cary and John Cook, who he knew trafficked in antislavery publications.

Instead, Key read long passages from the fiery rhetoric of the pamphlets, oblivious to the fact that the jurors were not so offended by their denunciation of slavery. One of the jurors, a grocer named George Crandle, had even signed one of Ben Lundy's petitions calling for the abolition of slavery in the District just a few years before.

Key gave way to the defense. Richard Coxe's junior counsel, Joseph Bradley, rose. Without introduction, he started reading from another pamphlet lamenting the cruelties of the slave trade. When Judge Cranch interrupted to ask him about the relevance, Bradley replied that the words actually came from the lips of the district attorney. He was quoting, he said, from Key's address to the American Colonization Society in 1827 in which Key cited the abuses inherent in slavery as justification for helping blacks move to Africa.

At the other table, Mr. Key was not amused.

Yet, Bradley went on, Mr. Key charged Crandall with libel for publications that used virtually the same language about slavery. Judges Cranch and Thruston laughed out loud at his cleverness. Key was on his feet spluttering that advocates of African colonization did not favor emancipation and did not incite the slaves to rebel, but the damage had been done.

Key's lack of preparation, his chief weakness as a lawyer, was showing. He focused on the language of the pamphlets, overlooking what Reuben had actually done. The district attorney managed to elicit testimony from Ralsaman Austin, the husband of one of Crandall's patients, that Reuben had once accepted shipment of a trunk full of antislavery pamphlets in New York from a "Mr. Denison."

Key did not seem to know that Denison was Charles Denison, the editor of the infamous antislavery broadsheet *The Emancipator* and a leader in the New York headquarters of the American Anti-Slavery Society. Austin's testimony suggested Reuben had previously acted in concert with leaders of the abolitionists, raising the possibility that he might have done so again when he brought pamphlets to the capital. The abolitionist press always said that Crandall had been railroaded. But it was also possible that Reuben had not only delivered pamphlets to the Post Office but had also passed copies to antislavery allies like John Cook and Isaac Cary for wider distribution. In any case, Key had missed an opportunity to bolster his case.

The newspapermen watching the trial found Key's argument weak, noting Key presented no evidence that Crandall sought to instigate rebellion or even circulate his publications among enslaved people. Whether or not the judges and jury had any sympathy for Crandall's antislavery views, the correspondents observed that they seemed to respect his right to hold them. Early on, a writer for the *Charleston Courier* said he would not be surprised if Crandall was acquitted. The three judges, he reported, wanted "to show their independence of these popular excitements." A New York correspondent said he expected the trial to end soon "in the acquittal of the accused."

As the proceedings wore on, Crandall took heart. Each day after the trial's session ended, he was walked across Judiciary Square by a guard and returned to his jail cell. He was comforted by Mr. Key's disarray.

"The evidence for the prosecution," he wrote in a letter to his brother, "is the most confused mess you ever saw."

42

I N THE FINAL two days of *U.S. v. Reuben Crandall*, Francis Scott Key and Richard Coxe addressed the jurors for the last time. Their debate in many ways crystallized how new ideas of rights introduced by the free people of color and their white allies had galvanized popular thinking in the mid-1830s. These same views divided Americans into broad political tendencies that would endure. Coxe and Key were exemplars of what would become known as blue and red politics.

The blues of the 1830s were the liberals of the day, the opponents of slavery, concentrated in the Midwest and Northeast. They had a presence in Congress, led by former president John Quincy Adams. They had made themselves known in Washington City, thanks to the efforts of Ben Lundy, William Lloyd Garrison, John Cook, Isaac Cary, and Reuben Crandall. The abolitionists had brought three radical ideas into the realm of American politics: no property in people; multiracial citizenship; and the freedom to advocate both.

These ideals still animate the American liberal tradition nearly two centuries later. Like the antislavery men and women of yore, twenty-first-century liberals believe that property rights can be limited for the common good; that American citizenship should be as inclusive as possible; and that freedom of expression is a prerequisite of a free society. Richard Coxe was no abolitionist and he did not argue in court for Negro equality in *U.S. v. Crandall* or discuss property rights. But he did lay out a "true blue" case for freedom of expression to protect those who wanted to advance such ideas.

In response, Key denounced Coxe on all counts. He dismissed his defense of the emancipationist fanatics and those who questioned the slave owners' expansive definition of property rights. Compared to the blue

Coxe, the red Key had a much narrower idea of freedom of speech. He argued that the antislavery publications could be suppressed in the name of public safety since they might incite violent rebellion. Key insisted that white men *did* have a constitutional right to own property in people. And he defended a narrower conception of American citizenship—that it was reserved for the native born and whites only.

This general set of ideas still animates American conservatism against the country's liberal tendencies. Conservatives no longer believe in slavery, but they retain a maximal definition of property rights (embodied in freedom from taxation and regulation); a narrower conception of citizenship (to be reserved for native-born Americans); and a belief that threats to public safety may justify limitations on civil liberties. In *U.S. v. Crandall,* Francis Scott Key argued the red agenda of the day.

Richard Coxe spoke first in closing arguments. Never, he said, had the performance of his professional duties aroused "feelings of more intense anxiety." Never, he went on, had he felt a deeper interest in the outcome. The issues decided here, he told the jurors, "may be brought to bear upon each member of this community, and upon our children's children. . . . Great principles are to be settled."

As for himself, Coxe said he felt a sense of duty to "the principles of liberty and of the constitution." He said that if any individual in the District of Columbia could, like Reuben Crandall, be arrested, have his personal papers seized and his most confidential correspondence exposed to public gaze, "then I say, this District is no place for me."

Coxe spoke of Reuben's plight: arrested and charged, held for eight months and denounced before the community. Coxe wanted to make clear that his position was very different from that of his friend Mr. Key.

"This process, thus illegally issued, thus illegally executed, has been justified by the District Attorney. He avows his participation in it, and avows himself ready, whenever required, to prove that it is lawful."

Coxe wanted to interpose himself forcefully.

"On the other hand, I pledge myself on all occasions, and whenever the question shall be presented for judicial decision, to brand it as tyrannical, oppressive, illegal, and unconstitutional."

Coxe denounced Mr. Key's case against Reuben Crandall.

"It is, gentlemen, preposterous. It is monstrous," he slashed. "It has no foundation in any principle of law—it can find no support in any dictate of reason. It is a reproach to our community—it is a slander upon our institutions, that an intelligent and highly accomplished individual should, under such circumstances and upon such grounds, have suffered what has already been inflicted upon him."

Coxe looked to Reuben in the dock.

"His books and papers were harmlessly reposing in his trunk and his office, neither injuring nor calculated to injure any one. From this quiet repose, both have been snatched by the lawless violence which has characterized the proceedings against him: language imputed to him which he never uttered, and bruited forth to rouse into action, and to stimulate to deeds of ferocity, a ruthless mob."

Coxe knew when to stop. He thanked the jury on behalf of his client.

"I submit him and his fate with entire confidence into your hands," he said. He sat down.

It was half past five o'clock and Judge Cranch called for the court to adjourn for the evening.

Washington City was heating up. The next day Anna Thornton, still worried about Arthur languishing in jail, reported that the thermometer rose thirteen Fahrenheit degrees between breakfast and dinner. In that same interval, Francis Scott Key summed up the U.S. government's case against Reuben Crandall.

"I consider this one of the most important cases ever tried here," he began. It presented a conflict of rights, he said: the white man's property rights versus the free-speech rights of an antislavery man who sought not only to deprive white men but also to degrade them with the notice that black and white were equal.

"We are to give up our slaves—not for compensation—not gradually as we may be enabled to substitute other labour . . . but absolutely, unconditionally, immediately," Key said. "Nor is this all. They are to remain among us—to be admitted immediately to a full and equal participation in all civil and social privileges. Then, if we do not like our new condition, we can go away—and the friends of human rights and amalgamation can come and take our places."

So the most important question facing the jurors, the district attorney said, was whether the pamphlets seized from Crandall's house were "libelous."

"They declare that every law which sanctions slavery is null and void . . . ," Key reminded them, "that we have no more rights over our slaves than they have over us. Does not this bring the constitution and the laws under which we live into contempt? Is it not a plain invitation to resist them?"

Key cited the sorry story of Arthur Bowen as evidence.

"Mr. Crandall was told shortly after his arrival here with these publications that the attempt on the life of his mistress by Mrs. Thornton's slave, for which he has been since convicted, was instigated by the New York abolition pamphlets, passages from which he had been heard to repeat."

Implacable in his desire to see Crandall hanged, Key asked the jurors to understand the threat to their own honor posed by the antislavery cause.

"Are you willing, gentlemen, to abandon your country, to permit it to be taken from you, and occupied by the abolitionist, according to whose taste it is to associate and amalgamate with the negro? Or, gentlemen, on the other hand, are there laws in this community to defend you from the immediate abolitionist, who would open upon you the floodgates of such extensive wickedness and mischief?"

Key waxed sarcastic in summing up.

"If he is an innocent man, cruelly imprisoned under an illegal warrant, and these vile, calumnatory libels, are actually this innocent, persecuted gentleman's property—stolen from him—then gentlemen return him his property and let him go free."

The district attorney's last words quieted the courtroom.

"It is with you, gentlemen," he said. "I ask of you but to do your conscientious duty."

The jury went into a separate room to deliberate. The attorneys, the crowds, the clerks, and the pensive defendant could only wait and wonder. Outside it was a beautiful spring day.

Less than three hours later, the jury foreman reappeared. The spectators stilled themselves. The judges entered. Cranch asked the foreman for the verdict on Reuben Crandall.

"Not guilty!"

43

O N THE ADVICE of Mr. Coxe, Reuben Crandall returned to his jail cell after the trial. He could have walked out the door into Judiciary Square anytime, but he and his friends worried there might be another mob lurking. So Reuben sat where he had sat for eight months. He was a free man, now self-imprisoned.

William Jackson, an antislavery congressman from Massachusetts, came to see Reuben in his cell to congratulate and comfort him. Once it was dark outside, Jackson proposed that Reuben come with him to his boardinghouse. At nine o'clock they walked out of the jail. For the first time since the evening of August 10, more than eight months before, Reuben had his liberty.

Spring nights in Washington come with a gentle embrace that even visitors appreciate as unique. As Crandall walked along with his friend, he faced the disorienting sight of normal life. The shopkeepers were sweeping the macadam dust from their doorsteps. The taverns were coming alive with conversation. Lobbyists were returning to the hotels. The hack drivers spat into the gutter and conferred noisily.

No one paid much attention as they walked along. Reuben had a new appreciation of freedom. In Jackson's room they rested, talked some more, and prepared their next move. At one o'clock in the morning, they set out again into the now-empty streets. Jackson accompanied Crandall to the stagecoach station outside of Gadsby's Hotel at the corner of Sixth and Pennsylvania. The National Eating House was open for business on the opposite corner. Crandall boarded the night mail coach headed north to Baltimore and then Philadelphia. He would reach his parents' home in Connecticut by nightfall the next day.

As Congressman Jackson saw him off, he thought it was a sad story.

"Thus an amiable and respectable young man's prospects are all overturned, his property sacrificed and his health greatly injured by long imprisonment," he said to a friend. "And after full proof of his innocence, he is compelled to flee from the capital of his country for his life, like a felon in the dark."

The next day Crandall's acquittal made headlines across the nation. "Crandall the Abolition *Botanist* has been acquitted," the acidic Duff Green wrote in the *Telegraph,* his italics signaling his suspicion of Reuben's true profession. "We never expected anything else.

"There is not an individual in the city who does not think he was an agent of the Abolitionists," Green went on. While many deprecated the antislavery movement as a tiny minority with no prospects of success, this experienced editor did not make that mistake. Crandall's acquittal, he noted, demonstrated the growing influence of the antislavery men. "The whole power of the Abolitionists, here and abroad, [was] exerted to save him," he wrote, "and they succeeded, as we predicted at the time they would do."

What Green, in his hatred of the abolitionists, could not imagine was that a jury of white men in Washington City could both believe that Reuben Crandall was an abolitionist *and* that he should go free. What Key could not imagine is that people would doubt his integrity.

Yet that was the case, according to a correspondent for the *Boston Courier.*

"I believe there is a feeling of sympathy for him and regret for his eight months imprisonment," the correspondent wrote. "There is much to answer for somewhere. Mr. Key, the Van Buren Attorney of the District, did his best against him."

"He has suffered for the public good," wrote a correspondent for the Philadelphia-based *Gazette of the United States,* "and must find his reward in the reflection that he will be placed by the side of the multitude of martyrs to political expediency."

In Boston, William Lloyd Garrison hailed the acquittal of "this excellent but suffering man." In the pages of *The Liberator,* he denounced Key, who, he said, "cherished a deep malignity of purpose toward Dr. C. and spared no effort to procure his conviction." Garrison noted that when the district attorney failed to prove that Crandall had circulated antislavery publications, "he offered to prove that the prisoner was a manager of the American Anti-Slavery Society!" Here the abolitionist editor poured on the sarcasm. "What a horrible crime, if true! And how richly would Dr. C. deserve to be gibbeted, could the charge have been sustained. . . .

"And this in a free country!" Garrison concluded in disgusted wonder. "At the seat of government!! In the city of Washington!!"

44

ARTHUR BOWEN REMAINED seated in his cell on the second floor of the City Jail, still in leg irons. The warming of the weather made his dank quarters slightly more hospitable. At night, the high windows of the cells could catch a breeze off the river or a whiff of jasmine or the pungent slaughterhouse nearby. With a steady supply of provisions delivered by his mother, Arthur ate better than his fellow inmates. But his appetite was not theirs. They were confined for their crimes. He was still due to be hanged. President Jackson's respite of February 25 had spared him from execution until June 3, a day fast approaching.

Anna Thornton still worried about him and wondered what she might do. And then she had a moment of inspiration. A woman of habit, she was rarely creative, but in her desperation to avert Arthur's execution she became daring. She wrote a letter to the notorious Richard Mentor Johnson, the senator from Kentucky, who had been nominated as Mr. Van Buren's running mate in the election coming in November. Anna knew Johnson might well be the next vice president of the United States, and she knew President Jackson admired him. Perhaps he could help.

Anna knew the stories about Johnson. His enemies in the South were telling the story to any newspaper editor who would listen. Southerners were balking at supporting a man known to keep a black "wench." Anna knew that he had taken Julia Chinn as a common-law wife and fathered two girls with her. She might have read Duff Green's outraged charge that Johnson's dalliance would win abolitionist votes for the Van Buren ticket because the antislavery voters approved of racial "amalgamation." But Anna also knew that Johnson had plenty of respectable defenders, including a friend who wrote a letter to the *Globe* arguing that Johnson had never married a Negro woman, merely kept house with several of them. Julia Chinn, the writer added, had been "one of the most exemplary and pious of women." Anna might have observed that if Johnson was a scandalous man to some, he was also a candidate for national office who enjoyed the personal blessing of Mr. Jackson, Mr. Van Buren, and Mr. Blair, three of the most powerful men in the capital. Senator Johnson had even appeared in a public platform with chief justice nominee Roger Taney back in January. Whatever Anna thought of Johnson's morality (and it probably wasn't much), she recognized he was a decent man, not intimidated by what people thought of him. If he loved his own mulatto children as he said he did, he might well sympathize with Arthur's plight.

A few days later, Johnson agreed to pay her a call.

When the senator arrived at the house on F Street, Anna was preparing another petition on Arthur's behalf for President Jackson. Johnson was an unusual visitor to Anna's parlor, less punctilious than most gentlemen and more expressive. "His countenance is wild though with much cleverness in it," observed Harriet Martineau when she met him. "His hair wanders all abroad, and he wears no cravat."

Anna gave Johnson her petition and he read it over. He could see that other reliable allies of Jackson had signed on, including *Globe* editor Francis Blair. "I hope the president will pardon the convict," wrote the *Globe* editor. "I believe he was the victim of the [drink] and that he had no design on the life of his mistress." Johnson needed no more persuading. "I have enquired into the facts of this case," he wrote on the petition, "and have no hesitation in strongly recommending the pardon of the condemned slave. . . . Most respectfully R. M. Johnson."

Jackson was swayed. On June 2, the president issued a two-month respite for Arthur, sparing him from execution until August 4. He also sent word to Anna via a friend hinting that he would eventually pardon Arthur. "He is favorably inclined towards him" was the message.

Anna did not relent. On June 13, Anna and Johnson called on President Jackson. They made an unusual pair, this conventional society lady and the roguish soldier turned politician. Jackson probably liked them all the more for it. He told them he wanted to pardon Arthur but said he would need a new petition and he needed the support of the district attorney.

Johnson welcomed this news but Anna was "greatly disappointed." She already had such a petition and she knew the pitiless Mr. Key would reject it. He would rather see Arthur hang than change his mind.

In her diary that night, Anna reflected on how her life had changed since the night of August 4. Once she worried about Mama's health, her debts, and her rents. Now she talked to the president of the United States about saving Arthur's life.

"What a strange business for me to have to do," she wrote.

J UNE 21 WAS yet another cool and rainy day in Washington's wettest spring in years. Mr. Key was at his desk on the first floor of City Hall. The court's spring session was over. He had prosecuted as much of the criminal docket as he could. He regretted that Reuben Crandall and his ilk had stirred up popular feeling in the capital. The blacks, he felt, faced only more control now than they did before.

Key welcomed the more leisurely tempo of summer. In one term, he had attended more than four hundred criminal appearances or cases in the courtroom. Now he was looking forward to going up to Terra Rubra, where he could finally spend some time with Polly and the children. Taney was sure to join them.

As Key worked, his son Daniel was walking on Sixth Street near Pennsylvania Avenue, spoiling for a fight. The most temperamental of the Key boys, Daniel was not a dandy like his oldest brother, the reprobate Frank Jr. Nor was he dutiful, like John Ross. He was not intellectually gifted like his younger brother Philip Barton. He was impulsive and brash.

Outside of Gadsby's Hotel, Daniel spotted a man he knew well, John Sherburne, who had been a fellow midshipman in the navy. He was waiting for a hack with some friends when Daniel approached him.

"You're a coward," he shouted.

He and Sherburne had met by chance earlier that year on a navy ship in the Pacific. While serving on the *Brandywine*, Key had defied an order and was arrested for insubordination. The captain sent him home on another ship to face disciplinary action. It was on this ship that Key had met Sherburne and taken an instant dislike to him. In their brief acquaintance, they fell into a discussion of steamboats, debating which of two famous vessels was faster. The argument turned into an exchange of insults that enraged both men and elevated their trivial differences into an affair of masculine honor. Key challenged Sherburne to a duel when the ship docked in Norfolk. Local authorities, warned of Key's intent, arrested him during shore leave. Sherburne proceeded to his family's home in Baltimore, while Key was informed that he been sentenced to a week in the brig in Biloxi, Mississippi.

He returned home to Washington in disgrace and stayed with his mother and father in their new house on C Street. He told his father about his sentence and said his quarrel with Sherburne was over. His father was delighted to see him, despite his troubles. He felt the navy had favored Sherburne and that his son was being bullied.

But when Daniel spotted John Sherburne outside of Gadsby's he could not help but renew his challenge, no matter what he told his father.

"You are a coward," he repeated. Sherburne and friends suddenly found themselves listening to a lethal challenge. Sherburne coolly told Key that his friend Mr. Mattingly would contact him to arrange a duel.

The next morning, Thomas Mattingly visited the Key house on C Street. Daniel was alone. His father was at the office. His mother was visiting relatives.

"I am calling as a friend of Mr. Sherburne's to make arrangements to close the unsettled difficulty between you and him," Mattingly said.

"There is no difficulty between me and Mr. Sherburne," young Key snorted. "He is a scoundrel, and I will not meet him."

"I did not come here to discuss Mr. Sherburne's character," said Mattingly. "I want you to say once and finally if you will meet Mr. Sherburne."

Daniel Key was silent for a few minutes, thinking about honor and his father.

"I will fight Mister Sherburne provided it is done immediately," he finally said.

"Would one hour from now suit you?" Mattingly asked.

"I need to provide myself with a friend," Daniel answered.

"At six o'clock tonight?"

Daniel nodded.

"Let's meet at the Good Hope Tavern."

At that time in America, duels of honor were common, if not respectable. They marked the culmination of an elaborate, commonly understood protocol. If a man's honor was insulted or even impugned, he could demand a duel to the death as redress. Friends, known as seconds, handled the time and place of the duel, selected the weapons, and determined the distance between the duelists. The practice of dueling was technically illegal but largely tolerated. Charges for dueling had been filed in Washington circuit court for the first time in October 1821, probably in response to the much-lamented death of Commodore Stephen Decatur the year before. But the law was observed mostly in the breach. Since becoming district attorney in 1833, Francis Scott Key had prosecuted only two men for sending or seconding challenges for duels, and they were each fined all of one dollar.

The Good Hope Tavern stood a mile and a half south of the city on a hill looking down at the Anacostia River and the Navy Yard. The establishment welcomed duelists, who settled their differences in the adjacent fields, not that a lot of room was needed. The standard duel was fought at ten paces, barely twenty feet. "A moderately skillful marksman could readily hit his adversary at that distance," said one historian, "provided he was not unduly nervous."

Daniel Key was not unduly nervous. Late on the afternoon of Wednesday, June 22, he and his cousin, a young man named Richard West, took a hack from Key's house down Pennsylvania Avenue, up to Capitol Hill and over to the rickety wooden bridge across the Eastern Branch. They passed through the village of Anacostia and followed Good Hope Road up to the tavern at the top of the hill. Washington City was visible in the distance.

John Sherburne was already there with his second. While the principals hung back, Thomas Mattingly again proposed reconciliation, this time to Richard West.

Daniel Key overheard the offer and scoffed. "It's useless to waste time talking about it," he jibed.

"We have come to fight, not to talk," said West, who was almost as obnoxious as his cousin Key, though not quite so audacious. "The sooner it is over, the better."

Mattingly pointed to the nearby meadow and the four men walked out into its green expanse. As they came to the spot, Sherburne spoke up.

"Mr. Key," he began, "I have no desire to kill you."

"No matter," Daniel barked back. "I came to kill you."

"Very well," finished Sherburne without pleasure. "I *will* kill you."

Ten paces were measured off between the two men. West gave the word, and both men raised their guns and fired. Both missed.

"Goddamnit," Key snapped. "Load up quickly and let us have another shot."

It was now twilight, and Mattingly's turn to give the signal. Key and Sherburne again took their stands, counted their steps, and turned to each other. A bullet slammed into the lower part of Daniel Key's chest, smashing through ribs and staggering him backward. He stumbled in reverse, toppled onto his rear, sat on the grass, and keeled over on his side.

Sherburne was unhurt. He rushed toward Key, offering his hand.

"Leave me. Leave me," Daniel cried, touching the wetness of the red blot growing on his white shirt. "I scorn and detest you."

Impetuous to the end, Key had not brought along a doctor as many duelists did. His cousin West didn't know how to bandage a wound any more than he knew how to cook an egg. The red stain grew. Daniel Key lived for another twenty minutes. He expired on the wet grass where he fell. He was twenty years old.

46

FRANK AND POLLY Key were at home on C Street that evening when they heard a knock on the door. A family friend was calling with alarming news: Daniel had been wounded in a duel and a doctor had been sent for. Frank was surprised. Daniel's fellow officers had assured him that the quarrel with Sherburne was over. Polly had been planning to take her son to visit his sister in Maryland. Frank hoped his son would serve his time in the brig and learn his lesson. Their hopes vanished when a group of men arrived with a stretcher bearing the body of Daniel Key. He was not wounded. He was dead.

Polly was frantic, then stunned. The men laid the lifeless body on a table in the house. It was the same room where Daniel had spoken with Mattingly that morning. The mother bent over the corpse in speechless agony. His sisters wrung their hands and wept.

At the same time Frank Key could not move. He thought of the little boy who lived so brightly and wrote so sprightly. When he was nine years old Daniel had composed a poem in a little booklet that his parents had saved:

I am a possum bred + borne
My name and birth I will not scorn
My father was a noble fellow
Who dwelt upon a weeping willow

That was Daniel on the table, but he was gone. Once again, Key had lost a son, this time to a duel of honor. To others Daniel might have been a surly rebel. To his bereft father, Daniel would always be that little possum, bred and borne in family happiness, who had lost his way.

231

Key was desolate. A man of ambition, idealistic and opportunistic, a man of Washington City, accustomed to fame and privilege, he was also sensitive and sinful. In looking at his son's body, he again felt his faithlessness and failure as a parent and as a Christian. He had chased the power of this world at the expense of His glory. The only way Key could live with the pain of losing another son was to believe that he deserved it, that it was God's will. Key's sense of shame and loss was so deep, he could not bring himself to write to his grown children that their younger brother was no more. He left that task to his niece Elizabeth, one of Roger Taney's daughters.

"The excitement caused by this tragedy can hardly be imagined," said one man who lived on C Street at the time. "The two families were so well known and the youth of the two midshipmen increased the interest in the affair."

"I need not tell you what a shock it was to us—so sudden & unexpected," Key wrote to daughter Ann later that week. "Our poor boy himself had no idea of it till the morning of the day on which it occurred."

Key wanted to believe the best of his son.

"It is some consolation to us to know that your poor brother was actuated by no malice," he went on, "but a generous disposition to give this young man, whose companions had treated him as disgraced by the quarrel, an opportunity to retrieve his character." Her brother, he wrote, "had no ill will toward him & would not attempt his life under any circumstances."

As always, Key sought the consolation of faith.

"I trust we shall endeavor to see even in this dark and mysterious providence, the chastening hand of our heavenly father and be enabled to say, 'Thy will be done.'"

The mourning of young Key was accompanied by pity for poor John Sherburne. He was mercifully called away for duty, leaving his father to defend his name and conduct. The elder Sherburne had worked in Washington City for decades. He was known and respected by the clerks and auditors and messengers of the government offices. He was pained for his son, who he believed had done everything possible to avoid the fatal engagement. And he was alarmed by a report in the *Baltimore Chronicle* that stated President Jackson had ordered his son's name stricken from the rolls of the navy. The elder Sherburne went to the President's House to ask if it was true. Jackson denied it. The president, who had once killed a man in a duel, said he had heard no complaints "on this painful subject."

Jackson shared in the "strong and universal" sympathy in Washington City for the Key and Sherburne families, and the tragedy of Daniel Key made the plight of Arthur Bowen more poignant. The president had Anna Thornton's latest pardon petition on his desk signed by his good friends Senator Johnson, Frank Blair, and others. He had not forgotten Anna's plaintive pleas that the execution of the boy would overwhelm her and her mother with "grief and horror unutterable." The time had come for mercy. He reached for his pen.

"Let the Negro boy John Arthur Bowen be pardoned to take effect on the 4th of July next," Jackson scrawled, a date that would imbue the pardon with the generosity of American patriotism.

Jackson gave the document to a messenger to take to the State Department. But for some reason, Jackson chose not to tell Anna Thornton that the tragedy of Daniel Key had prompted him to spare Arthur Bowen's life.

Unaware of Jackson's clemency, Anna continued to seek Arthur's pardon, not knowing it had already been secured. Then, on July 1, her mother's condition worsened. Anna, fearing Mrs. Brodeau was near death, called Reverend Hawley, the pastor at St. John's Church on President's Square, who came and prayed at her bedside. Her mother appeared to understand and be comforted. Between eight and nine o'clock on the morning of July 4, Mrs. Ann Brodeau died in her bed in the house on F Street. She was at least eighty years old. A few hours later, Anna learned that the president had pardoned Arthur.

"How much more thankful should I have been had he [Jackson] done so sooner," she wrote in her diary. At least then her mother would have had the comfort of knowing Arthur would live. Without that consolation, Anna had to face the inevitable.

"Now I have the painful task of selling him," she wrote in her diary.

That had been the bargain all along. Arthur would get to live but would have to be sold away. Maria Bowen succumbed to violent fits of crying at the thought that she would lose her son not to Judge Lynch or to the hangman, but to the slave traders and respectable man stealers living around President's Square. Her mistress, Anna, was a good woman, and Maria would be eternally grateful to her for saving Arthur's life. But they lived in a monstrous land, led by cruel, cynical hypocrites, and Maria Bowen had no reason not to say it to Anna's face.

Anna could only listen in silence.

"Now I am harassed and disturbed," she wrote in her diary. "Oh my god, support & strengthen me under all trials."

Anna grimly attended to the details. She sold Arthur for $750 to the president's friend John Eaton, who in turn sold him to a young white man named William Stockton, also an acquaintance of the president, who was going to Pensacola, Florida, to work his stagecoach and steamship business. Anna hoped he might get training to become a steward on a steamboat.

"I never intended to sell him for life, but could not now avoid it," Anna wrote. "I hope & pray that he may lead a new life and be happy."

On the second floor of the City Jail, the guards unlocked the leg irons that Arthur had worn since December. He was destined not for the gallows but the docks of Georgetown, where he met his new owner, Mr. Stockton. If Arthur was given a chance to say good-bye to his mother and to the woman who had saved his life, Anna did not record it. In any case, the affection between Arthur Bowen and Anna Thornton was unlikely. He might have killed her on that cool night in August. In his intoxicated state who could say what his intention truly was? And she could have delivered him to his death anytime after his conviction, if she only had put down her pen. But he did not and she could not. Through hate and love, they had both survived. The foolish boy whose bid for freedom ignited the capital's worst cataclysm since the British invasion of 1814 lived to see another day—as a young man in bondage bound for the Florida Territory. If Arthur looked back as he left the jail, he might have had one glance at the Capitol that William Thornton designed. At least he would not die in its shadow.

PART VII

THE EPICUREAN RECESS

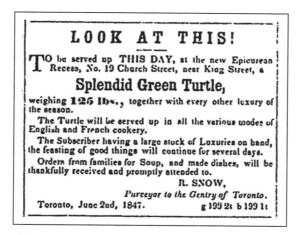

The irrepressible Beverly Snow advertised his favorite fare in Toronto's *Globe* newspaper on June 5, 1847.

47

OF ALL THE damn fool things Beverly Randolph Snow ever did in his long life, his decision to return to Washington City in the summer of 1836 had to rank high among them. Few other men, colored or white, would have even contemplated the notion, much less carried it to fruition. But Beverly did. Why was a question that confounded his friends and enemies alike. After all, less than a year before, a large assemblage of the local white citizenry had nearly lynched him, and the larger society of white people could not or would not stop them. Such was the rage of his assailants that when they could not lay hands on him, their fury could only be appeased by running riot over the whole capital city of the United States of America. He was a self-made man of pleasure, a disciple of Epicurus, who embodied an idea—multiracial citizenship—that disgusted and terrified many a white man and woman, a notion that was timeless yet decades, if not a century, ahead of the time.

Did he return to prove that he wasn't a fiend, merely a fellow American? Whatever possessed him to think anybody else would see the matter his way?

"Temerity and foolishness," said John O'Sullivan, who was no friend of the man. Those more disposed to Snow would have attributed the surprise visit to self-confidence and naïveté. Beverly had always made his way with wit and a sure conception of himself, relying on Epicurus as his mentor. Indeed, he returned to Washington City in the summer of 1836 so equipped. When asked later why he returned, Beverly said he intended to pay off some debts owed to his former business partner, William Walker, and to others. Shouldn't an honorable man pay his debts?

In the event, Beverly felt no compunction about walking down Pennsylvania Avenue on the evening of Friday, August 12. The city looked grander than when he first arrived from Lynchburg six years before. If he looked east, he saw the ever-present Capitol. If he looked west, he saw the new Treasury Building under construction on Fifteenth Street. But Congress was not in session, and the Avenue was uncrowded. The hotels were almost empty, the boardinghouses dark. Beverly walked down the street with a friend.

It was nearly dark when a group of four white men first recognized him. They called his name and started following him, speaking loudly. Beverly realized he might have overestimated his prospects, requiring him to accelerate his pace. At the corner of Eleventh Street, he turned right past Claggett's dry-goods store. As soon as he was out of the sight of the men, he took off running north at full speed. His companion, never identified, bolted in another direction. Beverly raced north past Mr. Dubant's barbershop and Mrs. Charles's boardinghouse, with the white men now giving chase. After he passed F Street he veered right into a hollow of trees on the grounds of St. Patrick's Catholic Church. Out of sight of his pursuers, he spotted a gully and dropped to lie down in it, covering himself with his cloak.

His pursuers, perhaps remembering how he escaped the mob by ducking under a bridge a year before, slowed down and found him lying in the darkness. They grabbed him with much threatening language. Now joined by others, the white men marched Beverly along Seventh Street, with some suggesting they take him to see Judge Lynch. Beverly spotted a passing constable and called out to him, asking that he be taken to the jail. Mr. Richard Burr, a veteran of the force, took control of the prisoner, escorting him to the jail for safekeeping. By the time they arrived in Judiciary Square, the crowd trailing them had grown to some two hundred people.

Clement Coote, the justice of the peace for the neighborhood, was called, and so was Mayor Bradley. Francis Scott Key was not. He was at Terra Rubra, still mourning Daniel's death. Mayor Bradley would not be rushed. He insisted the law be followed. Personally, his sympathies were with his friend Beverly. He saw no evidence that Snow, by law a free man, had violated any statute by walking down the street. He persuaded the crowd to disperse with the promise that Snow would be fully examined the next day.

Beverly spent the night in the City Jail. He was among the most famous prisoners ever to reside there and probably among the most popular, at least on the second floor. The man whose style ignited rage among whites also lit warm admiration among his fellow blacks. The sensational news of his arrest was now spreading around the city, evoking memories of the rioting a year before and its many causes.

"The name of Beverly Snow is inseparably associated with that excitement," said the *Metropolitan*, "and there are few, perhaps, in our community who are not so well acquainted with all the particulars of last summer's rioting, as to render even allusion to them unnecessary."

Beverly's white friends immediately came to his defense. John Hampden Pleasants, editor of the influential *Richmond Whig* newspaper, had known Beverly since he was a young man in Lynchburg cooking for John and Susannah Warwick.

"We know Snow, and shall be very much surprised if he has deserved in reality punishment designed for him," Pleasants wrote. "We have known him for some 16 years, and have always seen him, rather consequential and theatrical indeed, but perfectly respectful and unencroaching. We hope that the Districters will let him off."

In the morning, Beverly was brought out and escorted to the city council's chamber in City Hall. More than one hundred people had gathered, as well as a dozen constables, the entire city's police force. Beverly's ability to command attention was beyond dispute. While he was certainly reviled by many, including the mechanics, he also had his supporters. Members of both groups crowded into the chamber.

Magistrates Coote and Morsell opened the proceedings by questioning Beverly closely. He responded coolly but correctly. When did he come to Washington? Last night. What was his object? To satisfy his creditors. Whom did he meet with? Friends. Did he have incendiary publications in his possession? No. Did he have witnesses who could confirm his story? Yes. And so it went for more than two hours. Nobody wrote down the interrogation, but it was intense. Some in the audience were suspicious of his answers. John O'Sullivan detected "some prevarication and falsehood" in what Snow said. But the magistrates could find no legal fault with his answers or his conduct.

"There is no criminal charge against the prisoner," Mr. Coote finally said to the assembled crowd. "He must be dismissed from the custody of the officer."

Did that mean he was going to be turned over to the mob for summary justice? There was a lot of loud talk, but no one actually dared grab Beverly or even try to harm him. Mayor Bradley seized the moment to note that Snow's registry, required for all free people of color who lived in Washington City, had expired. By law he was required to leave the city immediately. Bradley was a decent man who would not have the city disgraced by lynch law. But he would not defy public opinion and the letter of the law by letting Snow stay in his adopted hometown.

Beverly had no problem telling the magistrates that he would leave. He had planned to do just that. Beverly departed from Washington City for the last time that day. He was headed for a destination he had already scouted, a city where an African in America might live freely. Beverly was bound for Canada.

48

Beverly Snow would never again figure in events as dramatic as the Snow-Storm of August 1835, not that he minded. He and Julia moved on from Washington City with considerably more dignity than some of his enemies retained in staying. He may have recalled what his friend Epicurus had said: The man "who is happy and immortal is no ways solicitous or uneasy on any account, neither does he torment nor tease others. Anger is unworthy of his greatness, and beneficence can not form the character of his majesty, for all these things are the property of weakness." Beverly would never be so weak as the white mob of Washington had proven to be.

In Toronto, Beverly and Julia found themselves in a sparkling city on Lake Ontario that was much smaller than Washington and much more pleasant, not the least because there was no slavery. The British parliament had abolished slavery in all its colonies three years before. When Snow arrived in Toronto, its ten thousand residents included about five hundred people of African descent, most of them, like him, American-born blacks seeking to escape the capricious laws of the slaveholding republic based in Washington. One of them was Thomas Cary, his friend and brother of Isaac, who had left Washington the year before. Now Cary was running his own ice business.

As the Snow family settled in for the coldest winter they had ever known, Beverly prepared to open another restaurant. Naturally, he gravitated to Church Street in the commercial center of the growing city. It was a neighborhood full of promise for an enterprising man. One British supporter of emigration to Canada exulted over Toronto's many charms, "its rows of splendid brick-built tin-covered houses; its magnificent churches, and number of places of worship; its banks; its floating palaces, its beautiful schooners; its magnificent stores, some of them rivaling those of the first city of the world, with their plate glass windows, their spacious areas, and their splendid contents."

Unlike in Washington City, Beverly did not need to mask his feelings about slavery in order to keep his customers. He had not been a public abolitionist in the American capital but he was now. In late 1837, Beverly joined a mass meeting that founded a new organization called the Upper Canada Anti-Slavery Society. When a local minister opened the gathering by offering a resolution calling for the "immediate and universal abandonment" of slavery, Beverly seconded the motion.

Beverly first opened a coffee shop on the northeast corner of Church and Colborne streets and settled into a new life of working, saving, and moderate pleasure. A few years later he opened a new eatery called the Epicurean Recess. As its name implied, the place offered refuge from the cold weather and stoic style of the north. He fitted it with the best furniture and sought out fresh oysters and other luxury items shipped in from the markets of New York and Boston.

Beverly had plenty of competition in the food business. On Church Street, Beverly's customers could also dine at the Peacock Tavern, William Phair's Inn, the Crown and Anchor Tavern, the Edinborough Castle Inn, and the Ontario Hotel. Within this bustling milieu Beverly expanded his business, becoming a caterer and wholesaler of foodstuffs and touting himself as "B. R. Snow, Purveyor to the Gentry of Toronto." His outgoing personality won him new friends. He fell in with George Brown, the editor of the city's newest newspaper, the *Globe*, which gave American antislavery forces a public forum. Brown enjoyed Beverly's fare and admired his style.

Beverly still relied on old advertising gambits, including that reliable command:

LOOK AT THIS!
To be served this day at the new Epicurean Recess . . .
Splendid Green Turtle

Although generous with friends, Beverly was known to drive a hard bargain, especially with those who did not share his republican politics.

When the local Tories, political conservatives, held a banquet in one of Beverly's smaller rooms, he offered them a limited menu for a dollar per man, wine included. Brown of *The Globe* knew Beverly well enough to be amused by his low quoted prices.

"Snow . . . with his whole soul (if he has one) despises of all things in the world, a cheap dinner," Brown observed as the bibulous scene unfolded. When the two dozen Tories gathered and got liquored up, they started calling lustily for more food and drink. Snow told the waiters to cut them off. "Snow had an abundance of good things remaining but not for a dollar," Brown reported. A "precious row" ensued.

The hungry Tories issued loud threats against the American caterer, which did them no good. They tried sweet blandishments to similar effect. Threats to annex the United States were ignored. Beverly simply refused to serve them. The Tories wound up paying him three dollars per man to finish their feast. He "knew the value of a dollar to the infinitesimal portion of a red cent," said Brown.

When a fire swept through the premises of the Epicurean Recess in 1847, *The Globe* reported that Snow, "with his usual liberality," paid a "handsome sum" to the neighborhood fire company that extinguished the flames. Beverly sold off the rest of the dining room furniture and kitchen accessories and put the proceeds into a new establishment called the Phoenix Saloon. He would rise from the ashes again. The new hotel and refectory, he boasted in a newspaper ad, "would be distinguished by its 'assiduity and attention,' with every comfort which 'Home' could possess."

The November 1848 opening of the Phoenix Saloon was no small affair. Beverly's debut was the annual Masonic Ball, attended by some seven to eight hundred Masons from across Ontario. To sate so many palates Beverly offered a rich bill of fare. It featured many of his culinary specialties, starting with oyster and turtle soup, then proceeding to cold dishes of impressive variety: boned mutton, stuffed turkey, geese (boned and jellied), and lobster salad.

The hot courses included venison with currant jelly, partridges with bread sauce, wild duck with claret sauce, and, of course, the final course of the turtle's delight, the calipash and calipee. At the end of the evening Snow's waiters brought out trays laden with desserts such as blancmange, an almond-flavored dish similar to vanilla pudding, as well as Málaga grapes from Spain, ice cream, and figs.

"A more elegant 'spread' could not be desired by any one," said the *British Colonist* newspaper. "Snow even surpassed himself on this occasion."

Among the city's legal elite, Snow's reputation as a caterer grew. The Law Society of Upper Canada, housed in an impressive two-story brick building called Osgoode Hall, often held functions for lawyers and judges and hired Snow to take care of the food. Beverly spent many gay and memorable nights working under the vaulted roof of the hall's beautiful library, commanding a squadron of cooks and waiters who wordlessly executed each course of his intricate menus.

As Beverly achieved a new level of professional success, he and his wife prospered. Back in 1843, the provincial government's tax man had assessed Beverly's worth at sixteen pounds in British currency, worth about seventy-five U.S. dollars of the day. Twelve years later, he was worth about twelve hundred U.S. dollars, a small fortune. Financially independent, he opened yet another eating house, the Exchange Saloon, in 1856. He was working there when he died suddenly on October 21, 1856, of unknown causes.

If Beverly realized during his brief illness that his allotted time on earth had come to an end, he might have thought one more time of his lifelong Greek friend who was said to have greeted death with constancy, if not joy. Suffering from a painful gallstone, Epicurus knew his time was not long. In the words of one eighteenth-century scholar, Epicurus contemplated his mode of thinking and what posterity would make of it.

"He had the satisfaction on one side to find nothing but what was praiseworthy in the past and nothing but what would be glorious to him in the future," said John Digby. "He therefore cheerfully embraced Death, as what would certainly suppress envy and render him immortal."

Beverly might have taken the same satisfaction for much the same reasons. After his passing, George Brown eulogized him in the pages of the *Globe* as a "long and favorably known . . . hotel keeper." A few days later, Julia Snow and friends laid Beverly Randolph Snow to eternal rest in the Toronto Necropolis.

As for the Snow-Storm of August 1835, Beverly apparently had never dwelled on it. Epicurus had recommended to his disciples a contempt for fame, a hearty dismissal of the notion that one's individual existence had more than atomic significance, and Beverly seemed to subscribe. Sometimes late at night at Osgoode Hall, after the plates had been cleared and the brandy poured, visiting attorneys from the wilds of Canada would question him about the famous statesmen he had entertained in the American capital. Beverly would regale them with amusing stories of John Calhoun, the stony apologist for slavery; Henry Clay, the cynical bon vivant; and Daniel Webster, the humane giant—all of whom he had seated at his tables in the Epicurean Eating House. He might have even told the story of Arthur Bowen, the young man whose thirst for freedom had upended the National Metropolis. He had many a tale to tell of Washington if anyone cared to listen. As for his own story of bondage freedom, respectability, notoriety, and redemption—that would have to wait for another time and another teller.

Epilogue

THE STRUGGLE FOR universal emancipation, which began about the time Beverly Snow arrived in Washington City in 1830, had taken root, broadened, and deepened by the time he left six years later. The core ideas of the new antislavery movement—that there was no property in people, that citizenship should be open to all Americans, and that freedom of expression was the cornerstone of a free society—had begun to transform American politics. As they spread, these ideas proved deeply unpopular in Washington and in many parts of the United States. But, after just six years, these same ideas were also much more commonly and respectably argued in many other places where they had never been heard before, including the halls of Congress. The fight against slavery that would cause and culminate in the Civil War was under way.

In barely half a decade, the abolitionists had established Washington City as a battlefield for their cause. In 1830, slavery was rarely debated in Congress. Six years later, it was the subject of fierce contention. The passage of the gag rule in May 1836 set off a three-year struggle, led by former president Adams and the small but determined antislavery bloc, to force the pro-slavery majority to accept petitions calling for abolition in the district. From December 1838 to March 1839, the Twenty-Fifth Congress received almost fifteen hundred petitions signed by more than one hundred thousand people. Eighty percent of the signatories supported abolition in the capital. Among the handful of congressmen who stood up for the petitioners' right to be heard was a first-term representative from Illinois, Abraham Lincoln. The pro-slavery majority ultimately prevailed, but the South's refusal to hear citizens petitioning their government did not go unnoticed among whites of the North and West. Most northern whites did not care much for the enslaved blacks, and even less for their

free brothers and sisters, but they did care about the threat that southern ambitions posed to their own civil liberties. Sectional hostility was
growing.

In 1830, the opponents of slavery had no national organization, no
champions in the popular press or the Christian pulpit. By 1836, the names
of William Lloyd Garrison and Arthur Tappan were known across the
land. Reuben Crandall was, at least for a few weeks, a nationally known
martyr to the cause. And on the eastern shore of Maryland, a young
enslaved man about the same age as Arthur Bowen made his first attempt
to escape from bondage. His name was Frederick Douglass. Within a
decade he would become the movement's most famous black leader.

In 1830, the free people of color in Washington City and the rest of the
United States were politically isolated and inert. That began to change
with the emergence of the anticolonization movement that met at the
AME Church on Capitol Hill in April 1831. The simultaneous emergence
of the Negro convention movement, joined by the likes of John Cook,
created a national network of activists seeking to improve the condition of
black people by education and emigration. With the arrival of Ben Lundy
in 1831, blacks and whites started to make common cause in the struggle
against slavery.

In 1830, African colonization was the most plausible and appealing
proposal to ameliorate the problem of slavery in America. By 1836, the
idea of universal emancipation had eclipsed colonization in popularity
and influence. In the interim, the upstart American Anti-Slavery Society
had attracted more followers, formed more chapters, and collected more
money than the well-entrenched American Colonization Society. Along
the way, the African colonization scheme lost its reputation as the most
realistic way to handle the bondage of several million people of African
descent. Among blacks, the idea of emigrating from the United States
retained appeal, as long as people of color, not the slaveholders and their
allies, would determine the destination. They chose Canada or the Carib-
bean much more often than they chose Africa.

The colonization society outdid its more radical rival in one area only:
support from elected officials. For example, Congressman Lincoln, while
he loathed slavery, was politically ambitious and prejudiced against blacks.
He declared himself a supporter of African colonization and he would

remain one even after he was elected president two decades later. But in April 1862, Lincoln, seeking to fortify the capital and gain advantage over the Confederacy's army, oversaw the abolition of slavery in the District of Columbia. Eight months later, on January 1, 1863, he issued the Emancipation Proclamation abolishing slavery in the rest of the country and settling finally the issue of whether emancipation or colonization was more realistic. Emancipation was.

Of course, the sudden coalescing of the antislavery movement in the 1830s had also triggered a wave of popular feeling that would become familiar in American politics: the white backlash. The revival of the revolutionary ideals of the Declaration of Independence by the new antislavery movement provoked a counterrevolution of majoritarian reaction that culminated in the violent summer of 1835.

The effects were especially pronounced within Washington City. Among white people, public support for the abolition of slavery evaporated. In the wake of the Snow-Storm of August 1835, the city council passed new restrictions on the free people of color, barring them from buying most commercial licenses needed to do business. In November 1836, Isaac Cary, blocked from renewing his license to sell perfume, sued to have the law overturned. Judge Cranch ruled in his favor, saying that while Negroes did not have all the political rights of whites, they had certain civil rights, including the right to pursue harmless professions. In 1836, the council passed an early curfew for all free Negroes. The legality of that was challenged too, but Judge Cranch upheld it.

In the District of Columbia and throughout the South, the pro-slavery forces, supported by most whites, suppressed the antislavery movement with a mixture of legality, intimidation, repression, and discrimination. But the acquittal of Reuben Crandall and the pardon of Arthur Bowen and the survival of Beverly Snow showed that the anti-abolition red majority could not always impose its will on the emancipationist blue minority, even in a southern bastion like Washington.

Resistance to slavery in Washington City would only increase. The number of enslaved and free blacks in the capital was roughly equal in 1836. By 1860, free blacks would outnumber bondsmen four to one. Antislavery sentiment in Congress remained a constant. While the movement's most public voice, William Lloyd Garrison, scorned the idea of working within the political system, more moderate antislavery leaders formed the Liberty Party in 1840, which evolved into the Free Soil Party and then, in the 1850s, into the Republican Party, which enlarged the antislavery bloc in Congress from an outgunned minority to a militant plurality.

Others in the National Metropolis spurned the legal tyranny of the U.S. government altogether. Thomas Smallwood, an ornery shoemaker from Prince George's County, and a white friend, Charles Torrey, began organizing large-scale escapes from plantations in the Chesapeake region. They arranged for groups of people, sometimes including whole families, to move from safe house to safe house, heading north to the free states, and they attracted support from respectable whites such as Joseph Bradley, the attorney who had defended Reuben Crandall. The flamboyant lawyer lent his house on Louisiana Avenue across from the courthouse to their efforts. While Bradley was away on legal business, Smallwood and Torrey would bring escaping slaves to stay in his rooms as they made their way north. Smallwood and Torrey were among the first conductors of what would be dubbed the Underground Railroad, and they were not alone. In 1848, abolitionists in Washington organized a mass escape of up to eighty slaves on a boat called the *Pearl,* which very nearly succeeded. The sheer scale of the *Pearl* endeavor increased the Chesapeake slaveholders' sense of insecurity.

The suppression of free speech in the capital city would not endure. In 1848, editor Gamaliel Bailey established *The National Era,* the first antislavery publication based in the capital since Benjamin Lundy ran the *Genius of Universal Emancipation* out of his office on E Street. The offices of the weekly paper would be mobbed and trashed, but the publication survived until the Civil War commenced.

Few could imagine the possibility in 1836, but within a generation the proud and vehement defenders of slavery in Washington City would be vanquished, self-exiled from Congress, defeated in national elections and then on the battlefield. Within half a lifetime, the genius of universal emancipation, once touted by only a few dreamers like Ben Lundy, Isaac Cary, and John Cook, would become national policy in the Emancipation Proclamation and the constitutionally sanctioned right to due process.

These ideas did not prevail simply because they were just or because of the might of the Union Army or the leadership of Abraham Lincoln. They prevailed because they were practical and attractive to growing numbers of Americans. Beverly Snow had proved by his menu, his hospitality, and his sheer Epicurean existence that all Americans deserved citizenship.

Washington City would experience another racially motivated riot in July 1919, with the unrest stoked by sexual rumors. The blacks, led by soldiers returning home from the Great War in Europe, fought back instead of fleeing, and at least six people were killed. Two generations after that, in April 1968, the assassination of Reverend Martin Luther King Jr. provoked black rioters to take revenge by rampaging up the same Fourteenth Street corridor where the white mechanics had attacked John Cook's school in August 1835.

By 2008, the capital had recovered again, emerging as a true national metropolis of marble and glass, and its early history had all but vanished beneath the architecture of power and influence. The only sign of Beverly Snow in the entire city was an unobtrusive plaque on the side of a downtown office building at the corner of Sixth Street and Pennsylvania Avenue. When Barack Obama, the country's first mixed-race president, rode in his ceremonial motorcade down the Avenue on Inauguration Day 2009, his limousine stopped and the new president emerged to stroll past the cheering crowds that thronged the very corner where Snow had tended his stove and greeted his customers 175 years before.

The formative history of the capital had been forgotten, and so had the secret of the Epicurean Eating House. The secret was that the struggle against slavery that culminated in the Civil War, the Emancipation Proclamation, and the passage of the Thirteenth and Fourteenth amendments had actually begun in Washington City about the time Beverly Snow came to town. The man from Lynchburg did not start this struggle, and he was not around to finish it. But in the fullness of time, his creation of a convivial meeting place open to people of all colors endured as an example that would eventually prevail in the life of Washington City, even as the man who invented it was all but forgotten.

Postscript: Who

In June 1837, the still-enslaved **Arthur Bowen** wrote to his mother from Pensacola, Florida, to complain about how his new owner, William Stockton, was treating him. The letters, Anna observed, left his Maria "very gloomy and dissatisfied." So Anna decided to arrange for Stockton to sell Arthur to a kinder master, an older man who worked in the Pensacola Navy Yard. Within a year, Arthur wrote to "say he was doing well and [was] liked on board the steamboat at Pensacola." Anna Thornton never mentioned Arthur Bowen again in her diary. What happened to the young man who detonated Washington City in August 1835 is not recorded in American history.

Reuben Crandall had contracted tuberculosis during his stay at the Washington City Jail. After winning his freedom, he booked passage to Kingston, Jamaica, thinking the tropical climate might help. He died there on January 18, 1838. Most people soon forgot his sacrifice for the antislavery cause, but not poet John Greenleaf Whittier. After the Civil War, Whittier wrote a poem called "Astraea at the Capital," in which the Greek goddess of justice visits Washington during the time of slavery. She stops at the City Jail.

> *Beside me gloomed the prison-cell*
> *Where wasted one in slow decline*
> *For uttering simple words of mine,*
> *And loving freedom all too well*

That was Reuben Crandall.

Francis Scott Key seemed to lose his ambition after his setbacks in 1835 and 1836. He continued to serve as district attorney for Washington City after the election of Martin Van Buren in the 1836 election, but he was no longer a presidential confidant. In May 1837 he suffered the painful loss of another son, John Ross, who succumbed to a quick-acting disease. Key resigned from the district attorney's job in 1840 and spent the rest of his years in private law practice, still a keen advocate of African colonization and sharp opponent of the antislavery movement. Key died of complications from pneumonia in his daughter's home in Baltimore on January 11, 1843.

The news of his death, said the *Intelligencer*, created "a very general painful sensation" in Washington. The U.S. Supreme Court suspended its proceedings for a day. At City Hall, Judge Cranch presided over a brief ceremony that was attended by the entire district bar, including Richard Coxe, Joseph Bradley, and Walter Jones. Cranch praised Key as one of the bar's "oldest and most respected members, and one of its brightest ornaments" who was always animated "by an overbearing sense of duty." In his eulogy Cranch did not mention "The Star-Spangled Banner."

Key's song was not formally adopted as the national anthem of the United States of America for another century. The designation came about after newly elected left-wing members of the Erie City Council in Pennsylvania opened a meeting in 1929 by singing the "The Internationale," a socialist anthem. A member of the American Legion took exception and organized a campaign to designate "The Star-Spangled Banner" as the national anthem so such a disgrace could never happen again. Congressman John Linthicum, a Democrat from Baltimore, introduced a bill to do just that. More than 150 organizations supported the move, and a petition attracted more than 5 million signatures. President Herbert Hoover signed the bill into law on March 3, 1931.

Roger Taney served as chief justice of the United States from 1836 to 1864. In 1856 his Supreme Court heard the case of *Dred Scott v. Sandford*. Scott was a middle-aged bondsman who had worked for the Sandford family in Illinois and the Wisconsin territory, where slavery was outlawed. Scott sued for his freedom, saying he lived in free territory. By a seven-to-two majority, the court dismissed Scott's argument and affirmed the plaintiff's right to coerce his labor. Taney took the lead in rejecting Scott's bid for freedom. In a passage that would become notorious, he declared that people of African descent

> had for more than a century before been regarded as beings of an inferior order, and altogether unfit to associate with the white race, either in social or political relations, and so far unfit that they had no rights which the white man was bound to respect.

The court's ruling effectively legalized slavery nationwide, even in states that had outlawed it for decades. Taney's ruling alienated public opinion across the North and hastened the coming of the Civil War in 1861.

The war was still raging when Taney died on October 12, 1864, but the North was winning. Three weeks later, slavery was officially abolished in his home state of Maryland. "His death at this moment," said one biographer, "seemed to mark the transition from the era of slavery to that of Universal Freedom." While his wisdom would be questioned, his influence would not. Roger Taney had shaped American law as surely as his brother-in-law Francis Scott Key had shaped American patriotic feeling.

John F. Cook returned to Washington in the fall of 1836 after spending one year teaching at a school in Columbia, Pennsylvania. In the words of one historian, "He resumed his work with broad and elevated ideas of his business." He would teach in the schoolhouse at Fourteenth and H streets for the next seventeen years, educating a generation of Negro children all by himself. Along the way, he founded the Union Bethel AME Church and the Fifteenth Street Presbyterian Church, located at Fifteenth and R streets, both of which still exist 175 years later. His two sons grew up to become professors and would play a leading role after the Civil War in the founding of Howard University, the first African American institution of higher learning. Cook died in March 1855. His funeral, said one account, was attended by "clergymen of no less than five denominations, many of the oldest and most respectable citizens, and a vast concourse of all classes, white and colored."

Benjamin Lundy published the *Genius of Universal Emancipation* from Philadelphia until 1838, when supporters of slavery destroyed his printing press and other possessions. Lundy moved to Lowell, Illinois, where he died on August 22, 1839.

Richard Mentor Johnson was elected vice president of the United States of America in 1836 under President Martin Van Buren. According to one historian, he "served without distinction and continued to scandalize his party by more dalliances with slave women."

Andrew Jackson retired from the presidency in March 1837. He died at his Tennessee estate, the Hermitage, on June 8, 1845. He bequeathed his property in scores of enslaved persons to his heirs.

John Sherburne was haunted by his slaying of Daniel Key. He took to drink, made lieutenant, and died in an asylum in Boston on November 2, 1849.

Maria Bowen and her mother, **Nelly,** were given their freedom in 1844 by Anna Thornton. Maria Bowen died in Washington City in March 1864. She was sixty years old.

Julia Snow, Beverly's widow, died on February 7, 1865. She was buried next to her husband in the Toronto Necropolis.

Beverly's friend **Isaac Carey** returned to Washington after the Civil War and became a deputy marshal and a member of the school board.

Anna Maria Thornton lived another thirty years after the Snow-Storm as her fortune slowly declined. She died in a rented room in Washington City on August 16, 1865. She was ninety years old. Mrs. Thornton was "remarkable for her beauty and accomplishments," said the *Intelligencer* and "one of the most distinguished ornaments of society." Her marriage was childless, the paper noted, "and she leaves no inheritor of her name and her virtue."

Postscript: Where

The home of John Marshall Warwick, where Beverly Snow lived until gaining his freedom in 1829, still stands on Court Street in Lynchburg, Virginia.

Where Francis Key's city residence once stood at Third and C streets is now the site of the E. Barrett Prettyman Federal Courthouse.

The riverside tract on Falls Street in Georgetown where Key lived from 1806 to 1835 is now a park named in his honor. A plaque in the park states inaccurately that Key was "active in anti-slavery causes."

The site of Terra Rubra, the Key family estate in Maryland, is still a country residence consisting of farm buildings and surrounding land.

Daniel Key is buried in Frederick, Maryland. The site of the Good Hope Tavern and dueling grounds where he died is now the intersection of Good Hope Road and Alabama Avenue, home to a fast-food fried-chicken restaurant.

Where City Hall (and its courtroom) once stood in Judiciary Square is now the Court of Appeals for the District of Columbia.

Where the City Jail stood at Fourth and F streets is now an office building of the D.C. courts.

Where the Jockey Club's racetrack stood from 1810 to at least the 1840s is now a block of apartment buildings near the intersection of Fourteenth Street and Columbia Road.

The Centre Market between Seventh and Ninth streets on Pennsylvania Avenue, where Anna Thornton and Maria Bowen did their shopping, is now the site of the National Archives.

Where Anna Maria Thornton, Ann Brodeau, Maria Bowen, and Arthur Bowen lived, on the north side of F Street between Thirteenth and Fourteenth streets, is now an office building with an Italian restaurant on the first floor.

The site of John Cook's Union Seminary near the corner of Fourteenth and H streets is now an office building.

President's Square, the park between Fifteenth and Seventeenth streets, G and H streets, is now known as Lafayette Square.

The northwest corner of Sixth Street and Pennsylvania Avenue, home to Beverly Snow's Epicurean Eating House from 1832 to 1835, is now occupied by a restaurant that caters to tourists and lobbyists.

The adjacent site of Isaac Cary's Emporium of Fashion from 1827 to 1841 is now a parking garage. Across the street where Gadsby's National Hotel once stood is now the media museum known as the Newseum.

William Thornton's Capitol building, topped with a dome after the Civil War, remains in use by the United States Congress.

The presidential mansion at Sixteenth Street and Pennsylvania Avenue, then home to the seventh president and now known as the White House, is home to the forty-fourth president of the United States.

Appendix
Beverly Snow's Menu

November 16, 1848
Masonic Ball, St. Andrew's Lodge, Toronto.
Supper at the two large dining rooms of Phoenix House, purveyed by
Mr. Snow.
Sponsored by the Provincial Grand Lodge. Between 700 and 800 attended.

Bill of Fare
Soups: Oyster, Mock Turtle

Cold Dishes: Boned Saddle of Mutton; Spiced Round; Bone forest
and Game stuffed Turkey; Boar's Head; bone forced and stuffed Hams;
Ducks (domestic); Geese, boned and jellied; Chickens; Tongue; Turkey
(plain); Oysters; Lobster Salad; Italian ditto; Walled Pie.

Hot Course: Saddle of Venison (Currant Jelly); Partridges (Bread
Sauce); Wild Ducks (Claret Sauce); Woodcocks (King of Odes); Quail
(Celery Sauce); Snipe (Spiced Gravy); Oyster Patties; Lobster; Patties;
Croquettes; Callabash; Calipee.

Pastry: Charlotte Russe; Blanc Mange; Jellies; Creams (Iced); Cus-
tards; Whips; Trifles; Malaga Grapes; Apples; Pippins; Nuts; Filberts;
Almonds; Raisins; English Walnuts; Cream Nuts; Prunes; Figs, &c.

Acknowledgments

I first wrote about the events of 1835–1836 in an article for *The Washington Post Magazine* in 2005. Sydney Trent's editing and enthusiasm perfected the article that, in retrospect, was the first draft of this book. Jodie Allen and Peter Perl encouraged me to pursue the story. Margot Williams provided invaluable research for both book and article.

George Briscoe and Bob Ellis of the National Archives staff helped me understand and navigate Record Groups 21 and 351. They also provided valuable insights into the workings of the Washington courts in the 1830s.

In the manuscript division of the Library of Congress, Jennifer Brathovde, Barbara Bair, and Jeff Flannery assisted my research, including the favor of a look at Anna Thornton's diaries.

At the archives of the District of Columbia, Director William Branch made available a wide variety of records.

The staff of the Kiplinger Library of the Historical Society of Washington aided my research with unfailing courtesy.

Jo-Ellen Bashir and the staff of the Moorland-Spingarn Research Center at Howard University helped me trace the remarkable story of John F. Cook.

Wayne Motts, executive director of the Adams County Historical Society in Gettysburg, Pennsylvania, showed me Clem Johnson's deed of manumission and shared his thoughts about its origins and implications. The interpretation presented here of Francis Scott Key's relationship with Clem Johnson is mine alone.

Bridgette Kamsler of the Historical Society of Frederick County helped me search the society's holdings on Key and slavery in Maryland.

Mary Williamson of York University provided invaluable information about Beverly Snow's time in Canada and the greatest gift an author can receive: a happy ending. Karolyn Smradz Frost introduced me to Williamson.

Jared Holloway of the University of Alabama assisted in unearthing the diary of Sarah Haynesworth Gayle. Paul Leatherdale, archivist of the Law Society of Upper Canada at Osgoode Hall in Toronto, provided Beverly Snow's bill of fare, which appears in the Appendix.

In Lynchburg, Joyce Mattox of Warwick House Publishing gave me a tour of the house where Beverly Snow lived in the 1820s. Kimeta Dover provided background on John Warwick and family. Ted Delaney shared insights into Lynchburg's racial history. Michael Lee showed me a long-lost slave cemetery.

Catherine Dixon, library director at Greenfield Library at St. John's College, gave permission to view Francis Scott Key material held at the Maryland State Archives.

Lynne Oliver, editor of the website foodtimeline.org, provided help on all food-related questions.

The manuscript was much improved by the superb line editing of Ronit Feldman and meticulous copy editing of Amy Ryan.

Catherine Talese perfected the illustrations. Agent Ron Goldfarb helped make it all happen.

My friends and family sustained me with their interest and encouragement throughout. Jeanette Noltenius was the first to say the *Post* article should become a book. When I doubted that, David Corn gave me a push. Jack Shafer shared his enthusiasm for the hidden history of the District of Columbia. David Talbot and Karen Croft infected me with enthusiasm. John Judis, Jim Campbell, Bruce Schulman, and Rosemarie Zagarri offered historical perspective and advice. Nesti Arene provided computer assistance. Anthony Morley did photo research. Diego Morley asked questions. Brad Knott, Kandace Kattar, Anya Schoolman, Barry Lynn, Clara Rivera, Ken Silverstein, Charles Sweeney, Stephanie Schehr, Mark Steitz, Mark Sugg, Rick Swartz, Patrice Lemelle, Steve Mufson, and Agnes Tabah all helped as only true friends can. Without the love and support of my wife, Teresa Arene, this book could not have been written.

Notes

Abbreviation Key

Key to Names, Places, Things
AJ: Andrew Jackson
AMT: Anna Maria Thornton
CHS: Columbia Historical Society
FSK: Francis Scott Key
RBT: Roger Brooke Taney

Key to Frequently Used Sources
AJP: Andrew Jackson Papers, University of Tennessee
AMT Diary: Diary of Anna Maria Thornton, Library of Congress
CFC: Charles Francis Cook papers, Moorland-Spingarn Center, Howard
    University
GUE: *Genius of Universal Emancipation*
MHS: Maryland Historical Society
MJQA: *Memoirs of John Quincy Adams*
National Archives
RG 21: Record Group 21
RG 351 Record Group 351
Sarah Haynesworth Gayle diary, Josiah and Amelia Gorgas Family Papers,
    Hoole Library, University of Alabama
Special Report: *Special Report of the Commissioner of Education on the Conditions
    and Improvements in the District of Columbia* (Washington, D.C., Govern-
    ment Printing Office, 1869)
TRC-DC: *Trial of Reuben Crandall*, Washington, D.C.
TRC-NY: *Trial of Reuben Crandall*, New York
WTP: William Thornton Papers, Library of Congress

Notes

Part I: The Disciple of Epicurus

Chapter 1

3   *John was the son:* "William Sidney Warwick, 1765–1832," Warwick Family file, Lynchburg Museum.

3   *Captain William Norvell, a veteran: Agora Journal for Undergraduate Scholarly Papers,* Lynchburg College, accessed October 2, 2010, http://www .agorajournal.org/x9368.html.

4   *Thomas Jefferson, who sold: The Jefferson Papers of the University of Virginia:* http://ead.lib.virginia.edu/vivaxtf/view?docId=uva-sc/viu00007.xml.

4   *Beverly, as a servant and cook:* City of Lynchburg, Will Book A (June 1809–1831), 41, contains a list of slaves owned by Norvell in 1824, including one named "Beverly," said to be worth $100. That relatively low figure is consistent with Beverly's limited term of servitude, which would have reduced his market value.

4   *his name appeared:* John's uncle, Daniel Warwick, supplied nails for the construction of Jefferson's "Academical Village" in Charlottesville, soon to be known as the University of Virginia. See University of Virginia Art Museum blog, "The Builders and Workers of Thomas Jefferson's Academical Village," accessed February 20, 2011: http://www.uvamblogs .com/jeffersons_academical_village/?p=235.

4   *a rich man well before:* Warwick's prosperity can be traced in the City of Lynchburg's Land Books, 1820–23, 1824–27, 1828–31, and 1832–35; City of Lynchburg Courthouse. At the beginning of 1825, Warwick reported owning two pieces of property in Lynchburg. A year later, he owned nine. See also "Mayor Waits 101 Years for Marker on Grave," *The News & Daily Advance* (Lynchburg), March 1, 1980.

4   *three of whom died:* "Plan of the Family Grave Yard Belonging to Estate of Wm Norvell, Dec'd," Warwick House Papers, Jones Library, Lynchburg, Va.

4   *"It is a stain":* Diary of Mrs. Susannah Caroline Warwick, 1829, John Warwick Daniels Papers, University of Virginia Library, Special Collections, series 9, Miscellaneous and Printed Material, box 33.

4   *Captain Norvell owned several Negro families:* City of Lynchburg, Will Book A (June 1809–1831), 4, 41.

5　*Susannah chose Beverly:* According to the City of Lynchburg Land Book for 1824–27, John Warwick owned two slaves over sixteen years of age in 1824. The next year he owned four. I conclude that Beverly Snow moved into John Warwick's house in 1825 at the latest.

5　*He also took a wife:* Judy Snow manumission, Lynchburg County Deed Book, 1824–1827, vol. K, 57.

5　*John became a member:* Christian W. Asbury, *Lynchburg, and Its People* (Lynchburg, Va.: J. P. Bell, 1900, 1967), 112.

6　*"I believe, sir":* Sketches and Recollections of Lynchburg by the Oldest Inhabitant (Richmond, Va.: C. H. Wynne, 1859), 120–21.

6　*John Warwick formed:* Asbury, *Lynchburg, and Its People,* 90.

6　*"Of all classes of our population":* Quoted in William Jay, *Miscellaneous Writings on Slavery* (Boston: John P. Jewett Co., 1853), 22–23.

7　*Johnson lived openly:* Thomas Brown, "The Miscegenation of Richard Mentor Johnson as an Issue in the National Election Campaign of 1835–36," *Civil War History* 39 (March 1993), 5–6.

7　*Johnson took up with:* Ibid.

8　*Virginia's eighth governor:* Governor's Information, National Governor's Association website, accessed June 1, 2010, http://www.nga.org/portal/site/nga/menuitem.29fab9fb4add37305ddcbeeb50101oao/?vgnextoid=24090d431dfb5010VgnVCM1000001a01010aRCRD. One reason I infer that Beverly Randolph Snow was named after Governor Beverley Randolph is because the former also sometimes spelled his first name "Beverley."

8　*only if a white man petitioned:* Ted Delaney and Phillip Wayne Rhodes, *Free Blacks of Lynchburg* (Lynchburg, Va.: Warwick House Publishing, 2001), 20, citing *A Collection of All Such Acts of the General Assembly of Virginia of a Public and Permanent Nature* (Richmond: Virginia General Assembly 1808), 95–98.

8　*A carpenter from the area:* Delaney and Rhodes, *Free Blacks of Lynchburg,* 11–12.

8　*only to be kidnapped and sold:* Jay, *Miscellaneous Writings on Slavery,* 48. The most famous case concerned Gilbert Horton, a free colored man and citizen of New York State, who had been snatched off the streets of the capital in 1826 and sold into slavery. Governor DeWitt Clinton of New

York addressed a public letter to President Adams demanding his immediate release, which was granted. Most kidnapping victims were not so fortunate.

9   *"emancipate, set free, and relinquish":* Deed Book, Lynchburg County Courthouse, vol. K, 46.

Chapter 2

10   *The stagecoach left Lynchburg: Lynchburg Daily Virginian,* February 28, 1829.

10   *"They may be likened":* Charles Dickens, *American Notes* (New York: St. Martin's Press, 1985), 119.

10   *the coach drivers were flamboyant:* Dickens, *American Notes,* 120.

10   *town of three thousand people:* Census.gov, accessed June 25, 2010, http://www.census.gov/population/www/documentation/twps0027/tab06.txt.

11   *by reputation, religious in tendency:* John T. Goolrick, *Historic Fredericksburg: The Story of an Old Town* (Richmond, Va.: Whittet & Shepperson, 1922), 151.

11   *The daily steamboat that went:* Advertisement, *National Intelligencer,* March 11, 1828.

11   *Long Bridge, a rickety wooden structure: Alexandria Gazette,* November 24, 1834.

11   *no other American city:* Constance McLaughlin Green, *The Secret City: A History of Race Relations in the Nation's Capital* (Princeton, N.J.: Princeton University Press, 1967), 53.

12   *enslaved people had outnumbered:* Mary Beth Corrigan, "Imaginary Cruelties? A History of the Slave Trade in Washington, D.C." *Washington History* 13, no. 2 (Fall/Winter 2001–2002), 6. According to George Watterston's *A New Guide to Washington* (New York: Robert Farnham, 1842), 19; in 1830, there were 6,152 free blacks and 6,119 enslaved people residing in Washington City.

12   *Franklin and Armfield, located:* Stanley Harrold, *Subversives: Antislavery Community in Washington, D.C., 1828–1865* (Baton Rouge: Louisiana State University Press, 2003), 30; *Virginia Landmarks Register,* 4th ed. (Charlottesville, Va.: University of Virginia Press, 2004), 80.

12   *"engaging and graceful":* E. A. Andrews, *Slavery and the Domestic Slave-Trade in the United States* (Boston: Light & Stearns, 1836), 136–37.

12   *slave pen at Third Street:* Corrigan, "Imagined Cruelties", 6–7. See also

Walter C. Clephane, "The Local Aspect of Slavery in the District of Columbia," *Records of the Columbia Historical Society* 4 (1899), 224–56.

12 *"See there. Ain't that":* Jesse Torrey, *A Portraiture of Domestic Slavery in the United States* (Philadelphia: John Bioren, 1817), 33.

12 *a dinner table conversation:* Fergus Bordewich, *Washington: The Making of the American Capital* (New York: Amistad, 2008), 21–52.

13 *Northerners and southerners alike:* Thomas Froncek, ed., *The City of Washington: An Illustrated History* (New York: Alfred A. Knopf, 1977), 47–51.

14 *"I doubt not it will be":* Letter, William Thornton to John Trumbull, January 6, 1796, William Thornton Papers (WTP), Library of Congress, reel 1.

14 *"I saw the dome":* Harriet Martineau, *Retrospect of Western Travel* (London: Saunders and Otley, 1838), 143.

14 *"We no longer say":* National Intelligencer, December 31, 1827.

15 *"scorching hot in the morning":* Dickens, *American Notes,* 105.

15 *"The whole affair":* The visitor was Basil Hall, author of *Travels in North America in the Years 1827 and 1828,* vol. 3 (Edinburgh: Cadell and Co., 1829), 1.

15 *lined with Lombardy poplar trees:* H. Paul Cammerer, *A Manual on the Origins and Development of Washington* (Washington, D.C.: U.S. Government Printing Office, 1939), Seventy-Fifth Congress, 3rd session, Senate document no. 178, 35.

16 *Seventy-five colored people:* Dorothy Provine, "The Economic Position of the Free Blacks in the District of Columbia, 1800–1860," *The Journal of Negro History* 58, no. 1 (January 1973), 68.

16 *less than the white messenger's: A Full Directory for Washington City, Georgetown, and Alexandria* (Washington, D.C.: E. A. Cohen and Co., 1834), 34.

16 *One could easily get drunk:* John Marszalek, *The Petticoat Affair: Manners, Mutiny and Sex in Andrew Jackson's White House* (New York: Free Press, 1997), 68.

Chapter 3

17 *The building, spanning 252 feet:* Wilhelmus Bogart Bryan, *A History of the National Capital* (New York: Macmillan, 1916), 80–81. Appearance: Francis Regis Noel and Margaret Brent Downing, *The Court-house of the District of Columbia* (Washington, D.C.: Judd & Detweiler, 1919).

17   *both in size and shabbiness:* Noel and Downing, *Court-house,* 24.

17   *settle for a license:* "Licenses for Races 5th Nov. 1830," Minutes of the Circuit Court, RG 21, microfilm 1021, reel 4.

18   *Brown boasted of fresh vegetables:* Jonathan Elliot, *Historical Sketches of the Ten Miles Square Forming the District of Columbia* (Washington, D.C.: J. Elliot, 1830), 315.

18   *"I have a delicious quarter of mutton":* Ben Perley Poore, *Perley's Reminiscences of Sixty Years in the National Metropolis,* vol. 1 (Philadelphia: Hubbard Brothers, 1886), 42.

18   *The big event took place:* The track "was on Columbia Road just west of 14th Street," according to Allen Clarke, "Dr. and Mrs. William Thornton," *Records of the Columbia Historical Society* 18 (1915), 71.

19   *While customers perched:* Walter Birkenhead, "Republicans, Democrats and Thoroughbreds," *Turf and Sport Digest,* January 1945, 44.

19   *"You must not be astonished":* Catherine Allgor, *Parlor Politics in Which the Ladies of Washington Help Build a City and a Government* (Charlottesville, Va.: University of Virginia Press, 2000), 86.

19   *Indeed the Jockey Club:* Elinore Stearns and David N. Yerkes, *William Thornton: A Renaissance Man in the Federal City* (Washington, D.C.: American Institute of Architects Foundation, 1976), 50.

19   *President Jackson's arrival:* Poore, *Perley's Reminiscences,* 190.

19   *he loved wagering large sums:* Benjamin Ogle Tayloe, *Our Neighbors on La Fayette Square: Anecdotes and Reminiscences* (Washington, D.C.: Junior League of Washington, 1982), 30.

20   *The* Telegraph *was as scrappy:* "About this Publication: United States Telegraph," Nineteenth Century Newspapers, Gale Databases, accessed March 15, 2010, http://gdc.gale.com/products/19th-century-u.s.-newspapers/.

20   *Beverly Snow:* Advertisement, *Telegraph,* December 15, 1830.

21   *what the French called:* British Concise Encyclopedia, 607.

Chapter 4

22   *"They consume an extraordinary quantity":* Frances Trollope, *Domestic Manners of the Americans,* 297.

22   *Mrs. Julia Seaton:* James S. Osgood, *William Winston Seaton of the National Intelligencer* (Boston: James R. Osgood, 1871), 217–19.

22 *"particular friend"*: *Paul Pry*, October 31, 1835, 2.

23 *"Look at This!"*: Advertisement, *National Intelligencer*, November 24, 1831.

23 *The surrounding streets housed*: Carol M. Highsmith and Ted Landphair, *Pennsylvania Avenue: America's Main Street* (Washington, D.C.: American Institute of Architects Press, 1988), 77.

23 *"One can tell the New England member"*: Martineau, *Retrospect of Western Travel*, 145.

23 *When a cholera epidemic struck*: "Authentic report of the Cholera in Washington, January 1, 1833," Board of Health Minutes, 1822–1848, Washington, D.C., Archives. "A large number of foreign Emigrants had recently arrived in the City and were employed upon the public works," the report concluded. "Most of these were from Germany and Ireland, men who understood not our language nor were accustomed to our climate, habits or modes of living. This manner of habitation and being as well as occupation probably exposed them to the disease. The cholera bore upon this class with great severity. It was also extremely fatal to our colored population and more specifically to the free blacks."

24 *Isaac Newton Cary, who owned*: Advertisements, *National Journal*, November 26, 1827; *Globe*, January 2, 1832.

24 *the son of a prosperous free black man*: Luther P. Jackson, "The Early Strivings of the Negro in Virginia," *The Journal of Negro History* 25, no. 1 (January 1940), 27. Thomas Cary's name is spelled "Carey" in this article, a spelling that Isaac also used on occasion.

24 *Known for his excellent sense*: *Provincial Freeman*, October 13, 1855.

24 *"Professor of Shaving"*: Advertisement, *Globe*, January 2, 1832.

24 *Cary had supported*: George W. Williams, *History of the Negro Race in America from 1619–1880*, vol. 2 (New York: G. P. Putnam's Sons, 1883), 65.

24 *his aunt, Lethe Tanner*: Tanner purchased the freedom of no less than twenty-three friends and relatives. They are named in A. N. Newton, *Special Report of the Commissioner of Education on the Conditions and Improvements in the District of Columbia* (Washington, D.C.: Government Printing Office, 1869), 197.

25 *"indefatigable application"*: Williams, *History of the Negro Race*, 188–89.

25 *"a matter of astonishment"*: Ibid.

25 *"seen nothing in all"*: Ibid.

25 *Cook organized a celebration*: "Exhibition No. 1 For the Benefit of A

young man, about to disenthrall himself from Slavery," October 17, 1832, Charles Francis Cook (CFC) Papers, Folder 10, at Howard University's Moorland-Spingarn Center.

25   *Cook would go on:* CFC Papers, Folder 10 contains Cook's lecture on tobacco addressed to the Philomathean or Young Men's Moral and Literary Society in 1834. Free people of color in other eastern cities also adopted Philomathean as their name for talking societies where opponents of slavery gathered. See also Dorothy Porter, "The Organized Educational Activities of Negro Literary Societies, 1828–1846," *The Journal of Negro Education* 5, no. 4 (October, 1936), 555–56.

25   *Benjamin Lundy, a white man:* Bruce Rosen, "Abolition and Colonization, the Years of Conflict: 1829–1834," *Phylon* 33, no. 2 (Second Quarter 1972), 183n.

25   *Lundy had grown up:* Thomas Earl, ed., *The Life, Travels, and Opinions of Benjamin Lundy* (Philadelphia: William D. Parrish, 1847), 13–16.

26   *He chose a headstrong:* Harrold, *Subversives,* 18–23.

26   *"Nothing is wanting":* Henry Mayer, *All on Fire: William Lloyd Garrison and the Abolition of Slavery* (New York: St. Martin's Griffin, 1998), 53.

26   *Their profession was hazardous:* "Garrison's Second Trial," *Genius of Universal Emancipation* (GUE), October 1830, 1.

27   *He moved south:* Earl, *Life, Travels, and Opinions of Benjamin Lundy,* 30.

27   *"to become more generally acquainted":* "Another Change of Location," GUE, October 1830, 97f.

27   *Lundy scoffed at such: Spectator* cited in GUE, December 1830, 144.

27   *When Lundy came:* Werner Sollors, Caldwell Titcomb, and Thomas A. Underwood, eds., *Blacks at Harvard: A Documentary History of African-American Experience at Harvard and Radcliffe* (New York: New York University Press, 1993), 47.

28   *He and his four children:* City of Washington, 1833 Tax Book, A–Z, Corporation of Washington, First and Second Ward, RG 351, entry 47, vols. 17 and 18.

Chapter 5

29   *The Potomac River froze:* Trollope, *Domestic Manners,* n223.

29   *an eclipse of the sun:* Anna Maria Thornton Diary (AMT Diary), vol. 1, 785.

29 *The Fourteenth Annual Meeting: National Intelligencer,* January 29, 1831.

29 *Colonization had been first proposed:* WTP, reel 1. Thornton corresponded about colonization with Granville Sharp, the English antislavery campaigner. See also Beatrice Starr Jenkins, *William Thornton: Small Star of the American Enlightenment* (San Luis Obispo, Calif.: Merritt Starr Books, 1982), 22–24.

30 *Paul Cuffe, a black sea captain:* James Oliver Horton and Lois E. Horton, *In Hope of Liberty: Culture, Community and Protest Among Northern Free Blacks, 1700–1860* (New York: Oxford University Press, 1997), 186–87.

30 *The society attracted gentlemen:* Jay, *Miscellaneous Writings on Slavery,* 150. Jay notes that of the society's seventeen vice presidents, five hailed from the free states. Of the group's twelve managers, all were slaveholders.

30 *On a windy Wednesday evening:* AMT Diary, vol. 1, 791.

30 *belonged to a network:* James T. Campbell, *Songs of Zion: The African Methodist Episcopal Church in America and South Africa* (New York: Oxford University Press, 1995), 32–36.

30 *The assembled crowd passed: National Intelligencer,* May 4, 1831.

31 *Withers, at age fifty-five:* "The Withers Family of Stafford, Fauquier, &c.," *The Virginia Magazine of History and Biography* 6, no. 3 (January 1899), 309–13.

31 *he used the profits of his mercantile firm to buy no less than seventeen different pieces of real estate:* 1833 Tax Book, Third and Fourth Wards, RG 351, entry 47, vol. 19.

31 *the greatest benefactor:* Harvey W. Crew, William Bensing Webb, and John Wooldridge, *Centennial History of the City of Washington, D.C.* (Dayton, Ohio: United Brethren Publishing, 1892), 506.

31 *building that Withers:* The building and its occupants in late 1835 are documented in "Blueprint, 6th Street and Pennsylvania Ave.," Forrest Sweet Papers, 1778–1864, accession #5976, University of Virginia Library, Charlottesville, Va. Also see the Directory for Washington City, 1834.

32 *"Snow's Epicurean Eating House":* Advertisement, *National Intelligencer,* October 26, 1832.

32 *"the most rational system":* Carl J. Richards, *The Founders and the Classics: Greece, Rome and American Enlightenment* (Cambridge, Mass.: Harvard University Press, 1994), 187.

33 *When Alexander Hamilton called:* Richards, *Founders and the Classics,* 93.

33 *"Of all the philosophers"*: *New-England Magazine*, October 1832, 353.

33 *Epicurus counseled avoidance:* John Digby, *Epicurus's Morals* (London: Sam Briscoe, 1712), xxiii.

34 *"No word has more"*: *Boston Masonic Mirror,* October 16, 1830.

34 *"Beverly Snow: The Disciple of Epicurus":* Advertisement, *Globe,* June 20, 1833. The identical phrase in the *Boston Masonic Mirror* and Beverly's advertisement two and a half years later may be coincidental. The literature of Epicurus often refers to his disciples. If a copy of the *Boston Masonic Mirror* reached Beverly's hands, it may have come from the black Masons he knew, such as Isaac and Thomas Cary or William Jackson, the Post Office messenger.

35 *Ben Perley Poore, a newspaperman:* Poore, *Perley's Reminiscences,* 179; Barry H. Landau, *The President's Table: Two Hundred Years of Dining and Diplomacy* (New York: Harper Collins, 2007), 11–12.

PART II: FRANK'S SONG

Chapter 6

39 *a two-story brick home:* Edward S. Delaplaine, *Francis Scott Key: Life and Times* (Stuarts Draft, Va.: American Foundation Publications, 1998), 46.

40 *Another child, Edward:* Ibid., 227.

40 *His practice, representing:* Francis Scott Key-Smith, *Francis Scott Key: What Else He Was and Who* (Washington, D.C.: National Capital Press, 1911), 39. The F. S. Key Papers, 1777–1843, Maryland Historical Society (MHS), MS 2199.

40 *On Sundays he prayed:* 1819–1852 Receipts General, F. S. Key Papers, MHS.

40 *"the Blacks' lawyer":* Marvis Olive Welch, *Prudence Crandall: A Biography* (Manchester, Conn.: Jason Publishers, 1983), 117.

40 *"a distinct and inferior race":* Delaplaine, *Life and Times,* 446.

40 *a distressingly serious man:* Victor Weybright, *Spangled Banner: The Story of Francis Scott Key* (New York: Farrar and Reinhart, 1934), 289. I'm borrowing from Weybright, who called Key a "distressingly serious layman" (289).

40 *Lancaster schools:* Delaplaine, *Life and Times,* 71 and elsewhere.

41 *He attended the annual General Convention:* Key-Smith, *What Else He Was,* 18.

41   *"His whole life is spent":* Hugh S. Garland, *Life of Randolph,* vol. 2 (Philadelphia: D. Appleton & Co, 1850), 64.

41   *Key was decent:* Weybright, *Spangled Banner,* 5–7.

41   *Key freed seven:* Early Lee Fox, *American Colonization Society 1817–1840* (Baltimore: Johns Hopkins Press, 1919), 10–17.

41   *"I have been thus instrumental":* Ibid.

42   *"the begging business":* Delaplaine, *Life and Times,* 201

42   *Key preferred not to respond:* See Key's speech of January 19, 1828, in *Eleventh Annual Report of the American Society for Colonizing the Free People of Color* (Washington, D.C.: Dunn, 1828), 21.

42   *a Negro servant:* William Seale, *The President's House: A History* (Washington, D.C.: White House Historical Association, National Geographic Society, 1998), 181.

42   *some of the rooms looked elegant:* Ibid., 181–83.

43   *"I want to tell you confidentially":* "Letters of Francis Scott Key to Roger Brooke Taney and Other Correspondence," *Maryland Historical Magazine* (1930), 25.

Chapter 7

44   *graduate of St. John's College:* Delaplaine, *Life and Times,* 30

44   *graduate of Dickinson College:* Taney manuscript memoir, written in 1854, handwritten, MHS, MS 645, box 8, 40–50.

45   *meshed in their differences:* Delaplaine, *Life and Times,* 47.

45   *Roger Taney and Ann Key married:* Weybright, *Spangled Banner,* 48; Delaplaine, *Life and Times,* 47.

45   *drew as close as brothers:* Bernard C. Steiner, *Life of Roger Brooke Taney, Chief Justice of the United States Supreme Court* (Baltimore: Wilkins & Wilkins 1922), 46–47.

45   *"a tall, square shouldered man":* John E. Semmes, *John H. B. Latrobe and His Times* (Baltimore: Norman Remington Company, 1917), 202.

45   *"ambition for legal eminence":* Taney manuscript memoir, 51.

45   *In 1819 he defended:* Samuel Tyler, *Memoir of Roger Brooke Taney, LL.D., Chief Justice of the Supreme Court of the United States* (Baltimore: John Murphy & Co., 1872), 126–31.

45   *Key had married Mary Tayloe:* Weybright, *Spangled Banner,* 43.

46   *the governor of Maryland:* Tyler, *Memoir of Roger Brooke Taney,* 165.

46   *"The worst men of a party"*: Quoted in Garland, *Life of Randolph*, 25.

46   *"You will put down"*: Garland, *Life of Randolph*, 29.

46   *Frank, as Key was known:* Virginia congressman John Randolph addressed Key as "Frank" in an affectionate letter in 1810. They would be close friends for the next twenty years. Garland, *Life of Randolph*, 11–12; see also Delaplaine, *Life and Times*, 91.

46   *held a barbecue:* Weybright, *Spangled Banner*, 234.

46   *"It is beautiful":* Gaillard Hunt, ed., *The First Forty Years of Washington Portrayed by the Family Letters of Mrs. Samuel Harrison Smith* (New York: Charles Scribner's, 1906), 294.

47   *Watkins was convicted: Niles' Weekly Register,* vol. 36 (June 20, 1829), 275; on the politics of the Watkins case, see Sean Wilentz, *Andrew Jackson* (New York: Henry Holt, 2005), 57.

47   *Margaret's flirtatious style:* The extensive Eaton literature is studded with intriguing, if apocryphal, details of her eventful love life. I consulted Queena Pollack's sympathetic *Peggy Eaton, Democracy's Mistress* (New York: Minton, Balch & Co., 1931), 38–39; Catherine Allgor's protofeminist *Parlor Politics*, 203–38; John Marszalek's entertaining *The Petticoat Affair*, 77–79; and Allen C. Clarke's judicious article "Margaret Eaton (Peggy O'Neal)" in the *Records of the Columbia Historical Society* 44/45 (1942–1943), 1–33.

47   *"the wildest girl":* Delaplaine, *Life and Times*, 281.

47   *Margaret Eaton was "very handsome":* Hunt, *The First Forty Years of Washington*, 252.

47   *"one of the most ambitious":* Ibid., 318.

48   *"She is as chaste":* Delaplaine, *Life and Times*, 286.

48   *Reverend John Nicholson Campbell:* Ibid.

48   *John Eaton wanted to challenge:* Clarke, "Margaret Eaton (Peggy O'Neal)," 13.

48   *Margaret took a swing:* Delaplaine, *Life and Times*, 283.

49   *Jackson dispatched his friend:* Afterward, Johnson and several former members of the cabinet published their accounts of the negotiations in the *National Intelligencer* and other newspapers, including the *Gettysburg Compiler*, August 30, 1831.

49   *the idea of the cabinet purge: Telegraph*, April 13 and 14, 1831.

49 *As a widower:* Robert V. Remini, *Life of Andrew Jackson* (New York: Harper Perennial, 1999), 193.

50 *"I expect that I am":* This and all subsequent dialogue is from "Letters of Francis Scott Key to Roger Brooke Taney and Other Correspondence," 24–25.

50 *Berrien resigned:* James Parton, *Life of Andrew Jackson,* vol. 3 (New York: Mason Brothers, 1860), 356–57.

50 *Before long he was:* Tyler, *Memoir of Roger Brooke Taney,* 168–73; Delaplaine, *Life and Times,* 294; Steiner, *Life of Roger Brooke Taney,* 103–4.

Chapter 8

51 *how he came to write:* I rely on Roger Taney's preface to Francis Key-Smith's *Poems of the Late Francis S. Key* (New York: Robert Carter & Brothers, 1857), 13–31, in which he recounts the story as Key told it to him. Taney's account serves as the "foundation of all further accounts," noted Oscar G. Sonneck, chief of the music division of the Library of Congress, in his definitive historiography *Report on "The Star Spangled Banner," "Hail Columbia," "America," "Yankee Doodle"* (Washington, D.C.: Government Printing Office, 1909), 7–42. I also consulted "'The Star-Spangled Banner' as Nation's Anthem," *New York Times,* July 15, 1917; Weybright, *Spangled Banner,* 98–106; and Delaplaine, *Life and Times,* 129–74.

51 *moved a flotilla:* William M. Marine, *The British Invasion of Maryland* (Baltimore: Society of the War of 1812 in Maryland, 1913), 87–103.

51 *offering freedom to enslaved:* Frank A. Cassell, "Slaves of the Chesapeake Bay Area and the War of 1812," *The Journal of Negro History* 57, no. 2 (April 1972), 144–55.

52 *"Mr. Francis Key informed me":* Weybright, *Spangled Banner,* 98.

52 *As the British forces approached:* Walter Lord, *The Dawn's Early Light* (New York: Norton & Co., 1972), 139–40.

53 *the British forces glided:* Weybright, *Spangled Banner,* 104.

53 *"Are you then":* William Thornton's self-serving account appeared in a letter to the *National Intelligencer,* September 14, 1814. See also Clarke, "Dr. and Mrs. William Thornton," 182; Stearns and Yerkes, *Renaissance Man,* 41; Jenkins, *William Thornton,* 90–91.

54 *then a tornado ripped:* Weybright, *Spangled Banner,* 104–5.

54   *"Key heard the voice":* Delaplaine, *Life and Times,* 146.

55   *He scrawled notes:* Taney's letter in Key-Smith, *Poems of the Late Francis S. Key,* 25–26.

57   *"beautiful and touching":* National Intelligencer, December 12, 1814.

57   *matched in popularity:* Sonneck, *Report on "The Star Spangled Banner,"* 47. Sonneck noted that in the annals of nineteenth-century American patriotic songs, "none except Key's 'Star Spangled Banner' and Reverend Smith's 'America' were destined to rival the popularity of 'Hail Columbia' for almost a century."

Chapter 9

58   *These verdant hills:* Weybright, *Spangled Banner,* 4.

58   *"The mansion was of brick":* Tyler, *Memoir of Roger Brooke Taney,* 101.

58   *Key delighted in his time:* Key-Smith, *What Else He Was,* 11–12.

58   *"Insurrection of the Blacks":* Frederick Town Herald, August 27, 1831; *National Journal,* August 27, 1831.

59   *Sixteen of the black rebels:* Telegraph, September 12, 1831.

59   *five-hundred-dollar reward:* National Journal, September 20, 1831.

60   *both came out:* Daniel Walker Howe, *What Hath God Wrought: The Transformation of America, 1815 to 1848* (New York: Oxford University Press, 2007), 325.

60   *Key gave the magistrate:* The record of Clem Johnson's manumission is found in the Collection of the Adams County Historical Society, Gettysburg, Pa. Wayne Motts, executive director, shared the original document with me as well as his thoughts about its origins and implications. He is not responsible in any way for my interpretation of Key and Johnson's relationship.

61   *One was called Big Round Top:* Weybright, *Spangled Banner,* 7.

Chapter 10

62   *"Are you Mr. Stanbery?":* Dialogue is drawn verbatim from three sources: the House trial testimony of Stanbery, published in the *National Intelligencer,* April 21, 1832; of bystander Jonathan Elliot, *National Intelligencer,* April 27, 1832; and of Senator Alexander Buckner, *National Intelligencer,* April 25 and April 28, 1832. Buckner's account is the most comprehensive. See also Delaplaine, *Life and Times,* 324.

63 *Stanbery had delivered:* Delaplaine, *Life and Times,* 325–26.

63 *resolution calling for Houston's arrest:* Ibid., 327.

63 *"vile attempt":* Globe, April 17, 1832.

64 *"On no occasion":* National Intelligencer, April 19, 1832.

64 *"ardent, zealous, fearless":* Delaplaine, *Life and Times,* 370.

64 *Key scorned the charge:* National Intelligencer, April 21 and 23, 1832.

65 *"Sir," he said to the House Speaker:* Joseph Gales, *Register of Debates in Congress: Comprising the Leading Debates and Incidents of the Second Session of the Eighteenth Congress:* [Dec. 6, 1824, to the First Session of the Twenty-Fifth Congress, Oct. 16, 1837] vol. 82 (Washington, D.C.: Gales and Seaton, 1837), 2597–2620.

65 *"his face reflected how deeply":* Weybright, *Spangled Banner,* 44–45.

65 *"I am proud":* Register of Debates in Congress, April 26, 1832, 2598.

65 *"A free Constitution":* Ibid., 2614.

66 *"a ruffian had brutally assaulted":* Delaplaine, *Life and Times,* 335.

66 *yearned for a roll call:* National Intelligencer, May 10, 1832, referring to the May 8 session.

66 *The vote was 106 to 89:* Delaplaine, *Life and Times,* 343.

66 *claiming vindication for pummeling:* Howe, *What Hath God Wrought,* 436; Parton, *Life of Andrew Jackson,* 385–92.

66 *lived the life of a young gentleman:* Isobel Davidson, *Real Stories from Baltimore County History* (Baltimore: Warwick & York, Inc, 1917), 91.

66 *told his mortified father:* Letter, FSK to Charles Howard, May 22, 1832, Howard Family Papers, Francis Scott Key Papers, MHS, MS 469 box 3.

67 *"Everybody is satisfied":* Letter, FSK to Charles Howard, May 25, 1832, Howard Family Papers, Francis Scott Key Papers, MHS, MS 469 box 3.

Chapter 11

68 *"I nominate Francis S. Key":* Journal of the Senate of the United States, Second Session of the Twenty-Second Congress (Washington, D.C.: Duff Green, 1832), 279.

68 *"not altogether to his taste":* Weybright, *Spangled Banner,* 241.

69 *increased the fines:* Bryan, *History of the National Capital,* 95.

69 *"There is no city":* National Intelligencer, November 13, 1833.

69 *a wage of fifty dollars:* Watterston, *A New Guide to Washington,* 166–67.

69 *reward money for capturing:* In 1832, Key's predecessor as district attorney,

Thomas Swann, prosecuted two constables, Gilson Dove and David Waters, for unspecified "illegal practices." Dove resigned and became a dealer of enslaved persons. Docket Book, vol. 69, RG 21, entry 6, Case Papers, box 492, March Term 1833, Criminal Appearances. Dove's new profession is identified in the *Directory for Washington City*, 1834, 16.

69 *proceeded to prosecute:* Ibid., Special Session, September 1833.

69 *forthright beauties:* George Watterston, *The L—— Family at Washington; or, a Winter in the Metropolis* (Washington, D.C.: Davis and Force, 1822), 104.

70 *The demimonde of the Washington:* All names and locations are found in Docket Book, vol. 70, RG 21, entry 6, Case Papers, box 493, September Term 1833, Criminal Appearances; Docket Book, vol. 70, RG 21, entry 6, Case Papers, box 502, November Term 1833, Criminal Appearances.

70 *a standard indictment form:* Docket Book, vol. 70., RG 21, entry 6, Case Papers, box 522, November Term 1834, Criminal Appearances.

Chapter 12

72 *dispatched him on another sensitive:* Delaplaine, *Life and Times,* 350–61; Weybright, *Spangled Banner,* 243–55; Thomas Chambers McCorvey, "The Mission of Francis Scott Key to Alabama in 1833," *Alabama Historical Society* 4 (1904), 141–63.

72 *The arrival of the famous author:* Alabama Department of History and Archives website: http://www.archives.state.al.us/timeline/al1801.html.

73 *"That is a pretty air":* Weybright, *Spangled Banner,* 250.

73 *twenty-nine years of age:* Elizabeth Fox-Genovese sketches Mrs. Gayle's winning personality in *Within the Plantation Household: Black and White Women of the Old South* (Chapel Hill, N.C.: University of North Carolina Press, 1998), 1–20.

73 *"He is very pleasant":* Sarah Gayle Diary typescript (Gayle Diary), 47. Sarah Haynesworth Gayle, series 5, Josiah and Amelia Gorgas Family Papers, W. S. Hoole Special Collections Library, the University of Alabama.

73 *"He has been around frequently":* Gayle Diary, 36.

74 *"And is it so?":* The entire poem appears in Delaplaine, *Life and Times,* 358.

74　*lamented in her diary:* Gayle Diary, 67. In her entry for October 4, 1834, she recalled their days as newlyweds. "I used to think then that Mr. Gayle loved me better than most men loved their wives—he had that sort of look which drew him to my presence constantly, that I cannot remember any time, that his eyes were not seeking me, and that the expression I always met there did not create and keep alive sun-shine in my bosom. I am sure I do not discover that same look in many countenances now."

74　*"I will set no wicked things":* Ibid., 50.

74　*he joined the Delphian Club:* The full text of Key's only known venture in erotic verse is found in Delaplaine, *Life and Times*, 230–31.

74　*"Few had stronger inward impulses":* Delaplaine, *Life and Times*, 182–83.

75　*"The Creek controversy":* Weybright, *Spangled Banner*, 258.

75　*"the gaunt man from Maryland":* Delaplaine, *Life and Times*, 295.

75　*"The African race":* Citing Carl Brent Swisher, *Roger B. Taney* (New York: Macmillan, 1935), 154. Howe, *What God Hath Wrought*, 442. Taney asserted, inaccurately, that blacks "were never regarded as a constituent portion of the sovereignty of any state." In fact, free Negroes held citizenship in several northern states after the Revolution. Taney also claimed they "were not looked upon as citizens by the contracting parties who formed the constitution," historically dubious for the same reason.

76　*Taney also encouraged:* Steiner, *Life of Roger Brooke Taney*, 120.

76　*He followed up with another letter:* Frank Otto Gatell, "Secretary Taney and the Baltimore Pets: A Study in Banking and Politics," *Business History Review* 39, no. 2 (Summer 1965), 217.

77　*Biddle, in the words:* Tyler, *Memoir of Roger Brooke Taney*, 207.

77　*Ellicott, an amoral Quaker:* Ibid., 162.

77　*"knew he would have to bail":* Gatell, "Secretary Taney and the Baltimore Pets," 217.

77　*"Insolvent you say?":* Remini, *Life of Andrew Jackson*, 189.

77　*a new financial regime:* Gatell, "Secretary Taney and the Baltimore Pets," 205–27.

78　*Taney's formal nomination:* Tyler, *Memoir of Roger Brooke Taney*, 221; Steiner, *Life of Roger Brooke Taney*, 166.

78　*they attended a political picnic:* Weybright, *Spangled Banner*, 261–63.

78　*"Never even in my boyhood,"* Delaplaine, *Life and Times*, 379–80.

79　*General Jackson had faced:* Esmeralda Boyle and Frederick Pinkney, Biographical Sketches of Distinguished Marylanders (Baltimore: Kelly Piet & Co., 1877), 255; Weybright, *Spangled Banner*, 263–64.

Chapter 13

80 *the grand jury indicted:* Docket Book, vol. 69, RG 21, entry 6, Case Papers, box 492, March Term 1833; Criminal Appearances; William Cranch, *Reports on Cases, Civil and Criminal, of the District of Columbia from 1801 to 1841 in Six Volumes*, vol. 4 (1830–1816), 303; Hillary Russell, "Underground Railroad Activists in Washington, D.C.," *Washington History* 13, no. 2 (Fall/Winter 2001–2002), 43.

80 *"There is neither mercy":* GUE 13 (June 1833), 127–28.

81 *Lundy reported another story:* Ibid.

81 *"to injure, oppress, aggrieve & vilify":* Docket Book, vol. 70.

82 *"never departed empty-handed":* Sollors, Titcomb, and Underwood, *Blacks at Harvard*, 47.

82 *the printer called two witnesses:* Ibid.; James Thomson, witness. *Directory for Washington City, Alexandria 1834*, 20. The directory lists a "James Thompson, Sea Captain, Duke near Water Street."

82 *The jury found Greer not guilty:* D.C. Circuit Court "Original Minutes," 1834–1836, RG 21, microfilm 1021, roll 4.

PART III: ANNA AND ARTHUR

Chapter 14

85 *lived next door:* Anna Thornton recorded many visits in her diary, such as on September 25, 1829, and November 3, 1829. On January 1, 1832, she noted that the Adamses were among her principal acquaintances. AMT Diary, vol. 1, 746, 748, and 813.

85 *The anniversary of their wedding:* Ibid., 238. In 1803, she wrote, "Our wedding day. Thirteen years."

85 *the anniversary of his passing:* Ibid., 760. On March 27, 1830, she wrote, "Another anniversary of my dreadful loss is arrived."

85 *bright eyes and sharp features:* Clarke, "Dr. and Mrs. William Thornton," 144.

85 *a friend of her late husband:* Gordon Brown, *Incidental Architect: William*

Thornton and the Cultural Elite of Early Washington, D.C., 1794–1828 (Athens: Ohio University Press, 2009), 66–67.

86 *The front parlor was adorned:* Memorandum, May 18, 1854, written by Anna Thornton listing all of her property. WTP, reel 1.

86 *she owned property:* In 1833 she and her mother owned at least 113 lots, which were located in every ward of the city. Tax Book 1833, A–Z, Corporation of Washington, First and Second Wards, RG 351, entry 47, vol. 18.

86 *She owned a five-hundred-acre farm:* Montgomery County Circuit Court Land Records, Grantee Index MSA-CE 217–290, Given Names L–Z, 1740.

86 *It was Anna's slaves:* Handwritten will, WTP. A published summary of Thornton's will in *District of Columbia Probate Records,* Will Book 2, compiled by Wesley E. Pippenger (Arlington, Va.: Family Line Publications, 1996), 144–45, states inaccurately that Thornton's will freed his slaves upon his own death.

86 *took care of the Bethesda farm:* AMT Diary, vol. 1, 747, 772, and 784.

86 *seven dollars a month:* Ibid., 846. When Thornton hired out Joe and Bill, she received only four dollars per month.

87 *Anna relied on George Plant:* His central role in the household and his residence in Georgetown is documented throughout the diary. See AMT Diary, vol. 1, 857, 859, 861, 869, and 874.

87 *"Races today + Arthur gone without leave":* AMT Diary, vol. 1, 728.

87 *"They are violent and unreasonable":* Ibid., 779.

88 *Anna was furious at him:* Ibid., 796.

88 *"Archy is dead":* Ibid., 847.

88 *at the southwest corner:* Wilhelmus B. Bryan, "A Fire in an Old Time F Street Tavern and What It Revealed." Records of the Columbia Historical Society 9 (1906), 198–215.

88 *jumped out of the window:* The incident scandalized Washington society and gave impetus to the creation of the American Colonization Society (ACS). See Torrey, *A Portraiture of Domestic Slavery in the United States,* 42.

89 *Anna hired him out to Mrs. Cochrane:* AMT Diary, vol. 1, 875.

89 *Anna hired him out to Mrs. Carlisle:* Ibid., 884–85.

89 *She hired him out to Mr. and Mrs. Fuller:* Ibid., 899.

89 *making new friends:* "He fell into bad company," Anna later told President Jackson. Letter, AMT to AJ, February 17, 1836. RG 59, General Records of the Department of State, Petitions for Pardons 1789–1860, Jackson Administration 1829–1837, box 25, file 1327.

89 *"It was obvious":* Ibid.

89 *left his clerk's job: Directory for Washington City,* 1834, 12.

89 *the Philomathean Talking Society:* Letitia Woods Brown and Elsie M. Lewis, *Washington from Banneker to Douglass, 1791–1870* (Washington, D.C.: National Portrait Gallery, Smithsonian Institution, 1971), 17–18.

89 *he began keeping "the company":* Letter, AMT to AJ, February 17, 1836.

Chapter 15

90 *"Mama poorly":* AMT Diary, vol. 1, 750, 763, and 767.

90 *"Mama better":* Ibid., 748, 787.

90 *"Mama unwell":* Ibid., 719, 801, and 876.

90 *"Mama a little better":* Ibid., 749, 922.

90 *"a great inconvenience":* Ibid., 770.

90 *Anna was annoyed:* Ibid., 785.

90 *Maria was not pleased:* Ibid., 808.

90 *warm and hazy days:* George and Arthur harvested potatoes; Anna read a book: Ibid., 799–801.

90 *While she complained:* Ibid., 818, 821, and 835.

90 *"I shall miss him":* Ibid., 793.

91 *With his winning design:* Brown, *Incidental Architect,* 7.

91 *they gave dinners and parties:* Ibid., 31.

91 *she saw Tudor House:* Stearns and Yerkes, *Renaissance Man,* 31, 35; *Caemmerer's Manual,* 173.

91 *which he had designed and built:* Tayloe, *Our Neighbors on La Fayette Square,* 5.

91 *he imagined what this:* Stearns and Yerkes, *Renaissance Man,* 27.

91 *he planted saplings and bushes:* Christian Hines, *Early Recollections of Washington City* (Washington, D.C.: Junior League of Washington, 1981), 86.

91 *two full-length unpublished novels:* The handwritten manuscripts of "Julia" and "Lucy" are found in the Papers of William Thornton, Library of Congress. In "Julia," the embattled heroine justifies her love affairs outside of her loveless marriage (WTP, roll 3).

92   *"Mr. Thornton, you don't know":* Tayloe, *Our Neighbors on La Fayette Square,* 76–77.

92   *"He knew many things":* Clarke, "Dr. and Mrs. William Thornton," 144.

93   *"His thirst for knowledge":* Ibid., 169.

93   *"a man of some learning":* John Quincy Adams, diary 31, 1 January 1819–20 March 1821, 10 November 1824–6 December 1824, 159 (electronic edition). *The Diaries of John Quincy Adams: A Digital Collection* (Boston: Massachusetts Historical Society, 2004), accessed September 21, 2010, http://www.masshist.org/jqadiaries.

Chapter 16

94   *"Luxury Luxury Luxury!":* Advertisement, *National Intelligencer,* September 12, 1834.

94   *The Avenue had been paved:* Bryan, *History of the National Capital,* 237.

94   *lived at Brown's:* Directory for Washington City, 1834, passim.

94   *The shiny blue carriages:* Advertisement, *National Intelligencer,* July 11, 1831.

95   *the mammoth orator:* Beverly himself said so. James Cleland Hamilton, *Osgoode Hall; Reminiscences of the Bench and Bar* (Toronto: Carswell Company Ltd., 1904), 133.

95   *prescribed by Mary Randolph:* Mary Randolph, *The Virginia Housewife; or, Methodical Cook* (Baltimore: Plakitt, Fite, 1838), 20.

96   *"the West Indian way":* Hannah Glass, *The Art of Cookery Made Plain and Easy* (London: 1778), 331–32.

96   *"Some of the most refined":* National Intelligencer, September 12, 1834.

96   *"Health Bought Cheap":* Advertisement, *Globe,* October 11, 14, 15, and 18, 1833.

97   *Beverly made the city tax rolls:* RG 351, entry 47, vol. 16, 1832 Tax Book, Third and Fourth Wards, RG 351, entry 47, vol. 22. 1834 Tax Book, Third and Fourth Wards.

97   *That distinction probably belonged:* Robinson declared five hundred dollars' worth of personal property in 1833, the most of any colored property owner in the city. Tax Book 1833, A-Z, Corporation of Washington, Third and Fourth Wards; RG 351, Entry 47, vol. 18. Her livelihood was revealed in April 1836, when she was convicted of running a house of ill fame. D.C. Circuit Court Original Minutes, 1834–1836, RG 21, microfilm 1021, roll 4.

97   *"The National Restaurateur":* Advertisement, *National Intelligencer,* December 12, 1832.

97 *herded groups of chained families:* Andrews, *Slavery and the Domestic Slave-Trade*, 136–37.

98 *posted a five-hundred-dollar bond:* D.C. Circuit Court "Original Minutes" 1834–1836, RG 21, microfilm 1021, roll 4.

98 *Beverly seems to have left:* Snow's absence is inferred from the notices of undelivered letters published in the *Globe*. Undelivered mail for Beverly Snow, *Globe*, September 2, 3; October 15–17; November 15, 18.

98 *"This man Snow":* Osgood, *William Winston Seaton of the "National Intelligencer,"* 217–19.

Chapter 17

99 *The mood was somber:* The attempt on Jackson's life is described in Martineau, *Retrospect of Western Travel*, 161–62; Delaplaine, *Life and Times*, 387; Remini, *Life of Andrew Jackson*, 201; Charles Francis Adams, ed., *Memoirs of John Quincy Adams: comprising portions of his diary*, vol. 9 (New York: J. B. Lippincott, 1876), 203.

100 *Judge Cranch gaveled the hearing:* The arraignment of Lawrence and Blair's stunt with the pistols is reported in the *Alexandria Gazette*, February 2, 1835, and the *Globe*, January 31, 1835.

101 *As district attorney, Key:* Delaplaine, *Life and Times*, 394.

102 *"rank with the fumes":* Edwin A. Miles, "Andrew Jackson and Senator George Poindexter," *The Journal of Southern History* 24, no. 1 (February 1958), 60.

102 *Jackson was certain:* Miles, "Andrew Jackson and Senator George Poindexter," 59–61.

102 *"He protested, in the presence":* Martineau, *Retrospect of Western Travel*, 163.

102 *a bricklayer who worked:* Account books showed Coltman had been paid forty-five dollars for a job at the President's House just a few days before. Andrew Jackson Papers (AJP), Library of Congress, no. 18260.

102 *The president invited:* The visit is recounted in Sam Southworth's letter reprinted in the *National Intelligencer*, February 28, 1835.

103 *"highly injurious to my moral character":* Stewart and Foy's testimony is found in the *Mirror*, April 4, 1835. See also Richard C. Rohrs, "Partisan Politics and the Attempted Assassination of Andrew Jackson," *Journal of the Early Republic* 1, no. 2 (Summer 1981), 159–61.

103 *"not a shade of suspicion":* Alexandria Gazette*, March 3, 1835.

103 *received with applause:* Ibid.

103 *passed two resolutions: National Intelligencer,* March 30, 1835.

103 *Some thought the Washington:* One such person was Philip Fendall, a Washington attorney who would later serve as district attorney. Adams, *Memoirs of John Quincy Adams,* 226.

103 *Key was more convinced:* Weybright, *Spangled Banner,* 267–68; Delaplaine, *Life and Times,* 388.

103 *"The whole transaction":* Adams, *Memoirs of John Quincy Adams,* 226.

Chapter 18

104 *balloon ascents: Alexandria Gazette,* November 11, 1834.

104 *Orang Utang: National Intelligencer,* April 19, 1832.

104 *the circus:* AMT Diary, vol. 1, 875.

104 *"Arthur came home":* AMT Diary, vol. 1, 927.

105 *"We pray God":* "Minutes of the Fifth Annual Convention for the Improvement of the Free People of Color" (Philadelphia: William P. Gibbons, 1835), 22. Found in the online Samuel J. May Anti-Slavery Collection, Library of Congress.

106 *She was born around 1800:* In the 1850 Census: Maria Bowen's age is given as fifty, suggesting she was born in 1800. In the 1860 Census, her age is given as fifty-six, indicating she was born in 1804. If she was born in 1804, she would have been eleven years old when Arthur was born, which seems improbable. More likely, Maria was born in 1800. See 1860 U.S. Census, population schedule. NARA microfilm publication, Census Place: Washington Ward 3, Washington, District of Columbia; Roll M653_102; p. 778; Image: 569; 1850 Census U.S. population schedule. NARA microfilm publication, Census Place: Washington Ward 2, Washington, District of Columbia; Roll: M432_56; 101A; Image: 208.

106 *nominated in May 1835:* Howe, *What God Hath Wrought,* 485; Elbert B. Smith, *Francis Preston Blair* (New York: Free Press, 1980), 100; Page Smith, *The Nation Comes of Age: A People's History of the Ante-Bellum Years,* vol. 4 (New York: McGraw-Hill, 1981), 123.

106 *had at least two African consorts:* Thomas Brown, "The Miscegenation of Richard Mentor Johnson as an Issue in the National Election Campaign of 1835–36," *Civil War History* 39 (March 1993), 6.

106 *"a colored person may have":* "Lucy" manuscript, WTP, reel 4, 2372. The

manuscript is not paginated or dated. From internal evidence, "Julia" was written in 1817 or after, because the text makes reference to the death of poet Joel Barlow, a friend of Thornton's who died in 1817.

Chapter 19

108 *he called on Benjamin Hallowell:* Hallowell testified to the meeting; see *The Trial of Reuben Crandall, M.D., Charged with Publishing and Circulating Seditious and Incendiary Papers* (TRC-DC) (Washington, D.C.: 1836), 31. The New York and Washington transcripts differ significantly, but neither is obviously superior to the other, so I have relied on both.

108 *He was the brother:* Suzanne Jurmain, *The Forbidden Schoolhouse: The True and Dramatic Story of Prudence Crandall and Her Students* (Boston: Houghton Mifflin, 2005), 55.

109 *Reuben was more cautious:* He called her "a very obstinate girl"; see *The Trial of Reuben Crandall, M.D., Charged with Publishing and Circulating Seditious and Incendiary Papers* (TRC-NY) (New York, H. R. Piercy, 1836), 35.

109 *the Tappans proved adept:* Lewis Tappan, *The Life of Arthur Tappan* (New York: Hurd and Houghton, 1870), 59–91.

109 *the procrastination of colonization:* Howe, *What God Hath Wrought*, 428.

110 *his friends Denison and Williams: Second Annual Report of the American Anti-Slavery Society (AAS)* (New York: William S. Dorr, 1835), 27.

110 *a million copies:* Bertram Wyatt-Brown, "The Abolitionists' Postal Campaign of 1835," *The Journal of Negro History* 50, no. 4 (October 1965), 228; Howe, *What God Hath Wrought*, 428.

110 *James Kennedy, a Post Office clerk:* TRC-NY, 29.

110 *Another clerk, Charles Gordon:* TRC-NY, 37.

110 *"A shower of Anti-Slavery":* Mirror, August 8, 1835.

110 *"Please to read and circulate":* TRC-DC, 10–11.

Chapter 20

111 *Green Turtleism:* Advertisement, *Mirror*, July 25, 1835.

111 *"shall not take upon him":* Digby, *Epicurus's Morals*, 34.

112 *the steam-driven cylinder press:* William Stanley Pretzer, "The Printers of Washington, D.C., 1800–1880: Work Culture, Technology, and Trade Unionism" (PhD dissertation, Northern Illinois University, 1986), 73–88.

112   *Rival bands of printers: National Intelligencer,* June 15, 1835; *Mirror,* June 6, 1835.

112   *The militia was headed:* Fannie Lee Jones, "Walter Jones and His Times," *Records of the Columbia Historical Society* 5, 145.

113   *one of the mechanics dared: Mirror,* May 23, 1835.

113   *His campaign against:* Docket Book, vol. 70, RG 21, entry 6, Case Papers, box 493, September Term 1833, Criminal Appearances; Docket Book, vol. 70, RG 21, entry 6, Case Papers, box 502, November Term 1833, Criminal Appearances.

113   *"I did not think it would":* Letter, FSK to Anna Key Howard, April 20, 1835, Key-Cutts-Turner Papers, Library of Congress, folder 1.

114   *Key soon found a new home:* Douglas Zevely, "Old Houses on C Street and Those Who Lived There," *Records of the Columbia Historical Society,* 5, 151–75.

114   *Eighteen-year-old Daniel:* Edward W. Callahan, ed., *List of Officers of the Navy of the United States and the Marines Corps from 1775 to 1900* (New York: Haskell House Publishers, 1969), 312.

114   *"I had a wakeful hour":* Gayle Diary, 213–14.

Chapter 21

116   *an uprising near the town: National Intelligencer,* July 29, 1835.

116   *"Horrible Conspiracy": National Intelligencer,* July 31, 1835. Sorting out the truth of what actually happened in Clinton, Mississippi, is difficult. A number of men were hanged. Evidence of a slave rebellion is slighter. Contemporary newspaper accounts, not always a reliable source, suggest that Murrell's white partners had concocted the story of an incipient slave rebellion as cover for their plans to get rid of Murrell. Some slaves had been enlisted. The leaders of the supposed rebellion were, in fact, mostly white men. The editors of the *Mississippian,* published in Jackson, said they were convinced "from all we can learn that not one negro in every five hundred ever dreamed of or was in the slightest way connected with it. It was confined to a single neighborhood, and set on foot and originated by a few degraded and lawless white men. The negroes generally had nothing to do with it." Yet a dozen people, black and white, were hanged without benefit of trial.

    One of them was a man named Tom Donovan, a native of Maysville,

Kentucky (the hometown of Henry Clay), who had been arrested for his
role in the supposed insurrection, which he said was known "among many
other whites." He wrote a last letter to his wife, published in his hometown newspaper and reprinted in the *National Intelligencer,* saying that he
had been accused falsely by both blacks and whites. "Before my maker and
Judge . . . I go into his presence as innocent of this charge as when I was
born," Donovan wrote. The planters forwarded the letter to his wife and
hanged him in the morning. One scholar, W. Sherman Savage, concluded
the Clinton conspiracy was "one of the most extraordinarily lamentable
hallucinations of that time." *National Intelligencer,* August 7, 1835;
W. Sherman Savage, *The Controversy over the Distribution of Abolitionist
Literature 1830–1860* (Jefferson City, Mo.: Association for the Study of
Negro Life, 1938), 10.

117 *"We would not have these": Alexandria Gazette,* August 1, 1835.

117 *Snowden disputed the* Boston Courier's: *Alexandria Gazette,* August 5, 1835.

118 *Anna noted in her diary:* AMT Diary, vol. 1, 931.

PART IV: THE PERILOUS FIGHT

Chapter 22

121 *about nineteen years of age:* Advertisement, "$100 Reward," *National Intel-
ligencer,* August 7, 1835.

121 *at the Union Seminary:* For the name of the school, see Newton, *Special
Report,* 200.

121 *a leafy redoubt:* Tayloe, *Our Neighbors on La Fayette Square* (Washington,
D.C.: Junior League of Washington, 1982), 10; Jeanne Fogle, *Proximity to
Power: Neighbors to the Presidents near Lafayette Square* (Washington, D.C.:
Tour De Force Publications, 1999), 22–23.

122 *"the country seat":* H. Paul Caemmerer, *A Manual on the Origins and Development of Washington* (Washington, D.C.: U.S. Government Printing
Office, 1959), 171.

122 *construction of a new driveway:* Seale: *The President's House,* 193–99.

122 *Arthur had actually seen:* AMT Diary, vol. 1, 750.

122 *accompanied by their household slaves:* On Jackson's property in people, see
Matthew Warshauer, "Andrew Jackson: Chivalric Slave Master," *Tennessee
Historical Quarterly* 54, no. 3 (Fall 2006), 203–29.

122   *"much intoxicated":* Watson's statement is found in RG 59, General Records of the Department of State, Petitions for Pardons 1789–1860, Jackson Administration 1829–1837, box 25, file 1327.

122   *"By drinking the sudden passion":* "Remarks: On the Subject of Temperance," John Francis Cook, delivered before the American Moral Reform Society, Philadelphia, August 16, 1837. Dorothy Porter, ed., *Early Negro Writing, 1760–1837* (Baltimore: Black Classic Press, 1995), 241–48. Cook had publicly advocated temperance as early as 1834.

124   *Arthur undid the catch:* Letter, AMT to AJ, February 17, 1836, Petitions for Pardons, Jackson Administration 1829–1837, box 25, file 1327.

Chapter 23

125   *The noise of the opening door:* This chapter is based on AMT Diary, vol. 1, 931; *Metropolitan*, December 18, 1835; and AMT letter to AJ, February 18, 1836. Petitions for Pardons, Jackson Administration 1829–1837, box 25, file 1327. All dialogue is taken from these three documents. The punctuation of the spoken words reported in these sources has been edited and some repetitions of documented language have been inserted.

125   *the moon almost full:* Jared Sparks and Joseph E. Worcester, et al., eds. & comps., *American Almanac and Useful Repository Knowledge for the Year 1835* (Boston: Charles Bowen, 1835), 45.

126   *he was a well-known physician:* Huntt biography: "Biographical Sketch of the Late Henry Huntt, MD," *Medical Examiner* 1, no. 23 (November 7, 1838), 363–65.

126   *Gibson, a retired general:* Website of the Congressional Cemetery, accessed June 19, 2010, http://www.congressionalcemetery.org /maj-gen-george-c-gibson.

126   *"If Philo Parker and the others":* Huntt and Gibson testified about Arthur's outburst at his trial: *Metropolitan*, December 18, 1835. Both testified that Arthur referred to a "Philo Parker." I find no references to any abortive slave rebellion led by a "Philo Parker" in the English-language literature of slavery.

Chapter 24

128   *"A dreadful night":* AMT Diary, vol. 1, 932.

128   *"It could save his life":* Anna's friend Margaret Bayard Smith had come to

visit, and she heard her conversation with Maria. Smith then recounted the story to a friend in a letter dated August 18, 1836. Margaret Bayard Smith Papers, Library of Congress, microfilm reel 7, 60892–60893.

129 *"$100 Reward"*: Advertisement, *National Intelligencer*, August 7, 1835.

129 *"First Fruit": National Intelligencer*, August 7, 1835.

130 *"Desperate Attempt at Murder": Metropolitan*, August 8, 1835.

131 *Henry King:* TRC-NY, 8–10.

131 *William Robinson:* TRC-NY, 11.

131 *George Oyster:* TRC-NY, 22. In the trial transcript Oyster's first name is given as "Jacob." In the *Directory for Washington City, 1834, Directory for Georgetown, 15,* he is identified as "George."

131 *On the third day:* We can be fairly sure he turned himself in because Anna's account books were detailed down to the penny. They do not show any reward payment in August 1835.

132 *Bayard Smith had found:* AMT Diary, vol. 1, 932.

Chapter 25

133 *the authorities had intercepted: Metropolitan*, August 12, 1835.

133 *"Look at This!":* Advertisement, *Mirror*, August 8, 1835.

134 *"I'm afraid of trusting":* AMT Diary, vol. 1, 931.

134 *Constable Madison Jeffers:* Arthur was arrested at 11:00 a.m. on Saturday, August 8, according to the *Mirror*.

134 *"What possessed you": Metropolitan*, December 18, 1835.

135 *passing by the "whipping machine":* GUE, supplement to vol. 11, April 1831, 105.

135 *"Oh this is dreadful":* AMT Diary, vol. 1, 931.

Chapter 26

136 *he had warm feelings:* Years later Adams wrote a poem dedicated to Anna, "my intellectual and benevolent friend," declaring: "Words! Never! Never can they tell / The soul's intense emotion! / Can never break the bosom's swell / The faithful heart's devotion."

The poem can be found in WTP, reel 3.

136 *"The theory of the rights": The Diaries of John Quincy Adams,* diary 40, 1 June 1835–5 December 1836, 61–62.

137   *"They said their object was":* Michael Shiner Diary, U.S. Navy Department Online Library: (Shiner Diary), 59–61.

138   *On Monday, Anna sent Bayard Smith:* AMT Diary, vol. 1, 931–32.

139   *He called in some former neighbors:* "Duplicate of the Warrant and Commitment in the Case of *United States v. Reuben Crandall*," RG 21, entry 6, Case Papers, box 544, November Term 1835, Criminal Appearances.

139   *William Robinson, a gentleman of means:* TRC-NY, 12.

Chapter 27

140   *His neighbors included:* Directory for Washington City, 1834, Georgetown Directory. "John Simpson, Music master" and "Alexander Simpson, Portrait Painter" are listed on p. 18 as living on "High Street, east side, north end." "Jacob Baltzer, butcher" is listed at the same location on p. 2.

140   *"Are you Crandall?":* All dialogue comes from the testimony of Jeffers, Robertson, and others as reported in the two published trial transcripts: TRC-NY, 10, 19–22, and 32–34; TRC-DC, 10–11, 18–20.

142   *"We ought to take":* Metropolitan, August 12, 1835.

142   *"What were you doing":* This quote, and the conversation in the carriage, are from TRC-NY, 26–27; TRC-DC, 19–20.

143   *an eight-foot-square cell:* Elliot, *Ten Miles Square*, 202.

143   *"nothing can be done":* AMT Diary, vol. 1, 932.

Chapter 28

144   *"An alarming crisis":* The letter, which first appeared in the *Hartford Courant*, was reprinted in the *Globe*, August 20, 1835.

144   *Laub proclaimed himself:* An arrest document says that Laub appointed himself "Head and leader" of the mob; Docket Book, RG 21, entry 6, Case Papers, box 545, November Term 1835.

144   *"Our hearts grew sick":* Metropolitan, August 12, 1835.

144   *Andrew Laub represented:* John Laub, career clerk, *Directory for Washington City, 1834*, 34.

145   *he was married with three children:* 1830 Census, District of Columbia, 177.

145   *authorities suspected him:* See OpenJurist.org: http://openjurist.org/37/us/1 /the-united-states-v-andrew-n-laub.

145   *he sold tickets:* Alexandria Gazette, July 26, 1834.

145   *had recently lost them:* Redemptions of Real Property Sold for Taxes 1825–1856, Corporation of Washington, RG 351, entry 49: "Sq 250, lot 16, sold in the name of Andrew M. Laub, sold for $10.80 on June 10, 1835."

145   *"one of the men":* Richmond Enquirer, August 1835.

145   *Moore Galway, an editor:* Galway is identified as a reporter for the *Telegraph* in *Directory for Washington City, 1834,* 23.

145   *"a great disposition manifested":* Telegraph, August 12, 1835.

145   *The whole of Sixth Street:* Mirror, August 15, 1835.

146   *"gloomy dominions":* Elliot, *Ten Miles Square,* 202.

146   *The noise of the mob:* TRC-NY, 25–27.

146   *"Crandall will be punished":* Richmond Enquirer, August 14, 1835.

146   *The district attorney's appeal:* Metropolitan, August 12, 1835.

147   *Bradley arranged for the Ordnance Office:* Metropolitan, August 12, 1835.

Chapter 29

148   *"a remark derogatory to the character":* James Croggon, "Old Washington—Forgotten Streams," *Evening Star,* January 12, 1913, 14.

148   *"Snow was reported":* Telegraph, August 14, 1835.

148   *"disrespectful language":* Mirror, August 15, 1835.

148   *Julia Seaton said she knew:* Osgood, *Seaton,* 219.

148   *"God knows whether":* Shiner Diary, 65.

149   *"insolent and overbearing effrontery":* Mirror, August 15, 1835.

149   *"A number of persons":* Telegraph, August 14, 1835.

149   *"All the gentlemen of the city":* Osgood, *Seaton,* 219.

149   *Even Mayor Bradley favored:* Paul Pry, October 31, 1835, 2.

150   *"kept the people amused":* Telegraph, August 14, 1835.

150   *"started a hunt for him":* The constable's story was retold in Croggon, "Old Washington," 14.

150   *Over the objections:* Globe, August 14, 1835.

150   *"gathered in Snow's restaurant":* Shiner Diary, 60.

150   *"Today the mob are parading":* Liberator, August 29, 1835.

150   *"The Mob-mania":* Metropolitan, August 12, 1835.

151   *Snow had ducked into a sewer:* Clephane, "Local Aspect of Slavery," 245.

151   *they approved a proclamation:* Globe, August 14 and 24, 1835.

151   *He took a carriage to Georgetown:* Metropolitan, August 12, 1835.

152 *"excited great indignation"*: *Telegraph*, August 13, 1835; *Globe*, August 14 and 24, 1835.

152 *"I feel unwell & nervous"*: AMT Diary, vol. 1, 932.

Chapter 30

153 *"The constable in seeking"*: Letter, MBS to Mrs. Andrew Kirkpatrick, August 18, 1835, Margaret Bayard Smith Papers, reel 7, 60892–60893.

154 *The mechanics engulfed*: *Globe*, August 14, 1835.

154 *they were challenged*: Newton, *Special Report*, 201.

154 *Key had helped Hutton*: RG 21, entry 6, Case Papers, box 344, May Term 1825, Civil Appearances.

154 *ransacked his room*: *Globe*, August 14, 1835.

154 *The mob came for Wormley and Lee*: Newton, *Special Report*, 211.

154 *"It seems there was some danger"*: Green, *Secret City*, 36.

155 *The only Negro school spared*: Newton, *Special Report*, 204.

155 *"The populace of Washington"*: *Metropolitan*, August 15, 1835.

155 *One gang gathered around*: *Boston Courier*, cited in *Telegraph*, May 5, 1836.

155 *"The property of every colored person"*: *Metropolitan*, August 15, 1835.

156 *The* Intelligencer *noted the mob*: *National Intelligencer*, August 14, 1835.

156 *The* Globe *chastely reported*: *Globe*, August 14, 1835.

156 *When the sentries*: *National Intelligencer* and *Globe*, August 14, 1835.

Chapter 31

157 *"The State of the City"*: *National Intelligencer*, August 14 1835.

157 *Blair expressed "extreme regret"*: *Globe*, August 14, 1835.

157 *"the excitement in our city"*: *Telegraph*, August 14, 1835.

158 *"a scoundrel scarce removed"*: *Metropolitan*, August 15, 1835.

158 *"We now hope there is an end"*: Ibid.

158 *Over the next few nights*: *National Intelligencer*, August 15 and 17, 1835.

158 *volunteers from Georgetown continued*: Jones, "Walter Jones and His Times," 146.

158 *"Noises in the street that alarmed me"*: AMT Diary, vol. 1, 932.

159 *cities and towns across the Upper South*: Wyatt-Brown, "The Abolitionists' Postal Campaign," 230.

159 *"The state of society is awful"*: *Niles' Weekly Register*, August 8, 1835, 393.

159 *"There is something extraordinary"*: Adams, *Memoirs of John Quincy Adams*, 255.

Chapter 32

160 *"This spirit of mob-law"*: Howe, *What God Hath Wrought*, 429.

160 *The day Jackson returned*: Globe, August 18, 1835.

160 *warm with a light breeze*: "Meteorological Register," *National Intelligencer*, September 11, 1835.

160 *"one of the largest and most"*: National Intelligencer, August 20, 1835.

161 *"We have viewed"*: Globe, August 19, 1835. *National Intelligencer*, August 20, 1835.

161 *James Haliday rose to offer*: Globe, August 19, 1835.

162 *"sent a message to those"*: Shiner Diary, 63.

162 *The president's response*: In the words of Edgar Snowden, Jackson gave "a peremptory answer in the negative." *Alexandria Gazette*, August 20, 1835.

162 *"What causes have produced"*: Globe, August 20, 1835.

163 *"You need not come"*: AMT Diary, vol. 1, 933.

164 *"The desperate fellow"*: Mirror, August 22, 1835.

Chapter 33

165 *Beverly reached Fredericksburg*: Fredericksburg Arena, August 19, 1835; *Virginia Herald*, August 19, 1835.

165 *The Mechanics Association of Fredericksburg*: Fredericksburg Arena, July 14, 1835.

165 *"Beverly Snow Taken!"*: Daily Virginian, August 24, 1835.

165 *"Snow, the obnoxious free mulatto"*: Alexandria Gazette story as reprinted in the *National Intelligencer*, August 19, 1835.

166 *"We think it probable"*: Fredericksburg Arena, August 19, 1835.

166 *free Negroes "who have"*: Ibid.

166 *That was probably an allusion*: Jackson, "Early Strivings," 25–34.

166 *"the dungeon," a basement cell*: Fredericksburg Jail Records, Rappahannock County Clerk's office, microfilm 1836, 453–64.

166 *"The Wisest of Men"*: Digby, *Epicurus's Morals*, 42.

167 *With Snow now in custody*: Fredericksburg Arena, August 20, 1835.

167 *"Gentlemen," he began*: National Intelligencer, August 26, 1835.

168 *resolved that Snow should*: Daily Virginian, August 29, 1835.

168   *"The sufferings of the poor fellow": Virginia Herald,* August 22, 1835.

168   *"He had better stay": Metropolitan,* August 22, 1835.

168   *"The public has had enough": National Intelligencer,* August 28, 1835.

PART V: THE TRIALS OF ARTHUR BOWEN

Chapter 34

173   *His dear friend, Sarah Gayle: National Intelligencer,* September 9, 1835.

173   *A mob of white men attacked:* Ibid., September 16, 1835.

173   *"The white men's shame":* Green, *Secret City,* 37.

173   *"We have already too many": National Intelligencer,* August 18, 1835.

174   *The common council passed:* Green, *Secret City,* 37.

174   *William Wormley and William Thomas Lee:* Newton, *Special Report,* 169.

174   *John Cook did not return:* Ibid., 202.

174   *fifty-three riots in 1835:* Leonard L. Richards, *"Gentlemen of Property and Standing": Anti-Abolition Mobs in Jacksonian America* (New York: Oxford University Press, 1970), 12.

174   *The South's violent reaction: Quarterly Antislavery Magazine* 1, no. 1 (October 1835), 66.

174   *At the beginning of the year:* Wyatt-Brown, "The Abolitionists' Postal Campaign," 236–37.

175   *results of the pamphlet campaign:* Andrews, *Slavery and the Domestic Slave Trade,* 125.

175   *"but he has put me":* AMT Diary, vol. 1, 935.

175   *"I am in very bad spirits":* Ibid., 936.

175   *Anna wrote a letter:* Ibid.

175   *Anna went to Judge Cranch's home:* Noel and Browning, *Court-house,* 43.

176   *Anna wrote a note to presidential secretary Andrew Donelson:* AMT Diary, vol. 1, 938.

176   *"will surpass in interest and brilliancy": National Intelligencer,* October 7, 1835.

176   *Opening day attendance:* Ibid., October 14, 1835.

176   *"I answered as favorably":* AMT Diary, vol. 1, 940.

176   *The hotels and the boardinghouses: Alexandria Gazette,* November 30, 1835.

176   *"the unexampled growth and prosperity":* Presidential message to Congress, December 7, 1835. Abridgment of the Debates of Congress, from 1789 to 1856: December 3, 1832–July 4, 1836, vol. 12 (New York: D. Appleton, 1859),

699. Jackson's message is also reprinted in *Niles' Weekly Register*, December 12, 1835, 256.

178   *"violation of civil liberty"*: Howe, *What God Hath Wrought*, 430.

178   *Maria brought in a note:* AMT Diary, vol. 1, 941.

Chapter 35

179   *Anna asked her friend:* AMT Diary, vol. 1, 941.

179   *Judge Cranch sat:* Collectively, the three judges served close to a hundred years on the bench. "It may be presumed the citizens were gratified [by their service]," said one unimpressed local. "But if so, there was no public expression." Bryan, *History of the National Capital*, 82.

179   *"partially insane but knows it":* Adams, *Memoirs of John Quincy Adams*, vol. 8, 31.

179   *He was "extremely well-dressed":* Metropolitan, December 19, 1835.

179   *Margaret Smith thought he:* Letter, MBS to Mrs. Kirkpatrick, December 8, 1835, Margaret Bayard Smith Papers, reel 7, 68100. The letter is dated before the trial began but was written, at least in part, after it was over.

179   *The district attorney rose to address:* The jurors' names are found in the Minutes of the District Court, 1834–1836, M 1021, roll 3; the jurors' occupations and addresses are from the 1830 and 1834 directories for Georgetown and Washington.

180   *"It will be proved that":* The account of the trial is drawn largely from the *Metropolitan*, December 12, 1835.

181   *"a small spare man":* Semmes, *John H. B. Latrobe*, 369.

182   *"He said that 'if Philo Parker'":* Metropolitan, December 18, 1835.

182   *"I'm not certain":* Letter, Cranch to AJ, February 23, 1836. RG 59, General Records of the Department of State, Petitions for Pardons 1789–1860, Jackson Administration 1829–1837, box 25, file 1327.

183   *"He was present that evening":* Costin quoted in the *Metropolitan*, December 19, 1835.

183   *"It was a debating society":* Metropolitan, December 19, 1835.

183   *the instruction of the jury:* Letter, Cranch to AJ, February 23, 1836. RG 59, General Records of the Department of State, Petitions for Pardons 1789–1860, Jackson Administration 1829–1837, box 25, file 1327.

184   *"I hereby give notice":* Metropolitan, December 19, 1835.

Chapter 36

185 *"A verdict of guilty":* Alexandria Gazette, December 14, 1835.

185 *Key turned his attention:* Docket Book, vol. 74, November Term 1835.

186 *coaxing an endorsement from:* Weybright, Spangled Banner, 266.

186 *Taney shared the president's:* Smith, Nation Comes of Age, 111.

186 *Key worked "day and night":* Weybright, Spangled Banner, 266.

186 *"He could only blame":* Metropolitan, February 24, 1836.

186 *if Arthur's cell sat:* The jail at Fourth and F streets was a rectangular two-story brick building with windows on each side. Elliot, Ten Miles Square, 202.

187 *"the first explicit and extended struggle":* William Lee Miller, Arguing About Slavery: John Quincy Adams and the Great Battle in the United States Congress (New York: Random House, 1995), 24.

187 *a thirty-four-year-old lawyer:* Charles S. Bradley, "The Bradley Family and the Times in Which They Lived," Records of the Columbia Historical Society, vol. 6 (1903), 134. Joseph Bradley's father, Abraham Bradley, had a brother, Phineas Bradley, who was the father of Mayor William Bradley.

188 *"a malicious, seditious and evil":* U.S. v. Reuben Crandall, a True Bill, RG 21, entry 6, Case Papers, box 544, November Term 1835, Criminal Appearances.

188 *Key asked for a bond:* Crandall told the story of the bail in the letter to his father. Welch, Prudence Crandall, 117.

189 *On Christmas Day Anna opened:* Letter, MBS to AMT, December 25, 1835, quoted in Clarke, "Dr. and Mrs. William Thornton," 204.

189 *"a most disagreeable and painful year":* AMT Diary, vol. 2, 957.

189 *She also wrote a note:* Ibid.

189 *Mrs. Brodeau, started to succumb:* Ibid.

189 *Mrs. Brodeau had admitted:* So the National Intelligencer reported after Anna Thornton's death thirty years later. National Intelligencer, August 18, 1865.

190 *Dodd's fondness for:* Gerald Howson, The Macaroni Parson (London: Hutchinson, 1973).

190 *Aided by a recommendation:* Franklin endorsed her boarding school in an advertisement in the Pennsylvania Gazette, December 6, 1775.

190   *In one scholar's account:* Claude Anne Lopez, *My Life with Franklin* (New Haven: Yale University Press, 2000), 82–83. Lopez notes that Franklin received a letter from Reverend Dodd in January 1777, just a few days before he forged the bond. In the letter, Dodd asked after an unnamed young woman who had recently come to America. Lopez writes, "My guess is that the reverend, ridden with debts and obsessed by the thought of his lost mistress and baby girl, forged the bond in a desperate attempt to escape to America and use the money to start a new life away from his creditors and his inadequate wife. Franklin might help him do this as he had helped Mrs. Brodeau." That baby girl would grow up to become Anna Thornton.

190   *forged a letter:* Percy Fitzgerald, *A Famous Forgery: Being the Story of the Unfortunate Doctor Dodd* (London: Chapman and Hall, 1865), 99.

190   *On June 27, 1777:* Ibid., 182.

190   *Anna Thorton was startled to learn:* AMT Diary, vol. 2, 957.

190   *General Jones, it seems:* Letter, Cranch to AJ, February 23, 1836. RG 59, General Records of the Department of State, Petitions for Pardons 1789–1860, Jackson Administration 1829–1837, box 25, file 1327.

191   *"Have you anything to say":* Cranch's speech was published in the *Mirror,* January 30, 1836.

192   *heavy leg irons:* Arthur mentions the leg irons in a letter to Anna Thornton, February 27, 1836, WTP, reel 3.

Chapter 37

193   *the steel clasps tight:* Letter, Arthur Bowen to AMT, February 27, 1836, WTP, reel 3.

193   *a white man who murdered:* His name was Jonathan DeVaughn; he was hanged in June 1827. *National Intelligencer,* June 23, 1827.

193   *General Jones was in Annapolis:* AMT Diary, vol. 2, 960.

193   *She drew up a petition:* Petition is found in the General Records of the Department of State, Petitions for Pardons 1789–1860, Jackson Administration 1829–1837, box 25, file 1327.

194   *"induce a counter-petition":* AMT Diary, vol. 2, 960.

194   *"John O'Sullivan, editor of the* Metropolitan*":* *Mirror,* February 24, 1836.

194   *Anna had composed eighteen pages:* Letter, AMT to AJ, February 17, 1836.

RG 59, General Records of the Department of State, Petitions for Pardons 1789–1860, Jackson Administration 1829–1837, box 25, file 1327.

195 *There was snow in the air:* "Meteorological Table," *Metropolitan,* February 22, 1836.

195 *"Get the recommendation":* AMT Diary, vol. 2, 960.

195 *"I write to ask and entreat":* Letter, AMT to Van Buren, undated. RG 59, General Records of the Department of State, Petitions for Pardons 1789–1860, Jackson Administration 1829–1837, box 25, file 1327.

196 *"She is miserable":* AMT Diary, vol. 2, 960.

Chapter 38

197 *"Farewell, farewell my young friends dear":* National Intelligencer, February 19, 1836.

198 *"very creditable":* Metropolitan, February 24, 1836.

199 *"Your Petitioner hopes":* Letter, AMT to AJ, February 17, 1836, RG 59, General Records of the Department of State, Petitions for Pardons 1789–1860, Jackson Administration 1829–1837, box 25, file 1327.

199 *"to meet my fate with resignation":* Letter, Arthur Bowen to AMT, February 27, 1836, William Thornton Papers. Microfilm Roll 3.

200 *"with unruffled resignation":* National Intelligencer, March 29, 1828.

Chapter 39

201 *"They have brought it":* AMT Diary, vol. 2, 961.

201 *delivered a four-page memo:* Memo is found in RG 59, General Records of the Department of State, Petitions for Pardons 1789–1860, Jackson Administration 1829–1837, box 25, file 1327.

201 *"Let the execution of the sentence":* Ibid.

202 *"Almost as grateful":* Metropolitan, February 26, 1836.

202 *Around three o'clock:* AMT Diary, vol. 2, 961.

202 *ten inches of snow:* "Meteorological Table," *Metropolitan,* March 1, 1836.

202 *Anna read about the respite:* AMT Diary, vol. 2, 961.

202 *"Respected Mistress," he began:* Letter, Arthur Bowen to AMT, February 27, 1836, William Thornton Papers. Microfilm Roll 3.

202 *"Well written and worded":* AMT Diary, vol. 2, 961.

203 *"This tempering of justice with mercy":* Metropolitan, February 27, 1836.

Part VI: A Dark and Mysterious Providence

Chapter 40

207 *"Oysters from Deep Creek":* Advertisement for National Eating House, *National Intelligencer,* March 25, 1836.

208 *"No! Positively no!":* Delaplaine, *Life and Times,* 410.

208 *"the only one under the government":* Letter, RBT to AJ, AJP, roll 4CK, 19476.

208 *Two weeks later:* According to the Office of the Curator, Taney presented his commission and the documentation that he had taken the oath of office to the clerk of the Supreme Court in August 1836. E-mail from the Public Information Office, Supreme Court, February 18, 2011.

208 *Key resumed his busy life:* Docket Book, vol. 75, RG 21, entry 6, Case Papers, box 556, March Term 1936, Criminal Appearances, Case Papers 1802–1863, box 556, March Term 1836, Criminal Appearance.

208 *he won a guilty verdict:* Minutes of the District Court, 1834–36, M 1021, roll 3.

209 *the jury returned a split verdict:* Cranch, *Reports on Cases,* 680.

209 *"No voluntary association":* Ibid., 680–81.

Chapter 41

211 U.S. v. Reuben Crandall *began:* AMT Diary, vol. 2, 964.

211 *he hoped to defeat:* Neil S. Kramer, "The Trial of Reuben Crandall," *Records of the Columbia Historical Society* 50 (1980), 123.

211 *"quite pale":* Metropolitan, April 18, 1836.

212 *He read the five counts:* TRC-NY, 3; TRC-DC, 5–8.

213 *Coxe was forty-three:* Coxe's legal career is summarized in an obituary published in the *Evening Star,* April 28, 1865.

213 *"I differ from":* TRC-NY, 7.

214 *"he listens to the discussion":* Metropolitan, April 18, 1836.

214 *"a correct man in all his habits":* TRC-DC, 22.

214 *"a very steady man":* TRC-DC, 23.

215 *Judges Cranch and Thruston laughed:* TRC-NY, 30.

215 *testimony from Ralsaman Austin:* TRC-DC, 34; TRC-NY, 36.

216 *"to show their independence":* Charleston Courier, reprinted in the *Telegraph,* May 5, 1836.

216   *A New York correspondent:* Article from *Hudson News Rooms,* reprinted in *The New York Herald,* April 19, 1836.

216   *"The evidence for the prosecution":* Crandall's letter is quoted in Rena Keith Clisby, "Canterbury Pilgrims," an unpublished thirty-seven-page manuscript dated 1947, Prudence Crandall Museum, 20.

Chapter 42

218   *Never, he said:* TRC-DC, 41; TRC-NY, 50. This chapter relies primarily on the New York transcript, incorporating some passages from the Washington transcript.

218   *"On the other hand":* TRC-NY, 50–53.

219   *"It is, gentlemen, preposterous":* TRC-NY, 59–60.

219   *It was half past five o'clock: Metropolitan,* April 27, 1836

219   *thirteen Fahrenheit degrees:* AMT Diary, vol. 2, 966.

219   *"I consider this one":* TRC-DC, 46; I have also incorporated some language from Key's version of his summation as presented in the *African Repository and Colonial Journal (1825–1849)* (November 1836), 12, 11; American Periodicals Series Online, 339.

220   *Less than three hours later:* The *Metropolitan* said the jury deliberated for "three hours." In a letter to his brother, Reuben said the jury was out "but a short time." Clisby, "Canterbury Pilgrims," 20.

Chapter 43

221   *William Jackson, an antislavery:* He recounted the meeting in *The Emancipator,* March 8, 1838.

222   *"Crandall the Abolition* Botanist": *Telegraph,* April 28, 1836.

222   *"I believe there is a feeling": Boston Courier,* April 25, 1836, reprinted in *Liberator,* April 30, 1836.

222   *"He has suffered": U.S. Gazette,* April 27, 1836, reprinted in the *Telegraph,* April 28, 1836.

222   *"this excellent but suffering": Liberator,* May 9, 1836.

Chapter 44

224   *She wrote a letter to the notorious:* AMT Diary, vol. 2, 967.

225   *"one of the most exemplary":* Brown, "The Miscegenation of Richard Mentor Johnson," 18–19.

225 *Senator Johnson had even appeared: Gazette,* January 21, 1836.

225 *agreed to pay her a call:* AMT Diary, vol. 2, 967–68.

225 *"His countenance is wild":* Martineau, *Retrospect of Western Travel,* 155.

225 *"I hope the president:"* RG 59, General Records of the Department of State, Petitions for Pardons 1789–1860, Jackson Administration 1829–1837, box 25, file 1327.

225 *"I have enquired":* Ibid.

225 *"He is favorably inclined":* AMT Diary, vol. 2, 968.

225 *On June 13, Anna and Johnson:* Ibid.

226 *"What a strange business":* Ibid., 969.

Chapter 45

227 *Daniel, was walking:* This chapter relies heavily on the account of Sherburne's second, Thomas Mattingly, as recounted in "The Fatal Duel Between Midshipmen Key and Sherburne," *National Era,* May 12, 1859. I also consulted Charles Oscar Paullin, "Dueling in the Old Navy," U.S. Naval Institute Proceedings 35, part 1, no. 132 (Baltimore: U.S. Naval Institute, 1909), 1155–98; Myra K. Spaulding, "Dueling in the District of Columbia," *Records of the Columbia Historical Society* 29/30 (1925), 183–85; "Old Days on C Street," *Washington Post,* December 8, 1901; and "Naval Duels at Bladensburg," *Washington Post,* August 21, 1921. The latter *Post* article implies incorrectly that the Key-Sherburne duel took place at the Bladensburg dueling ground and states that Daniel Key was killed with the first shot. Mattingly's account in the *National Era* is more credible on both points.

229 *Charges for dueling had been filed:* RG 21, entry 6, Case Papers, box 236, October Term 1821, "Appeals, Criminal Appearances," 21.

229 *Since becoming district attorney:* Docket Book, vol. 71, entry 6, Case Papers, box 545, March Term 1834, Criminal Appearances.

229 *"A moderately skillful marksman":* Paullin, "Dueling in the Old Navy," 1155.

229 *"We have come to fight":* "Fatal Duel," *National Era,* May 12, 1859.

230 *"Very well," finished Sherburne:* Spaulding, "Dueling in the District of Columbia," 184.

230 *"Goddamnit," Key snapped:* "Fatal Duel," *National Era,* May 12, 1859.

230 *"Leave me. Leave me":* "Sketches of War," *Advocate of Peace,* September

1837, APS Online, 77. I have slightly edited Key's reported words. The original reads, "Leave me, leave me," gasped Key, "[for, though dying] I scorn and detest you." I excised the bracketed words, which sound imputed.

230   *Daniel Key lived for another:* "Fatal Duel," *National Era,* May 12, 1859.

Chapter 46

231   *"I am a possum bred + borne":* Daniel Key, "Life of Possum," Key-Cutts-Turner Papers, Library of Congress, folder 3.

232   *He left that task to his niece:* Letter, FSK to Mrs. Daniel (Anna Key) Turner, June 26, 1836, Francis Scott Key Collection, MS 469, Maryland Historical Society (MHS).

232   *"The excitement caused":* "Old Days on C Street," *Washington Post,* December 8, 1901.

232   *"I need not tell you":* Letter, FSK to Mrs. Daniel (Anna Key) Turner, June 26, 1836, Francis Scott Key Collection, MS 469, MHS.

232   *he was alarmed: Niles' Weekly Register,* July 16, 1836, 350.

233   *"strong and universal":* Delaplaine, *Life and Times,* 428.

233   *"Let the Negro boy":* Memo, AJ, RG 59, General Records of the Department of State, Petitions for Pardons 1789–1860, Jackson Administration 1829–1837, box 25, file 1327.

233   *Anna, fearing Mrs. Brodeau:* AMT Diary, vol. 2, 970.

233   *She was at least eighty years old:* Mrs. Brodeau arrived with baby Anna in Philadelphia in 1775 when Ben Franklin vouched for her school. If she was twenty years old at the time, she was born in 1755 and thus eighty years old at the time of her death.

233   *"How much more thankful":* Ibid., 971.

234   *"Now I am harassed":* Ibid.

234   *She sold Arthur:* Ibid.

Part VII: The Epicurean Recess

Chapter 47

237   *"Temerity and foolishness": Metropolitan,* August 13, 1836, reprinted in the *National Intelligencer,* August 18, 1836.

238 *Claggett's dry-goods store: Metropolitan,* August 13, 1836.

238 *Dubant's barbershop: Directory for Washington City, 1834,* 16.

238 *Mrs. Charles's boardinghouse:* Ibid., 12.

238 *covering himself with his cloak: Metropolitan,* August 13, 1836.

239 *"We know Snow": Liberator,* September 24, 1836, quoting an undated *Richmond Whig* article.

239 *O'Sullivan detected "some prevarication": Metropolitan,* August 13, 1836.

Chapter 48

241 *Epicurus had said:* Digby, *Epicurus's Morals,* 113.

241 *One British supporter of emigration:* Thomas Rolph, *Emigration and Colonization: Embodying the Results of a Mission to Great Britain and Ireland, During the Years 1839, 1840, and 1842* (London: J. Mortimer, 1844), 334.

242 *In late 1837:* Thomas Price, *Slavery in America: With Notices of the Present State of Slavery and the Slave Trade* (London: G. Wightman, 1837), 207.

242 *opened a new eatery:* Advertisement, *British Colonist,* April 26, 1843.

242 *plenty of competition:* These Church Street eateries are listed in the 1843 Toronto City Directory, 35, 82.

242 *"B. R. Snow, Purveyor": British Colonist,* January 24, 1845.

242 *"Look at This!":* Advertisement, *Toronto Globe,* June 5, 1847.

243 *"Snow . . . with his whole soul":* Ibid., July 10, 1849.

243 *Snow, "with his usual liberality":* Ibid., June 26, 1847.

243 *"assiduity and attention":* Ibid., October 28, 1848.

243 *Beverly offered a rich: British Colonist,* November 17, 1848.

244 *The Law Society of Upper Canada:* Osgoode Hall website, accessed October 1, 2010, http://osgoodehall.com/buildingevolution.html.

244 *Beverly spent many gay and memorable:* Hamilton, *Osgoode Hall,* 40–41.

244 *"He had the satisfaction":* Digby, *Epicurus's Morals.* M. Du Roudel, "The Life of Epicurus," xxxii.

244 *"long and favorably known": Toronto Globe,* October 22, 1856.

244 *Julia Snow and friends:* Snow is buried in section K, lot 90, according to a card in the files of the Toronto Necropolis found by Mary F. Williamson of York University.

245 *Beverly would regale them:* Hamilton, *Osgoode Hall,* 133.

Epilogue

246   *From December 1838 to March 1839:* Dwight Lowell Dumond, *Antislavery: The Crusade for Freedom in America* (New York: W. W. Norton, 1961), 245–46.

246   *Among the handful of congressmen:* Ibid., 225.

249   *moderate antislavery leaders:* Ibid., 290–304.

249   *lent his house on Louisiana Avenue:* Harrold, *Subversives*, 20; *Directory for Washington City,* 1843, 8.

249   *Smallwood and Torry were among:* Harrold, *Subversives*, 20.

249   *Gamaliel Bailey established:* Dumond, *Antislavery*, 264.

250   *Washington City would experience:* "Race Riot of 1919 Gave Glimpse of Future Struggles," *Washington Post*, March 1, 1999.

250   *his limousine stopped:* Ibid., January 20, 2009.

Postscript: Who

251   *to "say he was doing well":* AMT Diary, vol. 2, 1022. The passage, in its entirety, reads: "I rec'd an [illegible] from Maria to Capt. Bolton saying he was doing well and liked on board the steamboat at Pensacola."

251   *Reuben Crandall had contracted tuberculosis:* "Canterbury Pilgrims," unpublished manuscript, 1947, Prudence Crandall Museum, 21.

251   *Whittier wrote a poem:* John Greenleaf Whittier, *The Complete Poetical Works of* John Greenleaf *Whittier* (Boston: Houghton, Mifflin Co., 1894), 338.

252   *"a very general painful sensation":* National Intelligencer, January 13, 1843.

252   *Cranch praised Key as one:* Ibid., January 16, 1843.

252   *President Herbert Hoover signed the bill:* Historian, U.S. House of Representatives.

252   *Roger Taney served as chief justice:* Steiner, *Life of Roger Brooke Taney*, 550–55.

253   *"had for more than a century before":* The Case of Dred Scott in the United States Supreme Court. The full opinion of Chief Justice Taney and Justice Curtis and abstract of the opinions of the other judges (New York: Horace Greeley & Co., 1860), 9, 11.

253   *Three weeks later, slavery:* Maryland State Archives website, Historical List, Constitutional Convention 1864, http://www.msa.md.gov/msa /speccol/sc2600/sc2685/html/conv1864.html.

253 *"the transition from the era"*: Steiner, *Life of Roger Brooke Taney*, 553.

253 *"He resumed his work"*: Williams, *History of the Negro Race*, 188–91.

254 *Benjamin Lundy published*: Fred Landon, "Benjamin Lundy in Illinois," *Journal of the Illinois State Historical Society* 33, no. 1 (March 1940), 57–67.

254 *"served without distinction"*: Brown, "The Miscegenation of Richard Mentor Johnson," 27.

254 *bequeathed his property in scores*: Warshauer, "Chivalric Slave Master," 225–29.

254 *died in an asylum*: *Register of the Commissioned and Warrant Officers of the United States Navy* (Washington: Bureau of Naval Personnel, U.S. Navy Department, 1849), 112.

254 *Maria Bowen and her mother*: AMT Diary, vol. 2, 540.

254 *Julia Snow, Beverly's widow*: Records of the Toronto Necropolis.

255 *She died in a rented*: *National Intelligencer*, August 18, 1865.

Bibliography

Archives

National Archives

Record Group 21, Records of the U.S. District Court for the District of
    Columbia

Record Group 351, Records of the Government of the District of Columbia

Record Group 29, Records of the Bureau of Census

Library of Congress, Manuscript Division

Andrew Jackson Papers, microfilm edition

Anna Maria Brodeau Thornton Papers

Key-Cutts-Turner Papers

Margaret Bayard Smith Papers

Samuel J. May Anti-Slavery Collection, online

William Thornton Papers

Maryland Historical Society

Francis Scott Key Papers

Howard Papers

Roger Taney Vertical File

Maryland State Archives

Francis Scott Key materials from the St. John's College Collection

Howard University Spingarn–Moorland Research Center

Charles Francis Cook Papers

University of Virginia Library, Special Collections

John Warwick Daniel Papers, including diary of Susannah Norvell

Forrest Sweet Papers
William Wormley Family Papers

Jones Library, Lynchburg, Virginia
Warwick House Papers

University of Alabama W. S. Hoole Special Collections Library
Josiah and Amelia Gorgas Family Papers, including the diary of Sarah Haynesworth Gayle

BOOKS

Adams, Charles Francis, ed. *Memoirs of John Quincy Adams: comprising portions of his diary.* Vol. 9. New York: J. B. Lippincott, 1876 (*MJQA*).

Allgor, Catherine. *Parlor Politics in Which the Ladies of Washington Help Build a City and a Government.* Charlottesville: University of Virginia Press, 2000.

American Almanac and Useful Repository of Knowledge for the Year 1835. Boston: 1835.

American Colonization Society. *Annual Report of the American Colonization Society.* Vols. 11–15. Washington, D.C.: Dunn, 1829.

Andrews, E. A. *Slavery and the Domestic Slave-Trade in the United States.* Boston: Light and Stearns, 1836.

Asbury, W. Christian. *Lynchburg, and Its People.* Lynchburg, Va.: J. P. Bell, 1900; c.1967.

Berlin, Ira. *Slaves Without Masters: The Free Negro in the Antebellum South.* New York: Free Press, 2007.

Bordewich, Fergus. *Washington: The Making of the American Capital.* New York: Amistad, 2008.

Brown, Gordon. *Incidental Architect: William Thornton and the Cultural Elite of Early Washington, D.C., 1794–1828.* Athens: Ohio University Press, 2009.

Brown, Letitia Woods. *Free Negroes in the District of Columbia, 1790–1846.* New York: Oxford University Press, 1972.

Brown, Letitia Woods, and Elsie M. Lewis. *Washington from Banneker to Douglass, 1791–1870.* Washington, D.C.: National Portrait Gallery, Smithsonian Institution, 1971.

Bryan, Wilhelmus Bogart. *A History of the National Capital*. Vol. 2, 1815–1878. New York: Macmillan, 1916.

Buckingham, James S. *America: Historic, Statistic, Descriptive*. Vol. I. London: Harper & Brothers, 1841.

Cabell, Margaret Couch (Anthony). *Sketches and Recollections of Lynchburg*. Richmond, Va.: C. H. Wynne, 1859.

Caemmerer, H. Paul. *A Manual on the Origins and Development of Washington*. Washington, D.C.: U.S. Government Printing Office, 1939, Seventy-Fifth Congress, 3rd session, Senate document no. 178.

Callahan, Edward W., ed. *List of Officers of the Navy of the United States and the Marines Corps from 1775 to 1900*. New York: Haskell House Publishers, 1969.

Campbell, James T. *Songs of Zion: The African Methodist Episcopal Church in America and South Africa*. New York: Oxford University Press, 1995.

The Case of Dred Scott in the United States Supreme Court. The full opinion of Chief Justice Taney and Justice Curtis and abstract of the opinions of the other judges. New York: Horace Greeley & Co., 1860.

Clisby, Rena Keith. "Canterbury Pilgrims." Unpublished manuscript, 1947, Prudence Crandall Museum.

Cole, Stephanie. "Domestic Service in Washington D.C., 1800–1835." Master's thesis, University of Florida, 1988.

Cranch, William. *Reports on Cases, Civil and Criminal in the United States Circuit Court of the District of Columbia*. Vol. 4. Boston: Little Brown, 1852.

Crapol, Edward. *John Tyler: The Accidental President*. Chapel Hill: University of North Carolina Press, 2006.

Crew, Harvey W., Webb, William Bensing, and Woolridge, John. *Centennial History of the City of Washington, D.C*. Dayton, Ohio: United Brethren Publishing, 1892.

Dabney, Virginius. *Pistols and Pointed Pens: The Dueling Editors of Old Virginia*. Chapel Hill, N.C.: Algonquin Books of Chapel Hill, 1987.

Davidson, Isobel. *Real Stories from Baltimore County History*. Baltimore: Warwick & York, Inc., 1917.

Delaney, Ted, and Phillip Wayne Rhodes. *Free Blacks of Lynchburg 1805–1865*. Lynchburg, Va.: Warwick House Publishing, 2001.

Delaplaine, Edward S. *Francis Scott Key: Life and Times*. Stuarts Draft, Va.: American Foundation Publications, 1998.

Dickens, Charles. *American Notes*. New York: St. Martin's Press, 1985.

Digby, John. *Epicurus's Morals with Comments and Reflections*. London: Sam Briscoe, 1712.

Dumond, Dwight Lowell. *Antislavery: The Crusade for Freedom in America*. New York: W. W. Norton, 1961.

Earl, Thomas, ed. *The Life, Travels, and Opinions of Benjamin Lundy*. Philadelphia: William D. Parrish, 1847.

Eleventh Annual Report of the American Society for Colonizing the Free People of Color. Washington, D.C.: Dunn, 1828.

Elliot, Jonathan. *Historical Sketches of the Ten Miles Square Forming the District of Columbia*. Washington, D.C.: J. Elliot, 1830.

Federal Writers' Project. *Washington City and Capital*. Washington, D.C.: Works Progress Administration, 1937.

Fitzgerald, Percy. *A Famous Forgery: Being the Story of the Unfortunate Doctor Dodd*. London: Chapman and Hall, 1865.

Fogle, Jeanne. *Proximity to Power: Neighbors to the Presidents near Lafayette Square*. Washington, D.C.: Tour De Force Publications, 1999.

Fox, Early Lee. *American Colonization Society 1817–1840*. Baltimore: Johns Hopkins Press, 1919.

Fox-Genovese, Elizabeth. *Within the Plantation Household: Black and White Women of the Old South*. Chapel Hill, N.C.: University of North Carolina Press, 1998.

Froncek, Thomas, ed. *The City of Washington: An Illustrated History*. New York: Alfred A. Knopf, 1977.

Frost, Karolyn Smardz. *I've Got a Home in Gloryland: A Lost Tale of the Underground Railroad*. New York: Farrar, Straus and Giroux, 2007.

Full Directory for Washington City, Georgetown, and Alexandria, A. Washington, D.C.: E.A. Cohen and Co., 1834.

Gales, Joseph. Register of Debates in Congress: Comprising the Leading Debates and Incidents of the Second Session of the Eighteenth Congress: [Dec. 6, 1824, to the First Session of the Twenty-Fifth Congress, Oct. 16, 1837] Vol. 82. Washington, D.C., Gales and Seaton, 1837.

Garland, Hugh S. *Life of Randolph*. Vol. 2. Philadelphia: D. Appleton & Co., 1850.

Glass, Hannah. *The Art of Cookery Made Plain and Easy*. London: [Multiple printers], 1778.

Goode, James M. *Capital Losses: A Cultural History of Washington's Destroyed Buildings*. Washington, D.C.: Smithsonian Institution Press, 2003.

Goolrick, John T. *Historic Fredericksburg: The Story of an Old Town*. Richmond, Va.: Whittet & Shepperson, 1922.

———. *Old Homes and History Around Fredericksburg*. Richmond, Va.: Garrett & Massie, 1929.

Green, Constance McLaughlin. *The Secret City: A History of Race Relations in the Nation's Capital*. Princeton, N.J.: Princeton University Press, 1967.

———. *Washington: Village and Capital 1800–1878*. Princeton, N.J.: Princeton University Press, 1962.

Grimsted, David. *American Mobbing 1828–1861: Toward Civil War*. New York: Oxford University Press, 1998.

Hall, Basil. *Travels in North America in the Years 1827 and 1828*. Vol. 3. Edinburgh: Cadell and Co., 1829.

Hamilton, James Cleland. *Osgoode Hall: Reminiscences of the Bench and Bar*. Toronto: Carswell Company Ltd., 1904.

Harris, Alfred Garrett. "Slavery and Emancipation in the District of Columbia, 1801–1862." PhD dissertation, Ohio State University, 1946.

Harrold, Stanley. *Subversives: Antislavery Community in Washington, D.C., 1828–1865*. Baton Rouge: Louisiana State University Press, 2003.

Highsmith, Carol M., and Ted Landphair. *Pennsylvania Avenue: America's Main Street*. Washington, D.C.: American Institute of Architects Press, 1996.

Hines, Christian. *Early Recollections of Washington City*. Washington, D.C.: Junior League of Washington, 1981.

Horton, James Oliver, and Lois E. Horton. *In Hope of Liberty: Culture, Community and Protest Among Northern Free Blacks, 1700–1860*. New York: Oxford University Press, 1997.

Howe, Daniel Walker. *What Hath God Wrought: The Transformation of America, 1815 to 1848*. New York: Oxford University Press, 2007.

Howson, Gerald. *The Macaroni Parson: A Life of the Unfortunate Mr. Dodd*. London: Hutchinson 1973.

Hunt, Gaillard, ed. *The First Forty Years of Washington Portrayed by the Family Letters of Mrs. Samuel Harrison Smith*. New York: Charles Scribner's, 1906.

Jay, William. *Miscellaneous Writings on Slavery*. Boston: John P. Jewett Co., 1853.

Jenkins, Beatrice Starr. *William Thornton, Small Star of the American Enlightenment*. San Luis Obispo, Calif.: Merritt Starr Books, 1982 (typescript).

Journal of the Senate of the United States. Second session of the Twenty-Second Congress. Washington, D.C.: Duff Green, 1832.

Julius, Kevin C. *The Abolitionist Decade, 1829–1838: A Year-by-Year History of Early Events in the Antislavery Movement.* Jefferson, N.C.: McFarland & Company, 2004.

Jurmain, Suzanne. *The Forbidden Schoolhouse: The True and Dramatic Story of Prudence Crandall and Her Students.* Boston: Houghton Mifflin, 2005.

Key-Smith, Francis Scott. *Francis Scott Key: What Else He Was and Who.* Washington, D.C.: National Capital Press, 1911.

Landau, Barry H. *The President's Table: Two Hundred Years of Dining and Diplomacy.* New York: HarperCollins, 2007.

Leiber, Francis, ed. *Encyclopaedia Americana: A Popular Dictionary of Arts, Sciences, Literature, History, Politics, and Biography.* Vol. 10. Philadelphia: Carey and Lea, 1830.

Livingston, John. *Portrait of Eminent Americans Now Living. With Biographical and Historical Memoirs of Their Lives and Actions.* New York: Lamport and Co., 1853.

Lopez, Claude Anne. *My Life with Franklin.* New Haven, Conn.: Yale University Press, 2000.

Lord, Walter. *The Dawn's Early Light.* New York: W. W. Norton, 1972.

Marine, William M. *The British Invasion of Maryland.* Baltimore: Society of the War of 1812 in Maryland, 1913.

Marszalek, John. *The Petticoat Affair: Manners, Mutiny and Sex in Andrew Jackson's White House.* New York: Free Press, 1997.

Martineau, Harriet. *Retrospect of Western Travel.* Vol. 1. London: Saunders and Otley, 1838.

Mayer, Henry. *All on Fire: William Lloyd Garrison and the Abolition of Slavery.* New York: St. Martin's Griffin, 1998.

McCain, Diana Ross. *To All on Equal Terms: The Life and Legacy of Prudence Crandall.* Hartford, Conn.: Connecticut Commission on Arts, Tourism, Culture, History, and Film, 2004.

Miller, William Lee. *Arguing About Slavery: John Quincy Adams and the Great Battle in the United States Congress.* New York: Random House, 1995.

"Minutes of the Fifth Annual Convention for the Improvement of the Free People of Color." Philadelphia: William P. Gibbons, 1835.

Newton, A. N. *Special Report of the Commissioner of Education on the Conditions and Improvements in the District of Columbia*. Washington, D.C.: Government Printing Office, 1869.

Noel, Francis Regis, and Margaret Brent Downing. *The Court-house of the District of Columbia*. Washington, D.C.: Judd & Detweiler, 1919.

Osgood, James S. *William Winston Seaton of the "National Intelligencer."* Boston: J. R. Osgood and Company, 1871.

Parton, James. *Life of Andrew Jackson*. Vol. 3. New York: Mason Brothers, 1860.

Peck, Taylor. *Round Shot to Rockets: A History of the Washington Navy Yard and the Naval Gun Factory*. Annapolis, Md.: Naval Institute Press, 1949.

Phillips, Ulrich Bonnell. *American Negro Slavery*. New York: D. Appleton, 1918.

Poems of the Late Francis S. Key, Esq. New York: Robert Carter & Brothers, 1857.

Pollack, Queena. *Peggy Eaton, Democracy's Mistress*. New York: Minton, Balch & Co., 1931.

Poore, Ben Perley. *Perley's Reminiscences of Sixty Years in the National Metropolis*. Vol. 1. Philadelphia: Hubbard Brothers, 1886.

Porter, Dorothy, ed. *Early Negro Writing, 1760–1837*. Baltimore: Black Classic Press, 1995.

Pretzer, William Stanley. "The Printers of Washington D.C., 1800–1880: Work Culture, Technology, and Trade Unionism." PhD dissertation, Northern Illinois University, 1986, 73–88.

Price, Thomas. *Slavery in America: With Notices of the Present State of Slavery and the Slave Trade*. London: G. Wightman, 1837.

Proctor, John Claggett. *Proctor's Washington and Its Environs*. Washington, D.C.: McGill and Witherow, 1949.

———. *Washington: Past and Present*. Vol. 1. New York: Lewis Publishing Company, 1930.

Randolph, Mary. *The Virginia Housewife; or, Methodical Cook*. Baltimore: Plakitt, Fite, 1838.

Remini, Robert V. *Life of Andrew Jackson*. New York: Harper Perennial, 1999.

Reynolds, David S. *Waking Giant: America in the Age of Jackson*. New York: Harper, 2008.

Richards, Carl J. *The Founders and the Classics: Greece, Rome and American Enlightenment*. Cambridge, Mass.: Harvard University Press, 1994.

Richards, Leonard L. *"Gentlemen of Property and Standing": Anti-Abolition Mobs in Jacksonian America*. New York: Oxford University Press, 1970.

Ripley, C. Peter, and Hermle, Mary Alice, eds.. *The Black Abolitionist Papers*,

Vol. 2, Canada, 1830 to 1865. Chapel Hill: University of North Carolina Press, 1986.

Roberts, Robert. *The House Servant's Directory; or, A Monitor for Private Families: Comprising Hints on the Arrangement and Performance of Servants' Work.* Boston: Munroe and Francis, 1827.

Rolph, Thomas. *Emigration and Colonization: Embodying the Results of a Mission to Great Britain and Ireland, During the Years 1839, 1840, and 1842.* London: J. Mortimer, 1844.

Savage, W. Sherman. *The Controversy over the Distribution of Abolitionist Literature, 1830–1860.* Jefferson City, Mo.: Association for the Study of Negro Life, 1938.

Seale, William. *The President's House: A History.* Washington, D.C.: White House Historical Association, National Geographic Society, 1998.

Second Annual Report of the American Anti-Slavery Society. New York: William S. Dorr, 1835.

Secundus, Dick Humelbergius. *Apician Morsels; or, Tales of the Table, Kitchen, and Larder.* London: Whitaker, Treacher and Co., 1829.

Semmes, John E. *John H. B. Latrobe and His Times.* Baltimore: Norman Remington Company, 1917.

Smith, Elbert B. *Francis Preston Blair.* New York: Free Press, 1980.

Smith, Page. *The Nation Comes of Age: A People's History of the Ante-Bellum Years.* Vol. 4. New York: McGraw-Hill, 1981.

Soller, Werner, Caldwell Titicomb, and Thomas A. Underwood, eds., *Blacks at Harvard: A Documentary History of African-American Experience at Harvard and Radcliffe.* New York: New York University Press, 1993.

Sonneck, Oscar G. *Report on "The Star Spangled Banner," "Hail Columbia," "America," "Yankee Doodle."* Washington, D.C.: Government Printing Office, 1909.

Sparks, Jared and Worcester, and Joseph E. et al., eds. & comps. *American Almanac and Useful Repository Knowledge for the Year 1835.* Boston: Charles Bowen, 1835.

Stearns, Elinore, and David N. Yerkes. *William Thornton: A Renaissance Man in the Federal City.* Washington, D.C.: American Institute of Architects Foundation, 1976.

Steiner, Bernard C. *Life of Roger Brooke Taney, Chief Justice of the United States Supreme Court.* Baltimore: Wilkins & Wilkins, 1922.

Strane, Susan. *A Whole-Souled Woman: Prudence Crandall and the Education of Black Women*. New York: W. W. Norton & Co., 1990.

Swisher, Carl Brent. *Life of Roger B. Taney*. New York: Macmillan, 1935.

Tappan, Lewis. *The Life of Arthur Tappan*. New York: Hurd and Houghton, 1870.

Tayloe, Benjamin Ogle. *Our Neighbors on La Fayette Square: Anecdotes and Reminiscences*. Washington, D.C.: Junior League of Washington, 1982.

Toronto Directory and Street Guide. Toronto: H. & W. Rowsell, 1843.

Torrey, Jesse. *A Portraiture of Domestic Slavery in the United States*. Philadelphia: John Bioren Printer, 1817.

The Trial of Reuben Crandall, M.D., Charged with Publishing and Circulating Seditious and Incendiary Papers. Washington, D.C.: 1836 (TRC-DC).

The Trial of Reuben Crandall, M.D., Charged with Publishing Seditious Libels. New York: H. R. Piercy, 1836 (TRC-NY).

Tyler, Samuel. *Memoir of Roger Brooke Taney, LL.D., Chief Justice of the Supreme Court of the United States*. Baltimore: John Murphy & Co., 1872.

Virginia Landmarks Register. 4th ed. Charlottesville, Va.: University of Virginia Press, 2004.

Watterston, George. *The L—— Family at Washington; or, A Winter in the Metropolis*. Washington, D.C.: Davis and Force, 1822.

———. *A New Guide to Washington*. Washington, D.C.: Robert Farnham, 1842.

Webb, James. *Born Fighting: How the Scots-Irish Shaped America*. New York: Broadway Books, 2004.

Welch, Marvis Olive. *Prudence Crandall: A Biography*. Manchester, Conn.: Jason Publishers, 1983.

Weybright, Victor. *Spangled Banner: The Story of Francis Scott Key*. New York: Farrar and Reinhart, 1934.

Whittier, John Greenleaf. *The Complete Poetical Works of Whittier*. Boston: Houghton Mifflin Co., 1894.

Wilentz, Sean. *Andrew Jackson*. New York: Henry Holt, 2005.

Williams, George W. *History of the Negro Race in American from 1619–1889*. Vol. 2. New York: G. P. Putnam's and Sons, 1883.

WEBSITES

American Memory, Slaves and the Courts 1740–1860, Library of Congress: http://memory.loc.gov/ammem/sthtml/sthome.html.

Congressional Cemetery: http://www.congressionalcemetery.org.

Decatur House on Lafayette Square: http://www.decaturhouse.org.

The Diaries of John Quincy Adams, A Digital Collection, Massachusetts Historical Society, 2004: http://www.masshist.org/jqadiaries.

Digital Library on American Slavery: http://152.13.187.140/slavery/index .aspx?s=3.

Feeding America, the Historic American Cookbook project: http://digital.lib .msu.edu/projects/cookbooks/index.html.

The Food Timeline: foodtimeline.org.

Openjurist.org.

Osgoode Hall: http://osgoodehall.com/buildingevolution.html.

Seat of Empire, a History of Washington, 1790–1861, by Bob Arnebeck: http://www.geocities.com/BobArnebeck/introduction.html.

Michael Shiner Diary, U.S. Navy Department Online Library: http://www.history.navy.mil/library/online/shinerdiary.html.

ARTICLES

"Biographical Sketch of the Late Henry Huntt, MD." *Medical Examiner* 1, no. 23 (November 7, 1838): 363–65.

Birkenhead, Walter. "Republicans, Democrats and Thoroughbreds." *Turf and Sport Digest*, January 1945.

Bradley, Charles S. "The Bradley Family and the Times in Which They Lived." *Records of the Columbia Historical Society*, vol. 6 (1903): 123–42.

Brown, Thomas. "The Miscegenation of Richard Mentor Johnson as an Issue in the National Election Campaign of 1835–36." *Civil War History* 39 (March 1993): 5–30.

Bryan, Wilhelmus B. "A Fire in an Old Time F Street Tavern and What It Revealed." *Records of the Columbia Historical Society* 9: 198–215.

Caldwell, Charles. "Thoughts on True Epicurism." *The New-England Magazine*, November 1832, 45–65.

Cassell, Frank A. "Slaves of the Chesapeake Bay Area and the War of 1812." *The Journal of Negro History* 57, no. 2 (April 1972): 144–55.

Clarke, Allen C. "Margaret Eaton (Peggy O'Neal)." *Records of the Columbia Historical Society*, vol. 44/45 (1942/1943): 1–33.

———. "Dr. and Mrs. William Thornton." *Records of the Columbia Historical Society* 18 (1915): 144–208.

Clephane, Walter C. "The Local Aspect of Slavery in the District of Columbia." *Records of the Columbia Historical Society* 3 (1900): 224–56.

Corrigan, Mary Beth. "Imaginary Cruelties? A History of the Slave Trade in Washington, D.C." *Washington History* 13, no. 2 (Fall/Winter 2001–2002): 3–27.

Croggon, James. "Old Washington—Forgotten Streams." *Evening Star,* January 12, 1913, 14.

Dillon, Merton L. "Lundy, Benjamin." American National Biography Online. February 2000.

Gatell, Frank Otto. "Secretary Taney and the Baltimore Pets: A Study in Banking and Politics." *Business History Review* 39, no. 2 (Summer 1965): 205–27.

Hite, Roger W. "Voice of a Fugitive: Henry Bibb and Ante-Bellum Black Separatism." *Journal of Black Studies* 4, no. 3 (March 1974): 269–84.

Jackson, Luther P. "The Early Strivings of the Negro in Virginia." *The Journal of Negro History* 25, no. 1 (January 1940): 25–34.

Jones, Fannie Lee. "Walter Jones and His Times." *Records of the Columbia Historical Society* 5 (1901): 139–50.

Kramer, Neil S. "The Trial of Reuben Crandall." *Records of the Columbia Historical Society* 50 (1980): 123–37.

Landon, Fred. "Benjamin Lundy in Illinois." *Journal of the Illinois State Historical Society* 33, no. 1 (March 1940): 57–67.

"Letters of Francis Scott Key to Roger Brooke Taney and Other Correspondence." *Maryland Historical Magazine* 5 (1910): 23–37.

McCorvey, Thomas Chambers. "The Mission of Francis Scott Key to Alabama in 1833." *Alabama Historical Society* 4 (1904): 141–65.

Miles, Edwin A. "Andrew Jackson and Senator George Poindexter." *The Journal of Southern History* 24, no. 1 (February 1958): 51–66.

"Naval Duels at Bladensburg." *Washington Post,* August 21, 1921, 44.

"Old Days on C Street." *Washington Post,* December 8, 1901.

Paullin, Charles Oscar. "Dueling in the Old Navy." Part I, *U.S. Naval Institute Proceedings* 35, no. 132 (1909): 1155–98.

Provine, Dorothy. "The Economic Position of the Free Blacks in the District of

Columbia, 1800–1860." *The Journal of Negro History* 58, no. 1 (January 1973): 61–72.

Register of the Commissioned and Warrant Officers of the United States Navy. Washington, Bureau of Naval Personnel, U.S. Navy Department, 1849.

Rohrs, Richard C. "Partisan Politics and the Attempted Assassination of Andrew Jackson." *Journal of the Early Republic* 1, no. 2 (Summer 1981): 149–63.

Rosen, Bruce. "Abolition and Colonization: The Years of Conflict, 1829–1834." *Phylon* 33, no. 2 (Second Quarter 1972): 177–92.

Russell, Hillary. "The Operation of the Underground Railroad in Washington, D.C. 1800–1860." Historical Society of Washington/National Park Service, July 2001.

"Sketches of War." *Advocate of Peace,* September 1837.

Spaulding, Myra K. "Dueling in the District of Columbia." *Records of the Columbia Historical Society* 29/30 (1925–1926): 117–210.

"Thruston Family." *William and Mary College Quarterly Historical Magazine* 6, no. 1 (July 1897): 3–18.

"Underground Railroad Activists in Washington, D.C." *Washington History* 13, no. 2 (Fall/Winter 2001–2002): 29–49.

Warshauer, Matthew. "Andrew Jackson: Chivalric Slave Master." *Tennessee Historical Quarterly* 54, no. 3 (Fall 2006): 203–29.

Wisenburger, Francis P. "The 'Atlas' of the Jacksonian Movement in Ohio." *Bulletin of the Historical and Philosophical Society of Ohio* 14 (1956): 283–311.

"Withers Family of Stafford, Fauquier, &c." *The Virginia Magazine of History and Biography* 6, no. 3 (January 1899): 309–13.

Wood, Kirsten E. "One Woman So Dangerous to Public Morals." *Journal of the Early Republic* 17, no. 2 (Summer 1997): 237–75.

Wyatt-Brown, Bertram. "The Abolitionists' Postal Campaign of 1835." *The Journal of Negro History* 50, no. 4 (October 1965): 227–38.

Zevely, Douglas. "Old Houses on C Street and Those Who Lived There." *Records of the Columbia Historical Society* 5 (1902): 151–75.

NEWSPAPERS

The Adams Sentinel
Alexandria Gazette
British Colonist

Fredericksburg Arena

Gettysburg Compiler

Globe (Toronto)

Lynchburg Daily Virginian

Metropolitan (Georgetown)

National Intelligencer

National Journal

Niles' Weekly Register

Paul Pry

Provincial Freeman (Ontario)

Richmond Enquirer

Richmond Whig

United States Telegraph

U.S. Gazette

Washington Globe

Washington Mirror

Washington Sun

Illustration Credits

INTERIOR

Frontispiece: Prints & Photographs Division, Library of Congress

page 1: Prints & Photographs Division, Library of Congress

page 37: Painting by Percy E. Moran, 1912. Prints & Photographs Division, Library of Congress

page 83: Painting by Gilbert Stuart, 1804. Andrew W. Mellon Collection. Image courtesy of the National Gallery of Art, Washington

page 119: Prints & Photographs Division, Library of Congress

page 171: Prints & Photographs Division, Library of Congress

page 205: Broadside Collection, Rare Book and Special Collections Division, Library of Congress

page 235: The Globe and Mail Inc.

INSERT

page 1, top: Historical Society of Washington/Kiplinger Library

page 1, bottom: Prints & Photographs Division, Library of Congress

page 2, top left: Prints & Photographs Division, Library of Congress

page 2, bottom left: Prints & Photographs Division, Library of Congress

page 2, right: Oberlin College Library

page 3, top: Cook Family Papers, Moorland-Spingarn Research Center, Howard University

page 3, bottom: Prints & Photographs Division, Library of Congress

page 4, top: Painting by Gilbert Stuart, 1804. Andrew W. Mellon Collection. Image courtesy of the National Gallery of Art, Washington

page 4, bottom: Historical Society of Washington/Kiplinger Library

page 5, top left: The New York Public Library

page 5, bottom left: Jones Memorial Library, Lynchburg, VA

page 5, right: The New York Public Library

page 6, top: Courtesy of the Maryland Historical Society

page 6, bottom: Painting by Henry Inman. Courtesy of Historical & Special Collections, Harvard Law

page 7, top: Prints & Photographs Division, Library of Congress

page 7, bottom: National Archives & Records Administration

page 8, top: City of Toronto Archives

page 8, bottom: Finn O'Hara

Index

abolitionists:
  and amalgamation, 7–8, 220, 224
  American Anti-Slavery Society,
    109–10, 116–17, 119, 141, 160, 174,
    205, 215, 247
  and blue-state politics, 217, 248
  in Canada, 242
  and Emancipation Proclamation,
    248, 249
  growing numbers of supporters,
    174–75, 222, 246, 249–50
  mobs as threat to, 153–56, 174, 187
  in Pennsylvania, 13, 60, 61
  publications of, 24–27, 89, 108,
    109–10, 116, 119, 121, 139, 141–42,
    146, 154, 158–59, 160, 163, 174, 175,
    177–78, 187, 212–13, 218, 220
  and *U.S. v. Reuben Crandall*, 211–16,
    217–20, 223, 248
  in Washington City, 108–10, 111, 187,
    246, 248–49
Adams, John Quincy, 9, 85, 93, 99, 103,
  136, 159, 179, 187, 217, 246
Adams, Louisa, 85
Adams administration, 46, 75
African Americans, *see* people of
  color

African colonization, 6–7, 29–31, 60,
  85, 247–48
  Key's support of, 30, 40, 41–42, 61,
    215, 252
  opponents of, 24, 105, 109, 247
Alabama, dispute settled in, 72–75
Allen, Richard, 30
amalgamation, 7–8, 220, 224
AME (African Methodist Episcopal)
  Church, 30, 42, 173, 247
American Anti-Slavery Society,
  109–10, 116–17, 119, 141, 160, 174, 247
  "Slave Market of America," 205
  and *U.S. v. Reuben Crandall*, 211–16,
    217–20, 223, 248
American Colonization Society, 29,
  30–31, 41–42, 60, 215, 247
American Spectator, 27
"American System," 6
Anti-Slavery Record, The, 108, 110, 141,
  213
Armfield, John, 12
Ashton, Henry, 137
Austin, Ralsaman, 215

Bailey, Gamaliel, 249
Bank of Maryland, 77, 138, 207

323

A Note About the Author

JEFFERSON MORLEY is the Washington correspondent of *Salon*. He has worked as an editor and reporter at *The Washington Post*, *The Nation*, *The New Republic*, and *Harper's Magazine*. His work has appeared in *The New York Review of Books*, *The New York Times Book Review*, *The Washington Post Book World*, *Reader's Digest*, *Rolling Stone*, and *Slate*. His first book was *Our Man in Mexico: Winston Scott and the Hidden History of the CIA*.